COGNITIVE DEVELOPMENT
an information-processing view

David Klahr
CARNEGIE-MELLON UNIVERSITY

J. G. Wallace
UNIVERSITY OF SOUTHAMPTON

 LAWRENCE ERLBAUM ASSOCIATES, PUBLISHERS
1976   Hillsdale, New Jersey

DISTRIBUTED BY THE HALSTED PRESS DIVISION OF

JOHN WILEY & SONS

New York   Toronto   London   Sydney

Lawrence Erlbaum Associates, Inc., Publishers
62 Maria Drive
Hillsdale, New Jersey 07642

Distributed solely by Halsted Press Division
John Wiley & Sons, Inc., New York

Library of Congress Cataloging in Publication Data

Klahr, David.
  Cognitive development.

  Bibliography: p.
  Includes indexes.
  1. Human information processing (Child psychology)
  I. Wallace, John Gilbert, joint author.
II. Title.
BF723.I63K58   1976   155.4'13   76-13901
ISBN 0-470-15128-5

Printed in the United States of America

To

Aeneas Vincent Seamus
Anna Lise
Ashley Richard Leslie
Caroline Victoria Louise
Gavin John Gilbert
Joshua Alexander

and

our collaborators in their production

Maybell and Pat

"The human IPS must grow itself to its adult normal state, starting from a primitive neonatal state that is not yet understood. At each moment of growth the ongoing changes in the cognitive system must be capable of being assimilated by the system that is already there, at the same time that the latter remains in reasonable working order. This requirement for a capacity to develop while performing may well imply certain structural similarities in all human cognitive systems [Newell & Simon, 1972, p. 866]."

". . . the automaton model that represents how . . . knowledge is actually stored, accessed, and utilized by a real human subject will have at least as much complexity of structure and function as the most powerful and flexible computer system presently imaginable. . . . Simple models will just not do for human cognition, regardless of their seeming advantages in regard to explicability and operational definition [Flavell & Wohlwill, 1969, p. 74]."

Contents

Preface

In this book we will describe both the general features and some specific examples of an information-processing view of cognitive development. In terms of recent trends in psychological research, our work represents an attempt to apply the theoretical and methodological approach of Allen Newell and Herbert Simon (1972) to the complex problems raised by empirical work in the Piagetian tradition. The general paradigm is to formulate precise models of performance of the organism at two different levels of development, and then to formulate a model for the transition or developmental mechanisms.

The rationale for this deceptively straightforward approach was sketched by Simon over a decade ago:

> If we can construct an information processing system with rules of behavior that lead it to behave like the dynamic system we are trying to describe, then this system is a theory of the child at one stage of the development. Having described a particular stage by a program, we would then face the task of discovering what additional information processing mechanisms are needed to simulate developmental change—the transition from one stage to the next. That is, we would need to discover how the system could modify its own structure. Thus, the theory would have two parts—a program to describe performance at a particular stage and a learning program governing the transitions from stage to stage [Simon, 1962, pp. 154–155].

Looking back over a 20-year period, Brown (1970) lists several of the forces that revitalized research in cognitive development in the late 1950s; among them are (1) computer simulation of cognitive processes: "Since machines—hardware—could accomplish information processing of great complexity, it was obviously perfectly scientific and objective to attribute such processing to the human brain. Why limit the mind to association by contiguity and reinforcement when the computer, admittedly a lesser mechanism, could do so much more? Computers freed psychologists to invent mental processes as complex as they liked

[Brown, 1970, pp. ix–x]"; (2) America's discovery of Jean Piaget: "Computer simulation, psycholinguistics, curriculum reform, and mathematical models altered our notions of the scientific enterprise in such a way to cause us to see Piaget as a very modern psychologist. To see that he was, in fact, the great psychologist of cognitive development [Brown, 1970, p. x] ."

However exciting the promised merger of these two areas may have appeared at the time, it is only quite recently that studies of the type suggested have been carried out (Baylor & Gascon, 1974; Klahr & Wallace, 1970a, b; Young, 1973). Several factors probably contributed to the frustrating search for the "programmable Piaget" (Quillian, Wortman, & Baylor, 1964). The information-processing methodology as it initially developed (Newell, 1968) was devoted to the creation of models derived from intensive analysis of verbal protocols generated by adult subjects. It is now clear that such an empirical base is not the only one that can be used to support process models. Response latencies (cf. Carpenter & Just, 1975), nonverbal protocols (cf. Baylor & Gascon, 1974; Newell & Simon, 1972; Young, 1973), and error patterns (cf. Farnham-Diggory & Gregg, 1975) are all amenable to process modeling. Early formulations of languages for describing these models were difficult to deal with from the view of the developmental psychologist. Perhaps it seemed that the language of Piaget, whether at the level of either comprehensive and general verbal statements or formal logicomathematical notation, bore no direct relationship to the forms of dynamic languages used by the information-processing theorists. Nevertheless, Piaget's steadfast insistence on the characterization of the child as an organism functioning under the control of a developing set of central processes led to an ever widening search for an appropriate descriptive language. At the same time, increasingly sophisticated experimental work was generating a complex web of interrelated empirical results that was inadequately accounted for by extant theoretical formulations.

In this book we present our view of the nature of cognitive development. After more than five years of revision and extension, this volume represents our responses to questions we initially hoped to answer brilliantly in a single summer's effort. The problems are more difficult than we expected at the outset, and our answers are often incomplete and speculative. However, we believe that an extensive statement of our view—an information-processing view—of cognitive development might be interesting and useful to others attempting to understand this central psychological phenomenon. These others might include developmental psychologists, cognitive psychologists, and people working on machine learning.

This book would be suitable for use in advanced undergraduate courses in cognitive development, and in any graduate courses that deal with modeling of cognitive processes, development, or learning. Our treatment of the issues in cognitive development is neither comprehensive nor elementary, and readers without background in this area may need to do some preliminary reading. For those unfamiliar with the Piagetian research, we suggest Ginsberg and Opper (1969) for an elementary introduction and Flavell (1963) for a very extensive description of almost all of Piaget's work prior to 1960. Two works by Piaget most relevant to our book are his books on number concepts (Piaget, 1952) and on classification (Inhelder & Piaget, 1964). A variety of experimental studies based upon Piagetian theory is presented in the collection of readings edited by Sigel and Hooper (1968), and a range of viewpoints on information processing in children is presented in the symposium proceedings edited by Farnham-Diggory (1972). An adequate background for the purposes of our book could be acquired simply by reading Ginsberg and Opper (1969) and a sample of papers in Sigel and Hooper (1968), while the other readings would provide a broad context.

Our treatment of information-processing models assumes very little background on the part of the reader, but we have made no attempt to give comprehensive coverage of the field. A very brief review of Newell and Simon's work can be found in Simon and Newell (1971). A full presentation is contained in the book on human problem solving (Newell & Simon, 1972). A broad treatment of human information processing is presented in the textbook by Lindsay and Norman (1972).

ACKNOWLEDGMENTS

Many people have made contributions to our work, contributions which we have so thoroughly assimilated as to be unable to be sure who did what. There are a few influences, however, about which there is no ambiguity.

It is unlikely that we will easily amortize our intellectual debt to our mentors and colleagues Allen Newell and Herbert Simon. For most of our professional careers, their pioneering work on the formulation of models of adult cognitive processes has profoundly influenced our attempt to understand developmental processes. In addition, Allen Newell has generously assisted us in our utilization of his simulation languages. A mixture of encouragement and pithy criticism from Walter Reitman, John Flavell, Tom Trabasso, and especially Allen Newell came at appropriate points in our research program, and we have attempted to take their wisdom to heart.

Several students in the Psychology Department at Carnegie-Mellon University helped to make the book more readable. Marshall Atlas purged an early draft of its more opaque passages; David Neves cleaned up some of the program listings; Glenn Lea did all the line drawings; and Mary Harris and Elaine Shelton helped with the reference list.

There have been several sources of support, both direct and indirect. In the passage cited earlier, Brown (1970) notes the Social Science Research Council's "wonderful ability to detect intellectual developments in an early 'critical period' when they can benefit maximally from a little enrichment [p. ix]." He cites their establishment in 1959 of the Committee on Intellective Processes Research, which in turn produced the now classic series of five Society for Research in Child Development Monographs (Society for Research in Child Development, 1970). Our own work has been influenced by the SSRCs on both sides of the Atlantic. In the summer of 1965, SSRC sponsored a Research Conference on Learning and the Educational Process at Stanford University, directed by Lee Cronbach, where we first met and began to consider the application of the information-processing paradigm to the area of cognitive development. In 1966, the British SSRC funded Wallace's initial proposal to do research in this vein and has supported his research ever since. In the area of computer simulation, SSRC sponsored several intensive summer seminars at the RAND Corporation in the late 1950s and early 1960s whose purpose was to stimulate the use of simulation programs and list processing languages.

From 1970 to 1973, Richard Cyert, now the President of Carnegie–Mellon University and then the Dean of its Graduate School of Industrial Administration and Department of Psychology, provided optimal administrative support for what would otherwise have been a geographically difficult collaboration. In addition to the SSRC support mentioned above, the final stages of this work have been generously funded by a 3-year grant to Klahr from the Spencer Foundation.

The two kinds of computer work in this book have been run on two distinct systems at Carnegie–Mellon University. The data analysis was done at the Computation Center, and the simulation work was done on the systems operated by the Computer Science Department. All of our experimental work on quantification reported in this book was done in collaboration with Michelene T. H. Chi.

The manuscript has gone through distressingly many revisions, ably typed by Ellen Duke, Marlene Naughton, Cheryl Hutton, and Eloise Swanson on the North American side of the Atlantic and by Shirley Clarke on the English side.

1
Toward an Information-Processing Solution to Some Problems in the Study of Cognitive Development

This chapter starts with a brief statement of two central problems in the study of cognitive development: the issues of stage and transition. Specific aspects of these problems will be presented in subsequent chapters, and an extensive discussion of research relating to these issues can be found in Wallace (1972a). In its most concise form, the stage issue can be stated as: "What does a child have when he 'has' conservation (or class inclusion or transitivity)?" The transition question is: "From where did 'it' (what he 'has') come, and how did it get there?"

The second part of the chapter describes the nature of the models we will use in formulating answers to these questions. The models are based upon a specific kind of information-processing system—a production system—and an associated language for constructing computer-simulation models of the child at different levels of development. We assume that most readers will be unfamiliar with production systems, and we have attempted to provide a sufficiently detailed and comprehensive description to enable the reader to understand all the models in this book.

Production systems provide a descriptive format for stating information-processing models, as well as an actual language for writing simulation programs that allow the models to be "run" on a computer. In addition, they encompass a collection of psychological assumptions about the nature of the human information-processing system. In this chapter we will describe many of these assumptions, and then modify and elaborate them in subsequent chapters.

PROBLEMS IN RESEARCH ON COGNITIVE DEVELOPMENT

The Problem of Stage

One fundamental problem in the study of cognitive development is the determination of the developmental relationship between particular cognitive skills. In the customary experimental paradigm, children are presented with a set of test items intended to tap the cognitive skills under investigation. The developmental sequence for any pair of items, A and B, can be determined by examining the fourfold table of passes and failures for the two items. For instance, if there are no occurrences in the pass A–fail B cell (Fig. 1.1a), then there exists strong evidence that the cognitive processes sufficient to pass item B are necessary to pass item A; or, if the empty cells are pass A–fail B and fail A–pass B (Fig. 1.1b), then there is evidence that both skills appear simultaneously. The complexity of the questions raised by this problem is clearly illustrated by the research literature centered on the concept of "stage" in Piaget's theory of intellectual development. A comprehensive review of this work has been recently provided by Pinard and Laurendeau (1969). One of the most controversial issues which they discuss stems from Piaget's contention that all of the groupings underlying the stage of concrete operations "appear at the same time without our being able to seriate (them) into stages [Piaget, 1941, p. 246]." Their review of the studies aimed at evaluating this assertion provides an inconsistent picture: some of the results support synchronism while others reveal asynchronism.

In a careful analysis of the conceptual ambiguities inherent in the traditional view of stages, Flavell (1971) argues that much of this inconsistency can be attributed to an oversimplified view of what synchronism might mean. To say that two items (skills, rules, strategies, etc.) develop in synchrony could mean "that they begin their development at the same time, or conclude it (achieve functional maturity) synchronously, or both, or even neither (that is, have developmental courses which show some chronological overlap, but only in the middle regions) [Flavell, 1971, p. 450]."

It is extremely difficult to design experiments to resolve this issue, as the following consideration of methodological difficulties encountered by Smedslund (1964) will indicate. Smedslund attempted to determine the nature of the interrelations within a set of test items regarded as tapping specific aspects of Piaget's level of concrete reasoning. Concrete reasoning is assumed to be reflected in certain types of inference patterns and, in Smedslund's view, the unitary nature of the construct requires that these patterns should be exactly related. The results, however, revealed that not one of the fourfold tables covering the pass–fail relations between pairs of items contained an empty cell and, thus, none of the pairs of items exhibited an exact relationship. In addition none of the items were free from inconsistent subitem responses.

In searching for an explanation of the wide variations in children's performance on the tasks, Smedslund hypothesized that the inconsistency and absence of exact relations might be due to the fact that the items could not be meaningfully compared, since they differed not only in the inference pattern involved, but also in the nature of the stimulus situations presented to the subjects and in the goal objects which they were instructed to attain. Exact relations between inference patterns might be discovered if goal objects and

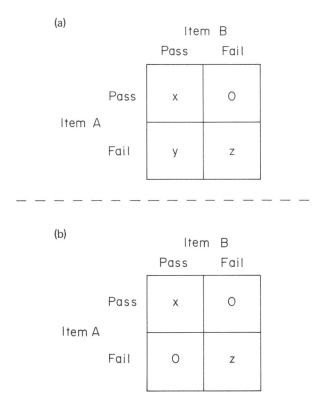

FIG. 1.1   (a) Hypothetical error pattern implying *A* acquired after *B*. (b) Hypothetical error pattern implying *A* and *B* acquired simultaneously.

stimulus situations were held rigidly constant. Smedslund (1966a, b, c) attempted to do this in a further series of experiments. Due to the difficulty of retaining identical stimulus situations while varying the inference pattern under consideration, the focus of the work was a comparatively narrow task area. It involved comparisons of children's ability to determine the effect of various combinations of addition and subtraction of one unit on the relative amount in two unseen collections which the subjects were informed were equal at the outset. Contrary to Smedslund's expectations, even with these narrow tasks exact relations between items proved to be nonexistent. The results demonstrated that the same logical task structure, with identical perceptual and conceptual contents, may yield radically different solution frequencies depending, for example, merely on position in the series of tasks.

The lesson to be learned from these findings, Smedslund believes, is that tasks must be analyzed in much more detail than is provided by a description of their conventional logical structure. The general problem is to determine exactly how the input is encoded by the subject and what transformations occur between encoding and decoding. The objective task structure alone does not yield a valid description of the solution performance, and it is necessary to diagnose the actual psychological processes in great detail to obtain minute descriptions or well-supported inferences about the actual sequence and content of the thinking processes.

The Problem of Transition

A second basic issue posing intractable methodological problems is the question of the nature of the transition rule in cognitive development, that is, the mechanisms or processes which govern the child's movement from state to state through the developmental sequence. The difficulties which characterize research on this theme are exemplified in the experimental studies aimed at determining the relative importance of the factors invoked by learning theories and Piaget's concept of "equilibration" in accounting for the process of transition. As Laurendeau and Pinard (1962) have pointed out, an overview of the results of these studies leads to pessimism about the outcome of an experimental approach to the transition problem. The existing experimental results appear to be compatible both with Piaget's position and with that of the protagonists of learning theory, and a solution is still awaited to the methodological problem of devising a series of critical experiments.

An important underlying cause of this situation appears to be the level of generality at which the theoretical accounts of transition are presented. The focus on change is, in general, imperfectly developed in Piaget's formulation of intellectual development. As Wohlwill (1966) has indicated, for all its formal elaboration and complexity, Piaget's system remains at base a structural analysis of children's performance on cognitive tasks at different levels of their development. His treatment of the functional side of the problem, the nature of the processes by which these changes take place, is much less complete. With the solitary exception of an account of the appearance of conservation of continuous quantity couched in terms of the typical test situation, Piaget's (1957, 1960) descriptions of the functioning of equilibration are highly general statements which do not deal with the particular mechanisms governing developmental changes or specify the conditions under which they take place.

The practical effects of this lack of an account of equilibration in specific process terms can be seen in the confusion surrounding the numerous experimental attempts to accelerate the appearance of the various conservations. Sigel and Hooper (1968) report a variety of competing acceleration treatments, all of which are regarded by their authors as being based on Piaget's description of the underlying processes concerned. The absence of a precise process—performance link contributes to the extreme difficulty of putting Piaget's account of transition to an experimental test, since the lack of specificity makes it all too easy to argue that a wide range of experimental results are compatible with his position.

These fundamental problems—stage and transition—are interrelated. The cognitive skills whose mastery defines a stage are operationally defined in terms of a set of tasks that have become classics in Piagetian literature (for example, class inclusion, transitivity, conservation). However, a careful analysis of the information-processing demands of the task variants indicates that we are dealing with a far from homogeneous entity, even when tasks are supposed to be identical. The difficulty compounds itself when procedural variations are introduced; for although we can record the gross effects of systematic procedural variations, we have no theoretical basis upon which to explain the effects of those variations or from which to derive new procedural variations. With respect to transition, in the absence of precise models of what it is that is going through transition, theories must remain vague and nonoperational.

THE INFORMATION-PROCESSING PARADIGM

Faced with a segment of behavior of a child performing a task, we pose the question: "What would an information-processing system require in order to exhibit the same behavior as the child?" The answer takes the form of a set of rules for processing information: a computer program. The program constitutes a model of the child performing the task. It contains explicit statements about the capacity of the system, the complexity of the processes, and the representation of information—the data structure—with which the child must deal.

Since the child's behavior can be represented as a finite time sequence of symbols, there are, in principle, an infinite number of different models one could construct to account for the child's performance. However, to gain even initial plausibility as psychological theories, such models might satisfy some general metatheoretical constraints. Simon (1972) lists four such criteria: (a) consistency with what we know of the physiology of the nervous system; (b) consistency with what we know of behavior in tasks other than the one under consideration; (c) sufficiency to produce the behavior under consideration; and (d) definiteness and concreteness.

With respect to the last criterion, one can view three levels of explanation in information-processing terms. At level I, the task-specific level, we have models that are designed to explain cognitive behavior for specific, narrowly defined, tasks, for example, playing games such as chess and checkers and solving problems such as series completion. Such models are usually stated as running programs that are sufficient to meet minimal performance criteria. At level II, the information-processing models are aimed at a general reformulation of a wider range of problems in terms of the requirements they impose on the organism. They also postulate some basic mechanisms that could explain a wide range of cognitive activities, for example, an EPAM-type discrimination net (Feigenbaum, 1963) or a model of semantic memory (Quillian, 1967). The emphasis at this level is not so much upon a running program as it is upon the analysis of cognitive activity in terms of internal symbolic representations and processes that operate upon these representations. An excellent example of this level of theorizing can be found in a reformulation of some stochastic learning theories in information-processing terms (Gregg & Simon, 1967).

At level III, the metaphorical level, the unique advantages of information-processing models begin to disappear. The notion of information-processing models of some sort has long had an appeal to psychologists, although it has only been with the recent invention of suitable languages to express ideas that any progress beyond vague verbal models has been possible. A prime example of the metaphorical use of information-processing terminology is Miller, Galanter, and Pribram's (1960) well-known book in which a wide range of cognitive activities are described in terms of a hypothetical information-processing device, called a TOTE unit. Examples of less extensive views of the process metaphor abound in recent discussions of cognitive development. For example, "If one does what is possible to do at the purely intensive level with logical operations of class and relation, one is behaving rather like a computer with a grouping program [Flavell, 1963, p. 188]." Or, another example, from Smedslund (1966c): "The difference in an error pattern from subject to subject indicates that the individual variability stems partly from differences in processing routines [p. 165]."

It is useful to keep these three levels in mind when evaluating information-processing theories, particularly those that purport to be models of cognitive development. For when stated only at the highest level of generality and metaphor, information-processing theories provide merely a different, rather than improved, mode of theorizing. Ultimately, one hopes to push all such theorizing down to the concrete level of a running program. In this book, as will become evident, this desideratum has been completely met only with respect to models of different performance levels. The model of the transition mechanism itself—although precise in some segments—still has many components that are stated at a metaphorical level. However, we believe that the precise formulation of the various stages of cognitive development makes it much more likely that a similarly precise model of the transition mechanism itself will soon be obtainable. In the next section, we will describe a form of modeling that enables us to make such precise formulations.

PRODUCTION SYSTEMS:
A LANGUAGE FOR PROCESS MODELS

In the past few years a new form for describing information-processing models of cognition has been proposed and successfully applied to a modest range of complex problem-solving activities (Newell, 1966; Newell & Simon, 1972). The models are posed in the form of a collection of ordered condition–action links, called *productions,* that together form a *production system.* The condition side of a production refers to the symbols in short-term memory (STM) that represent goals and knowledge elements existing in the system's momentary *knowledge state;* the action consists of transformations on STM including the generation, interruption, and satisfaction of goals, modification of existing elements, and addition of new ones. A production system obeys simple operating rules:

1. The condition of each production is matched against the symbols in STM. If *all* of the elements in a condition can be matched with elements (in any order) in STM, then the condition is satisfied.

2. If no conditions are satisfied, then the system halts. If more than one condition is satisfied, then some conflict–resolution principle must select which production to "fire." Typically, conflict is resolved by choosing the earliest production in the production system. Other resolutions are possible, but that is the one we will use at first.

3. When a production "fires," the actions associated with it are taken. Actions can change the state of goals, replace elements, apply operators, or add elements to STM.

4. After a production has fired, the production system is re-entered from the top; that is, the first production's condition is tested, then the second, and so on.

5. The STM is a stack in which new elements appear at the top (or front), pushing all else in the stack down one position. Since STM is limited in size, elements may be lost.

6. When a condition is satisfied, all those STM elements that were matched are moved to the front of STM. This provides a form of automatic rehearsal.

These rules operate within the framework of a theory of human problem solving extensively described in Newell and Simon (1972) and briefly summarized by Newell (1972b):

> Structurally, the subject is an information processing system (IPS) consisting of a processor containing a short-term memory which has access to a long-term memory (LTM). The processor also has access to the external environment, which may be viewed as an external memory (EM). . . .
> All action of the system takes place via the execution of elementary processes, which take their operands in STM. The only information available upon which to base behavior is that in STM; other information (either in LTM or EM) must be brought into STM before it can affect behavior. At this level the system is serial in nature: only one elementary information process is executed at a time and has available to it the contents of STM as produced by prior elementary processes. Seriality here does not imply seriality either of perception or of accessing in LTM [Newell, 1972b, pp. 375–376].

This general model and the verbal rules listed above have been precisely specified in a special programming language created by Newell (1972b) called

PSG (for production system, version G). Production systems written in PSG can be run on the PSG interpreter in a time-sharing mode under user (i.e., model-builder) control. The user can observe the sequential consequences of his model and provide inputs for as yet unspecified subprocesses.

Example 1

The following lengthy quote from Newell (1973) provides the best introduction to some specific details of PSG. Newell uses an abstract and meaningless example here in order to focus upon the PSG mechanisms:

> The overall architecture of the system is shown in Fig. [1.2]. All of the action in the system takes place in the Short-Term Memory (STM), which contains a set of symbolic expressions. STM is to be identified with the memory of Miller (1956) and Waugh and Norman (1965), its size is some small number of chunks (proverbially 7 ± 2).
>
> There is no direct representation in PSG of the various buffer memories that appear to be part of the immediate processor of the human: the visual icon of Sperling (1960), (possibly) the precategorical auditory store of Crowder and Morton (1969), and others. The interface to the senses is not represented as well, nor is the decoding on the motor side. Such deficiencies in the architectural model undoubtedly limit the scope and adequacy of the system. . . .

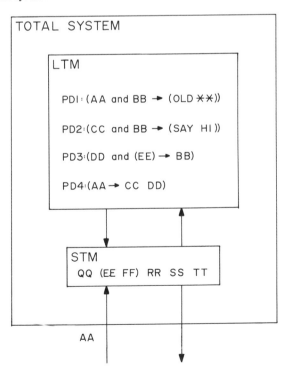

FIG. 1.2 Overall architecture of PSG. (From Newell, 1973.)

The STM holds an ordered set of symbolic expressions (i.e., chunks). The ordering shows up, as will be seen later, in that new expressions always enter STM at the front and that the conditions examine the expressions in order starting at the front (hence the frontal expressions may preempt later ones). As can be seen in Fig. [1.2], a symbolic expression may be simply a symbol (e.g., CC) or it may consist of an ordered collection of symbolic expressions [e.g., (EE(AA DD))]. Thus, symbolic expressions may be built up in a nested fashion, and we can represent them in the manner of algebraic expressions. STM may be taken as holding symbol tokens (i.e., pointers) to the expressions, or it may be taken as holding the expressions themselves. Operationally, there is no way of telling the difference. The degree to which an element in STM is opaque (Johnson, 1970) is determined by the conditions of the productions, which in essence are a description of what aspects of an expression can be responded to.

The Long-Term Memory (LTM) consists entirely of an ordered set of productions. Each production is written with the condition on the left separated from the action on the right by an arrow. In Fig. [1.2] only four productions are shown: PD1, PD2, PD3, and PD4. Some of the conditions (e.g., that of PD4) consist of only a single symbolic expression (e.g., PD4 has AA); others have a conjunction of two (e.g., PD1 has AA and BB). Some actions consist of a single symbolic expression (e.g., PD3 with BB), some have a sequence of expressions (e.g., PD4 with CC followed by DD), some have expressions that indicate operations to be performed (e.g., the SAY in PD2).

As the system stands initially, none of the productions is satisfied by the contents of STM and nothing happens. However, we have shown an AA about to enter into STM from the external world. When it does so we get the situation of Fig. [1.3]. Here we have shifted to the representation of the system we will use from now on. All the essential elements in Fig. [1.2] are represented, only the various enclosing boxes and input/output arrows are missing. STM now holds the AA and has lost the TT from the far right.

In Fig. [1.4] we show the trace of the run, as it is produced by the system. At each cycle the production that is true (i.e., the first whose condition is true) is noted, followed by each action when it is taken. Then the new state of STM is printed and the cycle repeats. The numbers to the left are a count of the number of actions that have occurred so far in the run.

Let us work through the trace, explaining how the conditions and actions operate. The only condition of the four productions satisfied is that of PD4, the AA on the left side of PD4 matching the AA in STM. This leads to the action of PD4 being evoked, first the CC then the DD. Notice that AA is still in STM but RR and SS have disappeared off the end. This can be seen in Fig. [1.4] at Line 500 where the contents of STM are printed after all actions for production PD4 have been taken.

A production (PD4) having been successfully evoked, the system starts the cycle over. PD4 is, of course, still satisfied since AA is still in STM. But PD3 is also satisfied since

```
00100   PS.ONE: (PD1 PD2 PD3 PD4)
00200
00300   PD1: (AA AND BB --> (OLD **))
00400   PD2: (CC AND BB --> (SAY HI))
00500   PD3: (DD AND (EE) --> BB)
00600   PD4: (AA --> CC DD)
00700
00800   STM: (AA QQ (EE FF) RR SS)
```

FIG. 1.3   Example production system PS.ONE. (From Newell, 1973.)

```
00100   0. STM: (AA QQ (EE FF) RR SS)
00200   PD4 TRUE
00300   0. ACTION- CC
00400   1. ACTION- DD
00500   2. STM: (DD CC AA QQ (EE FF))
00600   PD3 TRUE
00700   2. ACTION- BB
00800   3. STM: (BB DD (EE FF) CC AA)
00900   PD1 TRUE
01000   3. ACTION- (OLD **)
01100   4. STM: ((OLD AA) BB DD (EE FF) CC)
01200   PD2 TRUE
01300   4. ACTION- (SAY HI)
01400
01500   ********** HI
01600
01700   5. STM: (CC BB (OLD AA) DD (EE FF))
01800   PD2 TRUE
01900   5. ACTION- (SAY HI)
02000
02100   ********** HI
02200
02300   6. STM: (CC BB (OLD AA) DD (EE FF))
02400   PD2 TRUE
```

FIG. 1.4   Run of PS.ONE. (From Newell, 1973.)

the DD matches the DD in STM and the (EE) also matches the (EE (EE FF)) in STM. This latter follows from one of several matching rules in PSG. This one says that a match occurs if the condition matches completely, starting with the first symbol in the STM expression but optionally skipping some. Thus (EE) would match also match (EE (FF GG)), but would not match an expression without EE at the front, e.g., (FF EE).

When two productions are simultaneously satisfied, the rule for resolving such conflicts is to take the first one in order—here PD3. The result of PD3's action is to put BB into STM as shown at Step 2.

Notice that when PD3 was evoked the two items in its condition moved up to the front of STM in the same order as in the condition. Thus, attended items stay current in STM, while the others drift down toward the end, ultimately to be lost. This mechanism provides a form of automatic rehearsal, though it does not preclude deliberate rehearsal. It also implies that the order of the items in STM does not remain fixed, but flops around with the details of processing.

At the next cycle PD1 is evoked, being the first of the productions satisfied, which includes PD2, PD3, and PD4. The action of PD1 introduces a basic encoding (i.e., construction) operation. (OLD **) is a new expression, which will go into STM like any other. But ** is a variable whose value is the front element in STM. In the case in point the front element is AA, which was moved up by the automatic rehearsal when the condition of PD1 was satisfied. Hence the new element is (OLD AA). This element replaces the front element, rather than simply pushing onto the front. The net effect is to take the front element and embed it in a larger expression. . . . It is important that the AA no longer exists in STM . . . since it is necessary to modify STM so AA cannot reevoke a production.

The import of PD1's action is that it deactivates the STM item able to evoke PD4 (and itself, as well). On the next cycle only PD2 is satisfied. Its action involves SAY, which is a primitive operation of the system that prints out the expression following it in the element, i.e., it prints HI (as shown in the figure).

We see from Fig. [1.3] that the system continues to evoke PD2 and say HI. Nothing happens to modify STM so the condition of PD2 remains satisfied. If we had written

PD2:   (CC AND BB → (SAY HI (OLD **)))

then the production system would have turned off by marking CC as old.

There is a somewhat wider array of primitive operations and many more details of the matching operation for conditions (Newell, 1972[b]).

We can see, even at this stage, that many assumptions are required to specify a complete control structure. Some of them, such as the STM itself, its encoding, and the automatic rehearsal, constitute rather clear psychological postulates. Others, such as the details of matching, have psychological implications (presumably every aspect of the system does), but it is hard to know how to state them directly as independent postulates [Newell, 1973, pp. 465–471].

Example 2

Since PSG will figure so prominently in this book, it is worth presenting a second example. This time we use symbols whose names help to convey their function. Of course, to the system, these names are simply arbitrary unique symbols. The example to be presented in this section is intended not as a psychological model, but rather as a demonstration of some of the features of PSG *qua* programming language. Figure 1.5a shows a production system that represents the hammering of a nail into a board, and Fig. 1.5b shows a trace of a system as it is executed.

First, some PSG conventions. Text to the right of a semicolon is ignored: line 100 is merely a title. Everything else is in the form of a label, followed by a colon, followed by some sort of structure enclosed in parentheses. The first four of these structures (lines 200–500) are production rules. They consist of a condition written as a conjunction of elements, an arrow (– ->), and a series of actions. The details of these productions differ, but they are all of this same general form. We will return to the meaning of their particulars when we describe their execution. Line 600 contains a special structure, named LOOK, which requests input from the terminal; that is, LOOK represents a part of the model that has not yet been programmed and whose operation must therefore be "simulated" by the model builder. When LOOK is evoked as an action, the model builder must decide what information to give it before the system can continue to function. Line 900 contains the information that the system needs to get started: when PSG initializes the interpretation of a production system, it sets STM to be equal to STMI (STM initial). The structure named BUILD (line 800) determines the sequence in which the productions will be considered: thus, P4 will be tried first, then P1, and so on. Finally, the size of STM is determined by the size of STMI; in this case STM will have three "slots."

```
00100    ;DEMO OF PSG USING SIMPLE EXAMPLE
00200    P1:   ((GOAL * JOIN) AND (UP HAMMER) AND (NAIL UP) --> (UP ===> DOWN))
00300    P2:   ((GOAL * JOIN) AND (DOWN HAMMER) --> (DOWN ===> UP) LOOK)
00400    P3:   ((GOAL * JOIN) --> (DOWN HAMMER))
00500    P4:   ((GOAL * JOIN) AND (NAIL FLUSH) --> (* ==> +))
00600    LOOK:   (OPR CALL)
00700
00800    BUILD:   (P4 P1 P2 P3)
00900    STMI:   ((GOAL * JOIN) NIL NIL)
```

(a)

```
build start!

0.   STM:   ((GOAL * JOIN) NIL NIL)
P3 TRUE
1.   STM:   ((DOWN HAMMER) (GOAL * JOIN) NIL)
P2 TRUE
        OUTPUT FOR LOOK = (nail up)
4.   STM:   ((NAIL UP) (GOAL * JOIN) (UP HAMMER))
P1 TRUE
5.   STM:   ((GOAL * JOIN) (DOWN HAMMER) (NAIL UP))
P2 TRUE
        OUTPUT FOR LOOK = (nail up)
8.   STM:   ((NAIL UP) (GOAL * JOIN) (UP HAMMER)
P1 TRUE
9.   STM:   ((GOAL * JOIN) (DOWN HAMMER) (NAIL UP))
P2 TRUE
        OUTPUT FOR LOOK = (nail flush)
12.   STM:   ((NAIL FLUSH) (GOAL * JOIN) (UP HAMMER))
P4 TRUE
13.   STM:   ((GOAL + JOIN) (NAIL FLUSH) (UP HAMMER))
END:   NO PD TRUE
```

(b)

FIG. 1.5   A simple production system (a) and its trace (b).

Now for the dynamic behavior of the system (Fig. 1.5b). Everything in lower case letters is typed by the model builder, everything in upper case is typed out by the system. The command *build start!* initializes the production system interpreter: STM is set to STMI, the count of actions is set to zero, and a scan of the list of productions in BUILD commences. The first production to be considered is P4. It scans STM for two elements: (GOAL * JOIN), and (NAIL FLUSH). Only the first of these is currently in STM, so P4 is not satisfied. Next P1 looks for the three elements in its condition, and fails. P2 also fails; and finally P3 finds a match between its condition and the elements in STM. Since P3's condition is satisfied, the actions associated with it are taken. In this case the action consists of simply adding a new element (DOWN HAMMER) to the "front" of STM and pushing everything else in STM down one "notch." The current state of STM is printed out in Fig. 1.5 after "1." (to indicate that one action has been taken since the system started).

After a production has "fired," that is, after its condition has been matched and its associated actions have been taken, the production system is re-entered at the top. Thus, after P3 has completed its actions, the list of productions, as listed in BUILD, is tested sequentially once again. P4 and P1 fail again, but this time P2 is satisfied. The two actions in P2 are (DOWN ===> UP) and LOOK. The first of these is an action that modifies an element already in STM: the second element in STM is scanned for DOWN, and it is changed to UP. The action LOOK is, as described above, a call upon the terminal for the output of an as yet unprogrammed routine that is supposed to determine whether the nail is up or flush. At this point, the modeler decided that it was still up, entered (nail up), and returned control to the system. The state of STM after four actions is now printed out. The same basic control cycle is repeated with the determination of which production will fire being entirely dependent upon the contents of STM.

Production Systems in Cognitive Psychology

The above examples will provide the basis for our subsequent use of PSG. Although PSG is the language in which our models will be stated, it is important to note that PSG is not the only representation for stating production systems, and that even PSG allows wide latitude for the final configuration of specific assumptions about the human information-processing system. Two recent studies of the development of seriation skills in young children have used production systems in quite distinct forms. Both Young (1973) and Baylor and Gascon (1974) used production systems to model different levels of performance on seriation tasks; Baylor and Gascon developed a production system language specifically designed for seriation models (Gascon & Baylor, 1973). Both of these approaches are reviewed by Klahr (1976). The paper cited earlier (Newell, 1973) provides a basic introduction to production systems and to the use of PSG, while an extensive general treatment of production systems, independent of any particular programming language, can be found in Newell and Simon (1972). Yet another production system representation and language is utilized by Waterman's (1974) adaptive production systems.

SUMMARY AND OVERVIEW

During the course of cognitive development, the human information-processing system undergoes a sequence of state changes. Changes occur in the "hardware"—in the physical rates and capacities—and in the "software"—in the content and organization of processes and data structures. Since we have limited access to these states, we infer them from behavior. Some of the changes over time in children's performances are so striking, so qualitatively different from

Period 1 to Period 2, and so coherent across tasks presented during Period 1 or during Period 2 that we usually say the child is in a *stage* while within a period, and that he undergoes a *transition* between the two periods.

However, as indicated at the beginning of this chapter, the appealing notion of coherent stages does not withstand careful scrutiny. Performance is generated by interrelated sets of components, each of whose developmental course may be distributed over widely differing time periods. Task variations evoke unknown combinations of such component processes, producing anomalous results for those seeking chronological invariance. One can interpret the observed improvements in performance from one period to the next as the result of either a revolutionary reorganization of the system or as the completion of an incremental process of relatively localized state changes. In either case, the task of developmental psychology is to clarify the nature both of the system that generates the behavior during each period and of the transition process that moves the system from one state to the next.

A theory of transition can be no better than the associated theory of what it is that is undergoing that transition. In this book, we attempt to be explicit and precise about both kinds of theory. The system to be described takes the form of a self-modifying production system. As indicated above, we will describe some very explicit models for various states. The state models will all be cast as running production systems. However, the account of self-modification is not yet sufficiently refined to be a level I theory. Although its referents are the specific state models, it is itself stated at level III.

The substantive focus for this book is the set of tasks associated with the two substages of Piaget's concrete operational stage. These are usually labeled the *preoperational* substage and the substage of *concrete operations* proper. We chose them because the range of tasks on which the division into substages is founded all produce striking differences in children's performance with age. In addition, judging by the inconsistency of the experimental results, the tasks exhibit complex developmental interrelationships.

 Our strategy is to produce models sufficient to account for the patterns of success and failure on tasks that characterize a stage, and then to consider the type of transition process which might transform one such model into the next. Modifications and additions to the information-processing system as a whole will be made as they prove to be necessary in relation to task requirements.

The state theories of task performance are production systems which are sufficient to produce the types of performance they purport to explain. In dealing with each task, we will adopt a gradual approach in which the rationale and empirical background underlying the main features of the model are presented first followed by a full discussion of the details of the production system.

The plan of this volume is as follows: in Chapter 2 we describe an initial example of the formulation of a production system model for a substantively interesting task: quantitative comparison. In subsequent chapters, this model is used as a point of departure for extensions in two directions: (a) downward, to more specific models of the subprocesses utilized by quantitative comparison (Chapter 3); and (b) upward, into three contexts in which quantitative comparison takes place: class inclusion (Chapter 4), conservation (Chapter 5), and transitivity (Chapter 6).

At the end of each of these chapters (3 to 6), we summarize the implications of the task-specific theories for the structure and organization of the information-processing system as a whole. In the two final chapters we attempt to put it all together. Chapter 7 describes the overall nature of an information-processing system that is consistent with, but broader than, the specific models that precede it. Finally, in Chapter 8, we present a theory of the development of the information-processing system.

2
Quantitative Comparison:
A Production System Model

In this chapter we describe a model for quantitative comparison stated in the form of a production system. The didactic goal is to provide another instance of production system models and their dynamic behavior. The example to be presented will include extensions of both the psychological assumptions and the programming conventions of this form of modeling.

The substantive focus is the quantitative comparison process. It is of central importance to the theme of this book, for it provides the integrating thread for all the subsequent chapters. The basic version of the quantitative comparison model presented in this chapter will serve several purposes. First, it will convey the flavor and style of the approach when applied to a real psychological issue: What are the underlying processes required for a system to perform tasks requiring comparison of quantities? Second, it will demonstrate how the model-building enterprise, when performed at the level of exactness facilitated by production systems, enables us to ask new questions about the component processes, questions that would not have been asked if we had not attempted to work at this level. Finally, the model will provide a point of departure for later chapters in which we will extend both the generality and the precision of the initial model presented here.

QUANTITATIVE COMPARISON

The ability to make comparative judgments of quantity is logically required by a substantial proportion of the tasks that are used to assess cognitive development, and it is an explicit determinant of performance on three of the central Piagetian task areas: class inclusion, conservation, and transitivity. Each of these tasks is described and analyzed in great detail in subsequent chapters. For now, we present a very brief indication of the typical form of each task:

1. *Class Inclusion.* The child is shown a mixed collection of, say, 5 red and 2 blue blocks, and asked "Are there more red blocks or more blocks?"

2. *Conservation.* Two collections of pennies are arranged in two parallel rows in one-to-one correspondence. The child is asked to verify the initial quantitative equality of the two collections. Then the pennies in one row are spread apart, and the child is asked which of the two rows has more pennies, or if they are both the same.

3. *Transitivity.* Two upright rods, A and B, of slightly different length are presented, separated sufficiently to ensure that their relative lengths are not immediately discernable. The child is presented with a third rod, X, and told to directly compare A and X. This yields the discovery that $A > X$. Then the child is told to compare X and B, and he discovers that $X > B$. Then he is asked, which is longer A or B?

In this section we will examine—at first informally, and then with increasing exactness—the information-processing requirements of quantitative comparison tasks.

What processes does a child need in order to be able to make quantitative comparisons? In information-processing terms, what is required is the capacity to produce an internal symbol that represents the relative magnitude of two entities. The symbol itself might be represented in several forms: verbally, as an image, or as an abstract structure. Some process must produce this symbol: what subprocesses would a quantitative comparison process need?

First, it would need some way of communicating with its environment—some way to respond to verbal and visual stimuli. It would also need to recall or generate information about each of the quantities it was trying to compare, and finally it would actually need to generate the internal symbol representing the relative magnitudes of the items in question. Now we have a rough idea of the different kinds of processes required for quantitative comparison (QC), but things are still quite imprecise. We can refine this analysis by stating a series of conditionals for QC:

a. If you want to determine which is more, X or Y, then compare them.
b. If you want to compare two things, then determine the relative magnitude of their corresponding quantitative symbols.
c. If you want to relate two symbols, but you do not have two symbols to relate, then generate the appropriate quantitative symbols.
d. If you want to generate a quantitative symbol for X, then apply some quantification operator.

This conditional format is obviously going to facilitate the recasting of the verbal statements into production rules. But the format has another, more subtle, implication. Since the entire immediate knowledge state of a production system consists of symbols in short-term memory (STM), what the system "wants" to do must be explicitly represented. In our models, such information is represented by goals. Short-term memory can contain information not only about the actual results of operations, but also about goals and subgoals. These goals serve to guide the system through its problem-solving steps. The use of goals in problem-solving systems is very common (e.g., Ernst & Newell, 1969), and typically they are kept as distinct pieces of data on a "goal stack." As subgoals are generated, they are placed on top of the goal stack where they have priority, and older goals are temporarily interrupted while their respective subgoals are pursued. Such an approach implies a special memory for goals. In PSG, all goal symbols are intermingled with other symbols in STM. Thus, the entire state of knowledge is represented by the immediate contents of STM.

Before turning to a description of the production system, let us consider the level of analysis or "grain" that it attempts to capture. As noted above, quantitative comparison is pervasive in tasks designed to test for Piaget's stage of concrete operations, and the model for QC should apply to at least this range of tasks. In questions about subclass comparison or class inclusion, the steps outlined above are sufficient. However, in conservation, the idea is to avoid this entire process of quantitative comparison, relying instead upon the results of previous passes through QC and a conservation rule. Thus, we would need to modify the QC model above so that the first thing it tries to do is to use prior information to make an inference about the current situation. We would also need to generalize it to deal with *any* relative magnitude term, not just "more." At the other end of the model, we would like to be as explicit as possible about the form of the processes that produce the quantitative symbols—the quantification operators. It appears that these operators and their development play a central role in developing ability of the child to understand what are commonly termed "quantity concepts" (Gelman, 1972a, b; Gelman & Tucker, 1975; Klahr, 1973b; Klahr & Wallace, 1973). We will first introduce a simple model for QC—one without these additional features—written as a production system; in subsequent chapters we will make the appropriate extensions.

PS.QC1

PS.QC1, a PSG model for quantitative comparison, is listed in Fig. 2.1, and a trace of the model's behavior is shown in Fig. 2.2. In this description—as in all the production system descriptions throughout the book—we will first describe the model in terms of its static form (e.g., the listing in Fig. 2.1), and then describe its dynamic behavior (e.g., the trace in Fig. 2.2).

In some conditions, it is desirable to have variable elements. There are two general forms of variables. In the restricted case, we want to allow a variable to take on a limited and specified set of values. In Fig. 2.1, VAL and REL (lines 800–900) are examples of this type of variable. Whenever VAL appears in a condition element, it can be successfully matched with any member of its class:

```
00100  ;PSQC1
00800  VAL:(CLASS RED BLUE SQUARE ROUND WOOD)
00900  REL:(CLASS = > <)
01000  X1:(VAR)
01100  X2:(VAR)
01200
01300  PROBLEM:(OPR CALL); input (more) (val 1) (val 2).
01400  QUANTIFY:(OPR CALL); input quantitative value: (qs n val).
01500  RELATE:(OPR CALL); relate two symbols. (val rel val).
01600
01700  GOAL MANIPULATION
01800  PA:((GOAL *) (GOAL *) --> (* ===> %))
01900  PZ:((GOAL *) ABS (GOAL %) --> (% ==> *))
02000
02100  MAIN PRODUCTIONS
02200  P1:((GOAL + MORE) (X1 REL X2) --> (OLD **)(SAY X1)(SAY REL)(SAY X2))
02300  P3:((WORD MORE) --> (WORD ==> GOAL *))
02400  P4:((GOAL * MORE) --> (GOAL * COMPARE))
02500  P5:((GOAL + COMPARE) (GOAL % MORE) --> (% ===> +))
02600  P7:( (QS) (QS) (GOAL * COMPARE) -->
02700      (QS ==> OLD QS)(QS ===> OLD QS) RELATE)
02800  P6:((GOAL * COMPARE) (X1 REL) --> (* ==> +))
02900
03000  P9:((GOAL * COMPARE) (VALUE VAL) --> (VALUE ===> OLD VALUE)
03100      (GOAL * QUANTIFY VAL))
03200  P10:((GOAL * QUANTIFY VAL) (QS VAL) --> (* ==> +))
03300
03400  P11:((GOAL * QUANTIFY VAL) --> QUANTIFY)
03500
03600  PDVO:((WORD VAL) --> (WORD ==> VALUE))
03700
03800  PSTART:((GOAL * ATTEND) --> PROBLEM)
03900
04000  PSQC1:(PA PDVO P1 P3 P4 P5 P7 P6 P9 P10 P11 PZ PSTART)
04100  STMI:((GOAL * ATTEND) NIL NIL NIL NIL NIL NIL NIL NIL)
```

FIG. 2.1 PS.QC1: A production system for quantitative comparison.

RED, BLUE, and so on. Similarly, REL can be matched by =, >, or <. In the unrestricted case, any symbol will match the variable. X1 and X2 (lines 1000–1100) are examples of such variables. Their use will become apparent below.

The class variables VAL and REL provide a tiny semantic memory for PS.QC1, since, during the testing of conditions, any of the class members (e.g., RED, BLUE) will be recognized as instances of the class name (e.g., VAL). The matching of these variables is automatic in our models and does not require any explicitly stated search procedure. Although we will use this approximation in all of our running models, it is of questionable psychological validity, and in the final chapters we describe a system in which determination of values, attributes, class memberships, and relations are all accomplished by explicit production system operations.

In lines 1300 to 1500 are three "operator calls" (OPR CALL), named PROBLEM, QUANTIFY, and RELATE. Each one indicates a part of the model for which the model builder, rather than the model, must provide the result of the operator. (Recall that LOOK, in Fig. 1.5, was an operator call.) Operator calls provide an explicit indication of the boundaries of the model: PROBLEM is used to create a symbolic representation in STM of the initial problem statement; QUANTIFY is used to provide a quantitative symbol, as the result of some unmodeled quantification process; RELATE is used to determine the relative magnitude of two internal quantitative symbols. Their use will become clearer below in the description of the productions that use them.

Goal Manipulation

Next in Fig. 2.1 come the goal manipulation productions, PA and PZ (lines 1800–1900). These productions enable the system to treat goals in the same manner as other elements in STM. Their function is to distribute the goal stack throughout STM. If too many things enter STM, it is possible for a goal element to be lost and for the system to "lose track" of what it was trying to do. This seems psychologically plausible. Since goal information is explicitly represented, a STM capacity greater than the classic 7 ± 2 is usually required in these models. However, such estimates are based upon memory load imposed by symbols for task variables over and above the control information that is explicitly represented by goals in this model.

The goal manipulation productions are:

PA: ((GOAL *) (GOAL *) --> (* ===> %))

If there are two active goals in STM, then change the second of the two from an active state to an interrupted state. The most recent one—the first in STM—will remain active. This production ensures that the model is trying to do only one thing at a time. It works in the following way. First, STM is scanned for an element that starts with the subelements GOAL and * (our symbol for active). If it finds one, it then searches for another, different, element of precisely the same form. Suppose we had in STM: (AB (GOAL * XX) C (GOAL * YY) DE). Then PA would match on both of its condition elements. By the rule of automatic rehearsal of matched elements, both of the elements would be moved to the front of STM. Immediately preceding the instant when PA's action side fired, STM would be: ((GOAL * XX) (GOAL * YY) AB C DE). There is a single action for PA. It replaces the symbol * with the symbol %, in the second element in STM. (The first, second, and third STM elements in these replacement actions are indicated by ==>, ===>, and ====>, respectively. This is a clumsy, but convenient programming device. There are several other ways to effect the same result.) The symbol * is used to indicate an active goal. Other goal "tags" are "%" interrupted, "+" satisfied, and "−" failed.

PZ: ((GOAL *) ABS (GOAL %) − −> (% ==> *))

If there are no active goals, and an interrupted goal, then change the interrupted goal to an active goal. The function of PX is to reactivate a goal that had been temporarily interrupted by a higher priority goal—usually a subgoal. (The "ABS" symbol following a condition element means that the condition will not match unless the specified element is *absent* from STM.)

Main Productions

The main productions are listed from lines 2200 to 3400. The order in which they are considered is controlled by the list of production names in PS.QC1 (line 4000). These main productions produce, test, and coordinate the goals and other elements necessary to implement the set of four conditional statements listed at the start of this chapter. Since productions are considered sequentially, in addition to the explicit conditions stating what must be *true* of the current STM state, the location of a production implicitly adds the effective condition "and if all preceding conditions are *false.*" We will describe the productions in the order in which they are tested (the order in which they actually fire will be considered in the description of the trace in Fig. 2.2):

P1:   ((GOAL + MORE) (X1 REL X2) − −>
      (OLD **) (SAY X1) (SAY REL) (SAY X2))

If the goal MORE is satisfied and there is a relational symbol, then tag the satisfied goal as OLD, and output the result. P1 fires when the system has successfully completed its quantification attempt. It is the first of the main productions to be tested because on each pass the system wants to test for whether it has achieved its goal before it continues processing. The actions (OLD **) and (SAY) were described in Chapter 1. P1 uses both kinds of variables described above. In the condition element (X1 REL X2), the two free variables, X1 and X2, will match anything that is separated by a REL, and REL itself will match on =, >, or <. These variable assignments are then available for use by the action side of the production in which they were bound. Looking ahead to the bottom of the trace in Fig. 2.2, we can see the effect of three SAY actions when the matched element is (BLUE > RED).

P3:   ((WORD MORE) − −> (WORD ==> GOAL *))

If you just heard the word "more," then change its encoding into an active goal. P3 changes (WORD MORE) into (GOAL * MORE): its psychological effect is to transform a question into an imperative.

P4:   ((GOAL * MORE) – –> (GOAL * COMPARE))

If the active goal is MORE, then add an active goal COMPARE to STM. This corresponds directly to the first of the four verbal statements for quantitative comparison (see page 17).

P5:   ((GOAL + COMPARE) (GOAL % MORE) – –> (% ===> +))

If there is a satisfied comparison goal and an interrupted MORE goal, then satisfy MORE also. P5 fires when the system has successfully completed the comparison in the service of a MORE goal. Since comparison was successful, so is the attempt to determine which quantity is more.

P7:   ((QS) (QS) (GOAL * COMPARE) – –>
       (QS ==> OLD QS) (QS ===> OLD QS) RELATE)

If the active goal is comparison and you have two quantitative symbols, then mark the two symbols OLD and determine their relative magnitude (RELATE). Quantitative symbols (QS) are produced by quantification operators (to be described). If the system is attempting to compare two collections and it discovers that it has two quantitative symbols, then it executes the action RELATE, which determines the relative magnitude of the two quantitative symbols and produces a relational element [e.g., (RED > BLUE)] in STM. The presence of such a relational element is necessary to satisfy P6 and P1.

P6:   ((GOAL * COMPARE) (X1 REL) – –> (* ==> +))

If the comparison goal is active and there is a relational element, then satisfy the comparison goal. In the context of PS.QC1, the creation of a relational symbol is used to initiate the end of the comparison effort.

P9:   ((GOAL * COMPARE) (VALUE VAL) – –> (VALUE ===> OLD
       VALUE) (GOAL * QUANTIFY VAL))

If your goal is comparison and you have an element with the tag "VALUE," then mark the value OLD–so it won't be processed again–and add an active goal of quantifying that value. If STM had (VALUE RED), then after P9 fired, STM would get the new element (GOAL * QUANTIFY RED). The system only gets to P9 after P7 has failed–that is, when it does not yet have two quantitative symbols with which to determine a relationship. Thus, P9 attempts to remedy the situation by establishing a quantification goal. If quantification is eventually successful, a new QS will be added to STM.

P10:   ((GOAL * QUANTIFY VAL) (QS VAL) – –> (* ==> +))

If the active goal is to quantify some value (e.g., RED), and you have a quantitative symbol for that value (e.g., (QS 5 RED)), then since you have what you want, satisfy the quantification goal.

P11:   ((GOAL * QUANTIFY VAL) – –> QUANTIFY)

If the quantification goal is active (and there is no corresponding symbol, i.e., P10 has failed), then take the action QUANTIFY and attempt to produce an appropriate quantitative symbol.

PDV0:   ((WORD VAL) – –> (WORD ==> VALUE))

If there is an element containing WORD and a member of the class VAL, then change the tag from WORD to VALUE. This is a rudimentary verbal encoding production that transforms the initial encoding of the input statement into a form that is needed by the system.

PSTART is simply an arbitrary way to get the system started by calling upon the modeler, via PROBLEM, to input the starting conditions.

A Trace

A trace of PS.QC1 operating on a subclass comparison is illustrated in Fig. 2.2. The trace shows the state of STM each time that a production is satisfied and its associated actions have been taken. The numbers that precede each STM display indicate the total number of actions that have been taken since the system started. As described above, in several cases the system calls upon the terminal for the output of operators that are not included in programmed form in this production system. The model builder decides what these outputs should be and types them in (indicated by lower case in the trace).

When the system starts, STM is set to STMI. The only production whose condition side is matched by STM elements is PSTART. PSTART has an action named PROBLEM which calls upon the terminal for an input. The input for quantitative comparison is then provided. This input can be viewed as the result of (unmodeled) preliminary linguistic processing of the experimental instructions.

The state of STM after PSTART has completed its actions is shown at (1.). Then the simple verbal encoder, PDV0, changes the WORD tag, having detected that both RED and BLUE are members of the class VAL. Next, P3 converts

```
STMI:((GOAL * ATTEND) NIL NIL NIL NIL NIL NIL NIL NIL)
0.   STM: ((GOAL * ATTEND) NIL NIL NIL NIL NIL NIL NIL NIL)
        PSTART TRUE
        OUTPUT FOR PROCESS : (word more)(word red)(word blue)

1.   STM: ((WORD BLUE) (WORD RED) (WORD MORE) (GOAL * ATTEND) NIL NIL NIL NIL NIL)
        PDV0 TRUE
2.   STM: ((VALUE BLUE) (WORD RED) (WORD MORE) (GOAL * ATTEND) NIL NIL NIL NIL NIL)
        PDV0 TRUE
3.   STM: ((VALUE RED) (VALUE BLUE) (WORD MORE) (GOAL * ATTEND) NIL NIL NIL NIL NIL)
        PA TRUE
4.   STM: ((GOAL * MORE) (VALUE RED) (VALUE BLUE) (GOAL * ATTEND) NIL NIL NIL NIL NIL)
        PA TRUE
5.   STM: ((GOAL * MORE) (GOAL % ATTEND) (VALUE RED) (VALUE BLUE) NIL NIL NIL NIL NIL)
        P4 TRUE
6.   STM: ((GOAL * COMPARE) (GOAL * MORE) (GOAL % ATTEND) (VALUE RED) (VALUE BLUE) NIL NIL NIL NIL)
        PA TRUE
7.   STM: ((GOAL * COMPARE) (GOAL % MORE) (GOAL % ATTEND) (VALUE RED) (VALUE BLUE) NIL NIL NIL NIL)
        P9 TRUE
9.   STM: ((GOAL * QUANTIFY RED) (GOAL * COMPARE) (OLD VALUE RED) (GOAL % MORE) (GOAL % ATTEND)
            (VALUE BLUE) NIL NIL NIL)
        PA TRUE
10.  STM: ((GOAL * QUANTIFY RED) (GOAL % COMPARE) (OLD VALUE RED) (GOAL % MORE) (GOAL % ATTEND)
            (VALUE BLUE) NIL NIL NIL)
        P11 TRUE
        OUTPUT FOR PROCESS : (qs 1 red)

11.  STM: ((QS 1 RED) (GOAL * QUANTIFY RED) (GOAL % COMPARE) (OLD VALUE RED) (GOAL % MORE) (GOAL % ATTEND)
            (VALUE BLUE) NIL NIL)
        P10 TRUE
12.  STM: ((GOAL + QUANTIFY RED) (QS 1 RED) (GOAL % COMPARE) (OLD VALUE RED) (GOAL % MORE) (GOAL % ATTEND)
            (VALUE BLUE) NIL NIL)
        PZ TRUE
13.  STM: ((GOAL * COMPARE) (GOAL + QUANTIFY RED) (QS 1 RED) (OLD VALUE RED) (GOAL % MORE) (GOAL % ATTEND)
            (VALUE BLUE) NIL NIL)
        P9 TRUE
15.  STM: ((GOAL * QUANTIFY BLUE) (GOAL * COMPARE) (OLD VALUE BLUE) (GOAL + QUANTIFY RED) (QS 1 RED)
            (OLD VALUE RED) (GOAL % MORE) (GOAL % ATTEND) NIL)
        PA TRUE
16.  STM: ((GOAL * QUANTIFY BLUE) (GOAL % COMPARE) (OLD VALUE BLUE) (GOAL + QUANTIFY RED) (QS 1 RED)
            (OLD VALUE RED) (GOAL % MORE) (GOAL % ATTEND) NIL)
        P11 TRUE
        OUTPUT FOR PROCESS : (qs 2 blue)

17.  STM: ((QS 2 BLUE) (GOAL * QUANTIFY BLUE) (GOAL % COMPARE) (OLD VALUE BLUE) (GOAL + QUANTIFY RED)
            (QS 1 RED) (OLD VALUE RED) (GOAL % MORE) (GOAL % ATTEND))
        P10 TRUE
18.  STM: ((GOAL + QUANTIFY BLUE) (QS 2 BLUE) (GOAL % COMPARE) (OLD VALUE BLUE) (GOAL + QUANTIFY RED)
            (QS 1 RED) (OLD VALUE RED) (GOAL % MORE) (GOAL % ATTEND))
        PZ TRUE
19.  STM: ((GOAL * COMPARE) (GOAL + QUANTIFY BLUE) (QS 2 BLUE) (OLD VALUE BLUE) (GOAL + QUANTIFY RED)
            (QS 1 RED) (OLD VALUE RED) (GOAL % MORE) (GOAL % ATTEND))
        P7 TRUE
        OUTPUT FOR PROCESS : (blue > red)

22.  STM: ((BLUE > RED) (OLD QS 2 BLUE) (OLD QS 1 RED) (GOAL * COMPARE) (GOAL + QUANTIFY BLUE) (OLD VALUE BLUE)
            (GOAL + QUANTIFY RED) (OLD VALUE RED) (GOAL % MORE))
        P6 TRUE
23.  STM: ((GOAL + COMPARE) (BLUE > RED) (OLD QS 2 BLUE) (OLD QS 1 RED) (GOAL + QUANTIFY BLUE) (OLD VALUE BLUE)
            (GOAL + QUANTIFY RED) (OLD VALUE RED) (GOAL % MORE))
        P5 TRUE
24.  STM: ((GOAL + COMPARE) (GOAL + MORE) (BLUE > RED) (OLD QS 2 BLUE) (OLD QS 1 RED) (GOAL + QUANTIFY BLUE)
            (OLD VALUE BLUE) (GOAL + QUANTIFY RED) (OLD VALUE RED))
        P1 TRUE

********** BLUE

********** >

********** RED

28.  STM: ((OLD (GOAL + MORE)) (BLUE > RED) (GOAL + COMPARE) (OLD QS 2 BLUE) (OLD QS 1 RED) (GOAL + QUANTIFY BLUE)
            (OLD VALUE BLUE) (GOAL + QUANTIFY RED) (OLD VALUE RED))
```

FIG. 2.2   A trace of PS.QC1 on the question "More red or more blue?"

(WORD MORE) to the active goal (GOAL * MORE). Note that we are using automatic rehearsal in STM for those elements that fire a production. As new elements are added, any elements in STM that are *not* matched by condition elements get pushed further and further down until they eventually drop out of STM. For example, a scan of Fig. 2.2 from (6) to (22) shows the element (GOAL % ATTEND) being pushed down and out of STM. The interrupted goal (GOAL % MORE) is just about to drop out of STM (23) when P5 matches (and modifies) it (24).

Returning to (4), P3 moves (WORD MORE) to the front of STM and modifies it to (GOAL * MORE). Since this is a modification of an existing element, there are as many elements in STM at (4) as at (3). PA detects two active goals and interrupts the older one (5). P4 *adds* a new element to the front of STM, (GOAL * COMPARE), pushing all else down one "notch."

PA again detects two active goals, so now it interrupts MORE, leaving COMPARE active. Next, P9 detects both the active comparison goal and a value element. It fires, establishing the quantification goal, which then preempts comparison (via PA) as the active goal. At this point (10) we can describe the system's knowledge state as follows:

It wants to quantify the red things,	(GOAL * QUANTIFY RED)
because it's trying to do a comparison,	(GOAL % COMPARE)
in order to determine which is more,	(GOAL % MORE)
and it has used the value RED so far	(OLD VALUE RED)
but not the value blue.	(VALUE BLUE).

Now P11 is satisfied, resulting in the action QUANTIFY, an operator that calls on the terminal for the hypothesized output from a quantification operator. The element (QS 1 RED) is the result of a human simulation of a quantifier that scans the hypothetical display for red things and creates a quantitative symbol for one red thing. (Notice that at this level we have no model of quantification per se; however, we have indicated the necessity for quantification operators of some sort. We will return to this issue in detail at a later point.) The tag QS is the notation for a quantitative symbol, and the numeral 1 is an arbitrary (but convenient) symbol for a specific value. The tag will be used directly by other productions, while the value will be used by another terminal call for an operator that determines the relative magnitude of quantitative symbols.

The behavior of PS.QC1 between (4) and (12) can be summarized: Given a goal of determining which of two values is MORE, a subgoal of COMPARE is generated; this, together with a VAL, generates a subsubgoal of QUANTIFY for that value; this fires the quantification operator, which produces a quantitative symbol, which in turn satisfies the quantification goal. But two quantitative symbols are required for a comparison, and at this point only one exists; thus, the sequence is repeated (13)–(19).

Now P7 detects that the relationship between the two quantitative symbols can be determined by the operator RELATE. Since this is also a terminal call, the system asks for the result of the relational operator. Once this relationship is provided, the comparison goal is satisfied (23), then the goal of determining more is satisfied (24). Finally the system "says" the result (following P1 TRUE), and stops (28).

SOME COMMENTS ON THE MODEL

Having poured over this description (several times perhaps) the skeptical reader might begin to wonder just what the worth of the model is. In a model of quantitative comparison, two key processes remain unmodeled (i.e., terminal calls): quantification (QUANTIFY), and the determination of relative magnitude (RELATE). What then does PS.QC1 tell us?

First, it tells us that even something as "simple" as subclass comparison, when examined in detail, requires a nontrivial amount of information processing on the part of the child. In particular, goals and subgoals must be generated and coordinated, some minimal linguistic encoding must take place in order to "drive" the problem-solving, and some processes for the generation and coordination of quantitative symbols must be available. Second, PS.QC1 provides a specific explication of some of these functions in processing terms, and it tells us precisely what is yet to be modeled: those processes that are only terminal calls. Finally, at the conceptual level, a model like this enables us to make unambiguous distinctions between what would otherwise be nearly synonymous verbal labels: for example, between quantitative comparison (which is the function of PS.QC1), and the determination of the relative magnitude of two internal symbols (which is the function of RELATE).

The model is sufficient to do the task under consideration and simple variants. For example, if the system had knowledge about the two desired quantities from the outset, it would still function correctly. Suppose that the task were posed verbally in the form "If I have 3 reds and 2 blues do I have more reds or more blues?" If the initial encoding was STM: ((WORD MORE) (WORD RED) (WORD BLUE) (QS 3 RED) (QS 2 BLUE)), then the following sequence of productions would fire: PDV0, PDV0, P3, PA, P4, PA, P7, P6, P5, P1. Notice that this sequence contains none of the processing required to produce quantitative symbols that we saw in Fig. 2.2. For more extensive task variations, the model provides an adequate core of productions that can be modified to meet the new task demands. When PS.QC1 is expanded in later chapters to deal with class inclusion, conservation, and transitivity, the basic logic will remain unchanged.

By casting the model as a production system, we have an explicit statement of the requisite control information that determines what the model must do next at each step of processing. As we noted above, this model consists of almost nothing *but* such control statements, since the two processes that one might expect to be central to quantitative comparison are not even modeled.

The basic processing cycle in a production system is recognize–act. When the condition side of a production matches some elements in STM, that production has recognized some relevant aspects of the current knowledge state. The production then fires, acting upon that recognized state. In this sense, *all* information in STM is used as control information. PS.QC1 explicitly represents information about what processing to do next as well as the results of that processing. This representation is particularly well suited to modeling developmentally interesting tasks, for difficulties with the coordination and integration of basic elements appear to lie at the root of many developmental problems (Farnham-Diggory, 1970, 1972; Resnick & Glaser, 1976). It is clear from PS.QC1 that failure on a subclass comparison question could be generated by a system that has correct processes for both RELATE and QUANTIFY, but which lacks the appropriate coordinating productions.

This model has had value to us as a heuristic for guiding much of the research to be reported in this book. PS.QC1 grew out of our initial attempts to build a production system for class inclusion (CI) (Klahr & Wallace, 1972). In Chapter 4 we will offer an extensive treatment of CI. The interesting stage of development upon which we focused our model is one in which the child is successful with subclass comparisons (e.g., dogs versus cats) but unsuccessful with CI (e.g., cats versus pets). In such a model, one can begin to consider the exact location of the cause of failure with CI. As we shall argue in Chapter 4, the difficulty appears to be in the input to the quantification operators rather than in the goal manipulation productions or in the quantification processes per se. Consideration of these quantification processes raises the question of how the stimulus is encoded and internally represented. In PS.QC1, since quantification is not modeled, we avoided that issue. However, once we extended the model to directly quantify a symbolic representation of the stimulus, we had to make explicit statements about the interaction between the quantifiers and the stimulus being quantified. These questions led us to an investigation into the nature of quantification operators in children and adults, and in Chapter 3 we report the results of that inquiry.

Consideration of the stimulus representation issue also made it clear that direct quantification is not the only potential source of quantitative symbols in class-inclusion tasks. Depending upon the form of the CI task, the symbols could be directly provided, retrieved from LTM, or inferred from semantic categories (also in LTM). We have already provided an example of direct input (If I have 3 dogs and . . . etc.). Long-term memory retrieval would be adequate for questions where the subject has initial notions of the relative sizes of sets (e.g., Are there more trout or more bugs in the pond?) when, in fact, no direct quantification is possible. Semantic categories involve CI questions where the solution could be generated from set inclusion relations without either direct or indirect quantification (e.g., More animals or more bears?). The analysis in Chapter 4 is restricted to what we call *formal* class inclusion, as distinct from the semantically derivable relations. For example, when presented with some red and blue squares, the child cannot draw on preexisting semantic structure relating reds to squares. He must encode the presented stimulus. This distinction is rarely made in the CI literature (for an interesting exception, see Wilkinson, 1975), and we raise it here to suggest another advantage of formulating precise and detailed process models.

Finally, it seemed to us that one could view conservation and transitivity tasks as situations where the results of quantitative comparison had to be linked to some inferential rules—rules that would obviate the need for further quantifying or relating. In Chapters 5 and 6 we will describe models for conversation and transitivity based upon the initial model, PS.QC1, presented here. The linkage to those models involves an expansion of P3—the production that generates the COMPARE goal when faced with the MORE goal. If a child "has" conservation or transitivity, then he has rules which enable him to satisfy the MORE goal without necessarily going through the comparison processes of PS.QC1. The details of this argument will be presented in subsequent chapters.

3

Processes for Quantification

This chapter provides the basis for the next three in terms of its substantive focus, its formalisms, and its influence upon our overall theoretical orientation. The focus is upon quantification: the ability of humans to determine how much or how many or how big. The processes for quantification are—by definition—elementary with respect to the higher level tasks that utilize them (to be discussed in Chapters 4, 5, and 6). However, the characterization of any process as "elementary" is arbitrary and relative. Our models for quantification processes are production systems containing their own "elementary" components (productions), each of which is in turn composed of several complex components. Our discussion of the various quantification models will span several such levels; that is, we will consider both the contents of individual productions and their overall organization into a production system.

We will argue in this chapter and in later ones that the "elementary" quantification processes are of fundamental importance not only because higher level processes could not function without them, but also because they play a crucial role in the *development* of those higher level processes. Thus, in this chapter our description of quantification processes provides a developmental point of entry for subsequent chapters.

The models we propose to account for the empirical results of studies of quantification are ultimately cast as production systems. As we attempt to evaluate several production system models for different quantification processes we will extend the preliminary account of the overall system architecture provided in Chapter 1. In so doing, we will begin the first of a series of modifications to the structure and functioning of the basic information-processing system (IPS) that appear to be necessary to account for cognitive development. This general cycle of task analysis, production system formulation, and extensions to the basic IPS will be repeated throughout the book, culminating in Chapters 7 and 8 with a broad theoretical statement of the nature and development of the IPS.

This chapter is organized as follows: first there is a brief overview of the three main kinds of quantification operators: *subitizing, counting,* and *estimation.* Then follow extensive descriptions of the first two of these three: subitizing and counting. For both of these operators we first describe the experimental results and then present a series of models to account for those results. The models start as informal "black box" flow charts, and become, ultimately, running programs in PSG. In describing these models we have attempted to convey some of the flavor of how we have gone about refining, extending, and evaluating production system models. Following the subitizing and counting sections, the third operator, estimation, is treated at a less formal level, and then a sketch is provided of the developmental relations among these three operators. The developmental course of quantitative abilities is the central theme in this book, and the treatment of this chapter merely sketches the outlines of our theory. It will be extended in Chapter 5 and fully elaborated in Chapter 8. Following the initial discussion of the developmental relationships, we describe the core of the quantitative comparison process—relative magnitude determination—and its relation to the developing quantification operators. Next we discuss one—one correspondence and argue that it should not be viewed as a basic quantification operator. Finally, we end the chapter with a brief statement about the form of the necessary extensions to the basic IPS.

QUANTIFICATION OPERATORS: OVERVIEW

The necessity for the existence of quantification operators becomes apparent in the information-processing analysis of a wide variety of tasks, including the three to be considered in later chapters. In class inclusion, conservation, and transitivity tasks, the child is required to make quantitative comparisons between two or more collections. In order to carry out these comparisons he must have quantitative symbols corresponding to each of the collections, and in order to generate such symbols, he must have quantification operators.

A quantification operator is a production system which operates upon the information in the environment in accordance with a target to be quantified (such as "red dot") and as a result places a quantitative symbol corresponding to the target in STM. Quantitative symbols are semantic elements that constitute acceptable input to quantitative comparison production systems. Given two such symbols, the comparison systems can determine their relative magnitudes. In contrast, if two qualitative symbols are present in STM, comparison is confined to determining whether they are the same or different.

There is evidence that humans employ three distinct quantification operators: we will refer to them as subitizing, counting, and estimation. As a first step in introducing them we will attempt to provide a subjective impression of the differences in nature of the three quantification operators. The three displays presented later in this chapter constitute the necessary stimuli. Before turning to them, you should read this paragraph. Each of the displays consists of a number of dots. In order to obtain the appropriate subjective impression, you should first familiarize yourself with the task and then turn to the page indicated:

a. Determine as rapidly as possible how many dots the display on page 69 contains.
b. Determine the number of dots displayed on page 71 as rapidly as possible without making any errors.
c. Allowing yourself only a brief sight of the display lasting approximately a second, determine how many dots there are on page 73.

In the first task, people typically report that the answer is immediately obvious without any awareness of conscious calculation. This is indicative of the operation of subitizing. In the second task, there is usually a clear awareness of counting: attending to individual dots and sequencing through the list of number names. (Some people respond to this task by subitizing small groups of dots and adding the results to obtain the total. We will discuss this approach later.) The third task gives rise to introspective reports of some sort of "thinking," but it is unclear what has been considered in the process of producing an answer. This is typical of the functioning of estimation.

SUBITIZING: THEORETICAL AND EMPIRICAL BACKGROUND

The early psychological studies of what came to be called subitizing were centered upon the existence and extent of "immediate apprehension." The empirical question was whether the time required to quantify a collection of n items presented to view was independent of n, and if so, for what values of n. If a process such as immediate apprehension really existed, it would generate results like those shown in Fig. 3.1a, when reaction time (RT) was plotted as a function of n. The upper limit of the subitizing process—that is, the "span of apprehension"—would be the point at which B, the slope of RT versus n, became nonzero. Results from the very early studies seemed to support such a model with an upper value of n approximately equal to 6 or 7 (e.g., Jevons, 1871). Von Szeliski (1924) reported a continuous curve, such as that shown in Fig. 3.1b, arguing that there was no special subitizing process. During the late 1940s there was a brief controversy reported in a series of papers that presented evidence supporting or refuting these positions (Jensen, Reese, & Reese, 1950; Kaufman, Lord, Reese, & Volkmann, 1949; Saltzman & Garner, 1948). The final outcome of that exchange, reviewed by Woodworth and Schlosberg (1954) and further supported by experiments of our own (to be described below), is that two processes were operating to produce results such as those shown in Fig. 3.1c.

When we first began to attempt to determine the effect of different quantification processes upon children's performance on logical tasks, we found that for all its familiarity as a phenomenon, subitizing was essentially unexplained (and a bit unloved). For example, Beckwith and Restle (1966) found it "... amazing that although everyone knows that objects are enumerated by counting, most studies of enumeration or the judgment of number have attempted to rule out counting and ensure that only the primitive method of guessing is employed [p. 439]." However, after an empirical study of counting, they were forced to conclude that simple enumeration is inadequate to account for the fact that

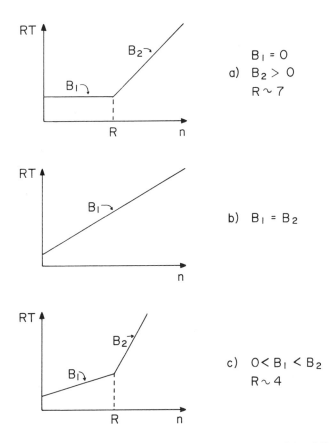

FIG. 3.1   Predicted reaction time as a function of n for three models of "immediate apprehension."

"assemblies of discrete objects are perceived in groups," and they retain the term "subitizing" for the "somewhat mysterious but very rapid and accurate perceptual method [p. 443]" of quantification.

Two different procedures have been used for investigating subitizing. In both procedures a collection of n items (usually a random dot pattern) is presented to view and subjects are told to respond by indicating (usually verbally) the number of items in the collection. In the *threshold* procedure, the items are exposed to view for brief periods and the subject's task is to respond as accurately as possible. The usual result of interest is the functional relation between exposure duration and the error rate for different values of n (e.g., Averbach, 1963). In the *latency* procedure, the display remains visible until the subject responds, and the subject is instructed either for speed or for accuracy. The important result from this latter procedure is the functional relation between n and reaction time (e.g., Fig. 3.1). Another measure that has been used in both procedures is the subject's report of his confidence in his own judgment (Kaufman *et al.*, 1949).

In almost every early study of quantification in the range $1 \leqslant n \leqslant 30$, striking discontinuities occur in the region of $n = 6 \pm 1$. This is true for plots of confidence versus n, reaction time versus n, and error rate versus n. These discontinuities define subitizing: it is the process that produces the results up to the point of discontinuity. After that point other processes are in operation.

There are two parameters associated with subitizing: (i) R, the upper limit of the range of n over which the subitizing process operates, and (ii) B, the slope of the least squares linear regression line of reaction time as a function of n, for $1 \leqslant n \leqslant R$. As mentioned above, the early studies of span of apprehension sought to determine the value of R for which B was zero. Even when it became apparent that B was nonzero, the focus was still upon the existence or nonexistence of a discontinuity in slope. None of the existing studies report the slope B, and one must extract it from the tables and figures of the early papers.[1]

The values of R and B have had varied estimates. Woodworth and Schlosberg (1954) estimate R to be 8, while Jensen *et al.* (1950) estimate $R \sim 5$ and 6. B has been found to be $\sim$50 msec by Saltzman and Garner (1948), 120 msec by Kaufman *et al.* (1949), and 130 msec by Jensen *et al.* (1950). The discrepant findings may be due to both procedural variations (e.g., speed versus accuracy instructions, different visual angles subtended by displays) and analytic variations (reports of means versus medians, inclusion or exclusion of error trials). Furthermore, for any collection of data, B is a function of the choice of R. Thus, we must specify a procedure for unambiguously determining R before we can precisely measure B.

Beyond R, in the range of approximately $7 < n < 30$, the slope has been found to be $\sim$340 msec by both Jensen *et al.* (1950) and Beckwith and Restle (1966).

---

[1] See Klahr (1973b, pp. 8–9) for the exact sources of these estimates.

Experiment 1

In order to further refine these parameters and to determine the effects of certain stimulus variables upon the subitizing operator, we ran a series of experiments. The first experiment was designed to determine whether or not the 50-msec and 300-msec slopes that can be teased out of the old data would be replicable. A secondary purpose was to accurately determine the value of R and the effects of visual angle and pattern density.

Subjects, materials, and apparatus. Three adult subjects were individually presented with patterns of 1 to 20 dots randomly generated (according to a scheme described below) on a standard video monitor controlled by a computer. Their responses triggered a voice-actuated relay which was sensed by the computer, yielding latency measurements accurate to the nearest millisecond, from the time the pattern appeared on the screen until the relay was activated. Dot patterns were generated by locating dots along the borders of a set of concentric squares formed by the perimeters of $m \times m$ grids ($m = 3, 5, 7, 9$). The grid lines were about 0.5 inches apart. Up to five dots were distributed randomly among the p possible locations on an $m \times m$ perimeter (the number of possible dot locations, p, on an $m \times m$ perimeter is $p = 4(m - 1)$. There were two display conditions. In the *inner* condition, for a given value of n, the first five dots were located on the innermost square, the next five dots on the immediately surrounding square, and so on, until n dots were distributed. In the *outer* condition, dots were distributed from the outside (9×9) square inward, five to a perimeter, until all n dots were distributed. Figure 3.2 shows the grid scheme and a few typical patterns in the inner and outer conditions.

Procedure and design. Subjects were seated about 2 ft in front of the video monitor, placed at eye level. At the start of each trial, the word "READY" was displayed in the center of the screen. The subject pressed the response button and the dot pattern appeared on the screen. The subject then responded by saying the number of dots he saw. This activated the relay and removed the pattern from the screen. The response was then entered through a keyboard connected to the computer. Then the next trial began. For each value of n there were eight patterns generated in the inner condition and eight in the outer. For each subject there was a total of 320 trials.

Results. The response latencies for errorless trials, averaged over the three subjects and both display conditions, are plotted in Fig. 3.3. There appears to be a slope discontinuity in the region of $n = 5$. The slope of the regression line for $n = 1$–4 is 57 msec and for $n = 5$–20 it is about 300 msec. If $n = 5$ is included in the lower regression, the slope is about 77 msec.

The effects of inner/outer display interacts with n as indicated in Fig. 3.4. For $n < 8$, the outer condition always takes longer, but above that, no consistent relationship emerges. As indicated in Fig. 3.2, there is a complex interaction

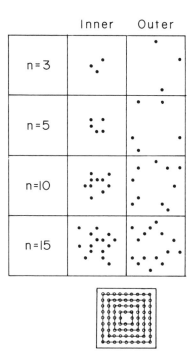

FIG. 3.2   Grid scheme and some typical patterns.

between visual angle, pattern density, and n. The inner grid subtends a visual angle of about $2.5°$, while the outer grids subtend about $8.5°$. For low n, the consistently greater latencies for the outer patterns could be the result of either additional eye movements, or more nonfoveal processing.

Experiment 1 indicated that indeed two processes are operating when subjects perform this task. The slope of the lower line (77 msec) and the point of slope discontinuity ($n = 5$) are similar to the scanning rate and capacity of STM, and they suggested to us that there might be a relationship between scanning STM and subitizing. This led us to explore the reliability of the empirical findings and their invariance over such perceptual factors as visual angle and eye movement, and cognitive factors such as the subjects' awareness of the range of n.

Experiment 2

In Experiment 2 in the series, we investigated the effect of varying the range of n and informing the subject of this range. We also wanted to get a larger group of subjects and further explore the effect of visual angle.

Subjects, materials, procedure, and design. Twelve subjects, students and faculty from our Psychology Department, served as volunteers. The same com-

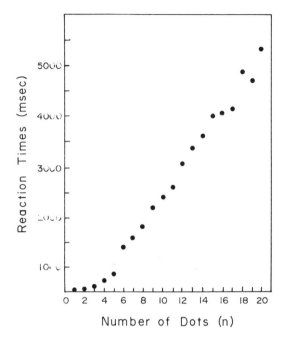

FIG. 3.3   Mean RT for 3 subjects with $n = 1$–20.

puter-controlled apparatus was used with three ranges of n: 1–5, 1–10, and 10–20. For each range the same inner/outer display condition was used. However, the subjects were now located so that the inner patterns for $n < 10$ were entirely within foveal view. For each of the three ranges of n there were 16 trials of each n value, appropriately randomized. At the start of a block of trials for a given range of n, the subject was told what that range would be.

The same general procedure was followed as in Experiment 1. The subject was instructed to fixate the "A" in "READY" before pressing the response button. After a delay of 1.5 sec, the dot pattern was displayed.

Results. The main result is shown in Fig. 3.5, a plot of mean error-free RT against n for the three ranges of n (the upper ranges have been omitted for display purposes). The slope of RT versus n for $n \leqslant 5$ is around 70 msec and for $n > 5$ it is about 270 msec. However, these results require closer analysis. We are attempting to determine the rate of two different processes as well as which process is operating. Thus, we did some curve fitting for different subranges of the range actually used. In particular, we systematically included or excluded the point $n = 5$ in the linear regressions. The results are shown in the top half of Table 3.1. When only points 1–4 are considered (Analyses 2 and 4), we get slopes of 66 and 72 msec for ranges of $n = 1$–5 and $n = 1$–10, respectively. These are not significantly different. When point 5 is included, the slope goes down to 58 msec for $n = 1$–5 (Analysis 1) and up to 110 msec for $n = 1$–10 (Analysis 5).

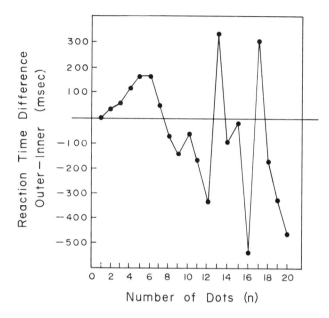

FIG. 3.4   Difference in mean RT between outer and inner conditions.

Our initial explanation for these results (Klahr, 1973a) was that in the case of $n = 1-10$, we were observing the effects of averaging trials and/or subjects for which $n = 5$ is sometimes subitized and sometimes counted. In the case of $n = 1-5$, we were observing an "end error." Once he determines that n is not 1, 2, 3, or 4, the subject responds "5" by default, rather than by a "positive" test for five items. If the time to make this decision were less than the subitizing rate, this would lower the regression slope.

If we look at the results for a single subject in order to eliminate the intersubject averaging, we still find the same effect. Figure 3.6 shows the results for a single subject over the range $n = 1-5$ in the conditions with $n = 1-5$ and $n = 1-10$, with the regression line for the first four points. This is typical of the analysis of individual subjects (see also Table 3.1, Analyses 10 and 11).

Finally, we used a more objective procedure to determine R. Separate analyses of variance and trend analysis were performed for $n = 1-3$, $n = 1-4$, and so on, until a significant quadratic component appeared. The subitizing range was defined by the first appearance of a quadratic trend. Then a linear regression was run independently over the upper and lower subranges of n.

A significant quadratic trend appeared for $n = 1-4$, but not for $n = 1-3$. Therefore, a least squares fit was applied to the first three points, yielding a slope of 46 msec and an intercept of 495 msec. For the upper curve, fit to the range $n = 4-10$, the slope and intercept are 307 msec, and -442 msec, respectively. The results are summarized in Table 3.1 (Analyses 3 and 6).

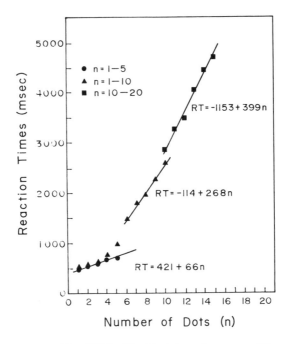

FIG. 3.5 Mean RT for 12 subjects in each range condition.

Errors are shown at the bottom of Fig. 3.8. Within the subitizing range, the overall error rate is 0.87%, and there are no significant differences among error rates for n = 1–3. Similarly, in the counting range, there are no significant differences in errors except for n = 10; however, the overall error rate for counting (8.9%) is significantly higher than for subitizing.

Experiment 3

Although the arrangement of the dot patterns within foveal view eliminates the necessity of eye movements, it does not directly control eye movements. In the third experiment in the series, Michelene Chi (Chi, 1973) used eye movement recording apparatus. This enabled us to analyze only those trials on which no eye movements occurred, thus giving a subitizing rate uncontaminated by eye movement latencies. Stimuli in the range n = 1–5 were used in essentially the same configuration as in the earlier experiments. Some changes in procedure were required by the eye movement recording equipment (see Chi, 1973), and a subject who had served in the previous two experiments was used. A videotape was made of a superimposed image of the stimulus field and the subject's fixations within the field using equipment designed by John Gould (Gould & Peeples, 1970). An analysis of the tapes allowed us to detect those trials on

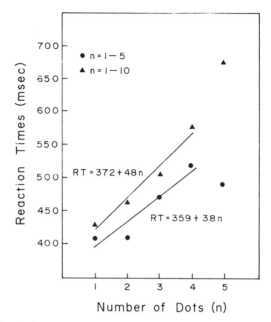

FIG. 3.6 Mean RT for single subject in Experiment 2 with n = 1–4 in conditions n = 1–5 and n = 1–10.

which eye movements did not occur and to treat them separately in the analysis.

In the inner condition, eye movements occurred on less than 10% of the trials, while in the outer condition they occurred on about 45% of the trials. If we include only those trials with a single fixation, we get the results shown in Fig. 3.7. These results are summarized in Table 3.1 (Analyses 12 and 13), along with other slopes for this same subject in Experiment 2 (Analyses 10 and 11). For this subject, the slope for subitizing is 25 msec per item.

Experiment 4

In this experiment, we studied the quantification rates of children. Twelve 5-year-old children participated, and the same general procedure was followed as in Experiment 2. (See Chi & Klahr, 1975 for details.) The latency results obtained with dot patterns in the range n = 1–8 are presented in Fig. 3.8, along with the final analysis from Experiment 2.

The break in the curve seems to occur between n = 3 and 4. This is supported by the fact that a significant quadratic component exists for n = 1–4, whereas no significant quadratic trend exists for n = 1–3. Hence, a linear regression was fit to the first three points, yielding a slope of 195.2 msec and intercept of 744.4 msec. Least square fit was also applied to the upper curve (n = 4–7) with n = 8

TABLE 3.1

Results of Linear Regression for Experiments 2, 3, and 4

Analysis	Subjects	Stimulus range	Analysis range	Intercept (msec)	Slope (msec/dot)	R^2	RMSD[a] (msec)
1	Exp. 2	1–5	1–5	436	58	97.6	12.7
2	(12 adults)		1–4	421	66	99.0	7.2
3		1–10	1–3	495	46	94.3	3.4
4			1–4	451	72	91.6	24.3
5			1–5	375	110	87.0	57.9
6			4–10	−442	307	98.0	65.0
7			6–10	−114	268	99.4	30.3
8			1–10	10	247	95.5	153.7
9		10–20	10–20	−1153	399	98.9	134.0
10	Exp. 2	1–10	1–4	372	48	97.0	9.7
11	(single adult)	1–5	1–4	359	38	89.0	14.9
12	Exp. 3	1–5	1–4[b]	342	25	97.9	4.1
13	(single adult)		1–4[c]	308	60	90.1	22.2
14	Exp. 4	1–8	1–3	744	195	94.2	39.4
15	(12 children)		4–10	−1774	1049	99.1	109.6

[a] Root-mean-squared deviation.
[b] Single fixation.
[c] More than one fixation.

excluded because the children tended to guess or estimate that a pattern of dots was 8 whenever 7 or 8 dots appeared. This is supported in part by the observation that the error rate for 7 is much greater than for 8 (41.4% versus 29.1%). The slope and intercept for $n = 4$–7 are 1049 msec and −1774 msec (Table 3.1, Analyses 14 and 15).

The overall error rate within the subitizing range ($n = 1$–3) is 1.57%. Error rates in the range $n = 1$–4 are not significantly different from each other (although the RTs are much slower for $n = 4$). For $n = 4$–7 there is a significant increase in error rates, and the overall error rate, 22.8%, is significantly higher than the error rate in the subitizing range.

Summary of the Four Experiments

It is clear that there are at least two quantification processes operating in the range studied here. Figure 3.8 summarizes the most important findings. The

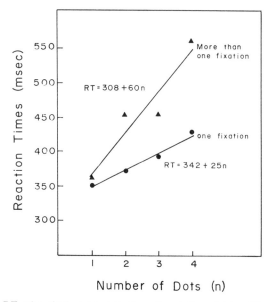

FIG. 3.7 Mean RT of a single subject in Experiment 3 on trials with and without eye movements (n = 1–5).

adult results are from Experiment 2 in the n = 1–10 condition; and the children's results are from Experiment 4. For adults "the" average subitizing rate is 46 msec, while for children it is 195 msec.[2] If we maintain the strict definition of subitizing as the point beyond which a nonlinear trend appears in the regression analysis, then the range for both adults and five-year-old children is n = 1–3.[3]

A MODEL FOR SUBITIZING

In this section we describe a model that accounts for the adult reaction times in subitizing. We defer until Chapter 8 a discussion of the child–adult differences. The model to be presented differs in several fundamental ways from an earlier

[2] Although for two subjects in Experiment 3 the rate without eye movements was 26 msec, the procedure used there makes those results somewhat subjective. Since the subjects had to use a bite bar to maintain a stable head orientation, they could not respond verbally. Instead, they pressed a button to indicate that they thought they were done quantifying. When told the correct answer, they indicated with a hand movement whether they had correctly quantified the stimulus. Thus we have chosen to use the 46-msec average from Experiment 2, even though Experiment 3 suggests that it is inflated by eye movements.

[3] It is, of course, possible that the adult or child subitizing limit might be as high as 4 or 5, and that the nonlinearity is introduced by averaging over values of n for which the pattern is on some trials subitized and on others counted.

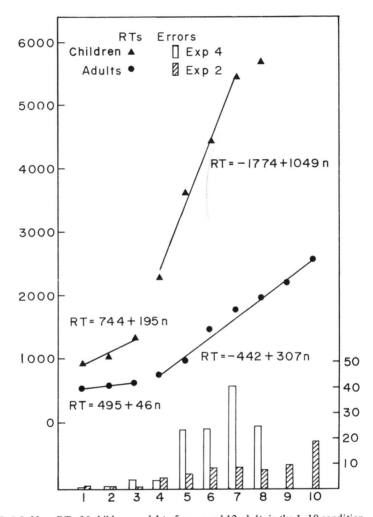

FIG. 3.8 Mean RT of 6 children aged 4 to 5 years and 12 adults in the 1–10 condition.

model (see Klahr, 1973b, for its details) that was built within the orthodox assumptions about production systems described in the first two chapters.[4] We have found those assumptions to be too restrictive to allow us to account for our data, and we have extended the basic system architecture.

[4] We use the term "orthodox" advisedly. There have been too few models built in PSG for any such orthodoxy to be seriously implied or understood. Furthermore, Newell (Newell & McDermott, 1974) has provided an almost bewildering array of options for the PSG model builder. A huge variety of optional timing, control, and architectural assumptions can be made in the current version of PSG. However, both Newell's (1972b, 1973) models and our own (Klahr, 1973a, c) have been based upon the set of default options about timing, and so forth, described earlier.

An Extended Model of System Architecture

There is abundant empirical evidence that suggests the existence of at least one extremely short-term memory ahead of STM in the visual chain (Neisser, 1967; Sperling, 1960). Sternberg (1969), Posner (1969), Chase and Calfee (1968), and Cavanagh and Chase (1971), among others, all have studied the effects of processing images (auditory or visual) versus processing names. Posner (1973) convincingly argues that the results of these studies demonstrate that multiple internal codes are used by subjects. However, he does not focus upon the locus of utilization of these codes. In the model we will describe below, different codes are processed in different buffers. The full model can be deferred until Chapter 7; in this chapter we describe only the addition of a single buffer in the context of revised models of quantification.

The basic extension is the addition of a visual short-term memory (VSTM) and the further specification of what was previously called STM to Semantic STM (SSTM). Corresponding to VSTM are a class of productions (still located in LTM) whose conditions refer to VSTM, and whose actions affect either VSTM or SSTM. The outlines of such a system are sketched in Fig. 3.9. The function of these *visual encoding productions* is to take the crudely processed information from a prior stage of processing in iconic memory (to be described in Chapter 7) and selectively transfer it from VSTM to SSTM. The subitizing systems to be described below consist almost entirely of this type of visual encoding production.

PSG extensions. In order to be precise about the revised set of systemic assumptions, we will first describe the *programming* modifications to the PSG system that facilitate the implementation of the new assumptions. Then we will describe the *psychological* correlates of the new model.

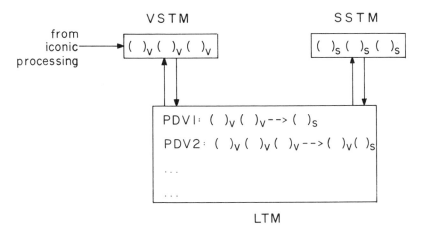

FIG. 3.9 An IPS with both visual and semantic STMs.

VSTM is a list of elements, just like SSTM, that can be scanned and modified semi-independently of SSTM. The contents of VSTM can be discovered by the condition SEE (X). This searches VSTM for the element X. If X exists in VSTM, then SEE (X) is true. The system can also keep track of where it is in VSTM, and can modify selected elements and insert new ones. The action (A =VS=> B) replaces A with B in the VSTM element that has most recently been seen by SEE. The action (IVS X) inserts the element X into VSTM.[5]

Another PSG feature which we will be using is an action of the form (PS X). This action causes production system X to be executed until it is complete (that is, until no condition in any of X's productions are true). Thus, (PS X) is like a subroutine call in that it suspends activity in the "calling program" until the subroutine is completed. We view this kind of action as an activation of a production system, about which we will have more to say in Chapters 7 and 8. A variant of (PS X) is (PS.1 X) which makes only a single pass through production system X, firing at most only one of its productions.

PS.SUB2

In PS.SUB2 we use all of these extensions to the basic model. Visual encoding productions, with SEEs in their conditions, search VSTM for their targets (Fig. 3.10, lines 1000–1300). Each of the visual encoding productions, called PDVSn (e.g., PDVS0, PDVS1, etc.), tests for the existence of precisely n target elements (called XLMs, for "external elements"). For example, PDVS2 has two conditions that do SEE (XLM) and another that tests for the *absence* of any further XLMs. If PDVS2's conditions are satisfied, the corresponding quantitative symbol (QS 2) is placed in SSTM. Thus, the PDVSs look at VSTM and place an encoded version of what is there into SSTM. Each of the PDVS productions can be viewed as a naming scheme. The pattern in VSTM discovered by the condition side produces a quantitative symbol in SSTM. Each unique pattern produces its own name.

The stimuli are represented as a cluster, or group, of elements that is first detected at a global level and then "unpacked." The determination of what constitutes a group is a function of spatial properties of the stimulus, such as symmetry, compactness, proximity, density, and so on, that are not represented explicitly in our models. In the examples below, all within the subitizing range, we assume that the entire stimulus field is encoded as a single group. The system

---

[5] Our operations on VSTM correspond to the task environment (TE) operations in PSG (Newell & McDermott, 1974). Our SEE is similar to NTCTE (notice task environment), except that the matched element does not automatically enter STM as it does with NTCTE. The actions (=VS=>) and (IVS) correspond directly to (=TE=>) and (ITE), respectively.

can detect the presence of a group, but it cannot determine its size until it unpacks it. Unpacking can be viewed as a detailed attending act in which the gross features of the visual field are examined more precisely. It is analogous to zooming in on the fine structure of an area previously noticed at a gross level. A group of two elements would initially be represented as

VSTM: ((GRP (ELM DOT1) (ELM DOT2))).

After unpacking, the VSTM representation would be

VSTM: ((ELM DOT1) (ELM DOT2) (OLD GRP)).

Then the PDVS productions would be able to detect elements.

The PDVS productions have two actions each. We have already mentioned the naming action: the placement of a quantitative symbol (QS n) into SSTM. The other action, SAT, satisfies the active subitizing goal (Fig. 3.10, line 300).

Notice that these productions have "mixed mode" conditions. The GOAL element tests SSTM, while the SEEs test VSTM. The actions modify both VSTM and SSTM. We can extend the contol of VSTM scanning by SSTM elements by using what we call *parameterized encoding productions*. For example, we could have

PDVS1:   ((GOAL * SUBIT T) (SEE(ELM T))(SEE (ELM T))ABS - ->

as the condition. If SSTM had (GOAL * SUBIT RED.DOT), then during the testing of PDVS1, the variable T would get assigned the value RED.DOT, and the SEEs would seek RED.DOTs. The production systems in this chapter will

```
00100   XLM:(CLASS ELM OBJ)
00200   X:(VAR)
00300   SAT:(ACTION (* ==> +))
00400
00500   ;GROUP UNPACKER
00600   PDUN:((SEE (GRP (XLM X))) --> (GRP (XLM X) =VS=> GRP) (IVS (XLM X)))
00700   PDUNX:((SEE (GRP)) --> (GRP =VS=> OLD.GRP))
00800   PSUN:(PDUN PDUNX)
00900
01000   PDVS0:((GOAL * SUBIT) (SEE (XLM)) ABS --> SAT  (QS 0))
01100   PDVS1:((GOAL * SUBIT) (SEE (XLM)) (SEE (XLM)) ABS --> SAT  (QS 1))
01200   PDVS2:((GOAL * SUBIT) (SEE (XLM)) (SEE (XLM)) (SEE (XLM)) ABS --> SAT  (QS 2))
01300   PDVS3:((GOAL * SUBIT) (SEE (XLM)) (SEE (XLM)) (SEE (XLM)) (SEE (XLM)) ABS --> SAT  (QS 3))
01400   PSVS:(PDVS0 PDVS1 PDVS2 PDVS3)
01500   PSUBIT:(PDSUB)
01600   STMI:((GOAL * SUBIT) NIL NIL)
01700   PDSUB:((GOAL * SUBIT)(SEE (GRP)) --> (PS PSUN)(PS.1 PSVS))
01800   VSTMI:((GRP (ELM DOT1)(ELM DOT2)))
```

FIG. 3.10   PSG model for PS.SUB2.

not contain any such parameterized productions, but they will be used in subsequent chapters.

A trace of PS.SUB2. Before looking at the actual trace of PS.SUB2 on quantification, it might be helpful to study the diagram in Fig. 3.11, where the processing stages are shown in flow chart form. First the group of elements is noticed; then it is unpacked, one element at a time. Next the template-matching visual encoding productions are tested, until a match is found and the corresponding quantitative symbol is placed in SSTM. In Fig. 3.12, we show two traces of PS.SUB2, first subtizing 2 dots and then 3 dots. For each initial configuration, after listing the initial VSTM and STM, the trace shows the sequence of true productions. For 2 dots it is PDSUB, PDUN, PDUN, PDUNX,

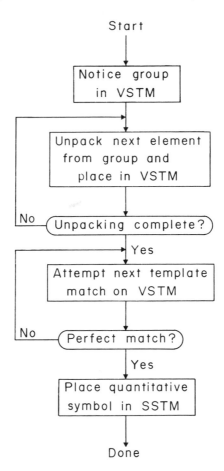

FIG. 3.11   Flow chart showing processing stages for PS.SUB2.

```
0000.   STM: ((GOAL * SUBIT) NIL NIL)
        VSTM: ((GRP (ELM DOT1) (ELM DOT2)))
0001.   TRUE: PDSUB: ((GOAL * SUBIT) (SEE (GRP)) --> (PS PSUN) (PS.1 PSVS))
1002.   TRUE: PDUN: ((SEE (GRP (XLM X))) --> (GRP (XLM X) =VS=> GRP) (IVS (XLM X)))
3003.   TRUE: PDUN: ((SEE (GRP (XLM X))) --> (GRP (XLM X) =VS=> GRP) (IVS (XLM X)))         (a)
5005.   TRUE: PDUNX: ((SEE (GRP)) --> (GRP =VS=> OLD.GRP))
7010.   TRUE: PDVS2: ((GOAL * SUBIT) (SEE (XLM)) (SEE (XLM)) (SEE (XLM)) ABS --> SAT (QS 2))
10010.  STM: ((QS 2) (GOAL + SUBIT) NIL)
        VSTM: ((ELM DOT2) (ELM DOT1) (OLD.GRP))
```

```
0000.   STM: ((GOAL * SUBIT) NIL NIL)
        VSTM: ((GRP (ELM DOT1) (ELM DOT2) (ELM DOT3)))
0001.   TRUE: PDSUB: ((GOAL * SUBIT) (SEE (GRP)) --> (PS PSUN) (PS.1 PSVS))
1002.   TRUE: PDUN: ((SEE (GRP (XLM X))) --> (GRP (XLM X) =VS=> GRP) (IVS (XLM X)))
3003.   TRUE: PDUN: ((SEE (GRP (XLM X))) --> (GRP (XLM X) =VS=> GRP) (IVS (XLM X)))         (b)
5004.   TRUE: PDUN: ((SEE (GRP (XLM X))) --> (GRP (XLM X) =VS=> GRP) (IVS (XLM X)))
7006.   TRUE: PDUNX: ((SEE (GRP)) --> (GRP =VS=> OLD.GRP))
9012.   TRUE: PDVS3: ((GOAL * SUBIT) (SEE (XLM)) (SEE (XLM)) (SEE (XLM)) (SEE (XLM)) ABS --> SAT (QS 3))
12012.  STM: ((QS 3) (GOAL + SUBIT) NIL)
        VSTM: ((ELM DOT3) (ELM DOT2) (ELM DOT1) (OLD.GRP))
```

FIG. 3.12   Trace of PS.SUB2 on 2 and 3 dots.

PDVS2, and for 3 dots it is PDSUB, PDUN, PDUN, PDUN, PDUNX, PDVS3. The final state of SSTM and VSTM is also shown.

Time calibration. How should we coordinate the number of steps that the model executes with the reaction time data from our experiments? There are two parts to the calibration. The first consists of the global assumptions about the locus of seriality and parallelism in a production system. The second consists of estimating the actual duration of those things that are supposed to take some time, and whose repeated execution is stimulus dependent.

Suppose we assume that only actions take time, and that all actions take equal time. Each of the PDVSs has two actions. The only incremental contribution to total time comes from (PS PSUN) which fires PDUN (see line 600) once for each item in the display. When PDUN fires it executes two actions on VSTM, one effectively deleting the first remaining element in the group, the other inserting that same element into VSTM. The action-only interpretation of timing attributes all of the 45-msec slope to these two VSTM actions. There are, however, several problems with this interpretation. First, it would seem that the actions on the VSTM should be much more rapid than actions on SSTM. Visual short-term memory is closer to the sensory end of the processing chain, and for processing reasonably complex stimuli, the estimate of 22 msec per VS action would appear to be much too high. Although this argument may seem somewhat ad hoc at this point, it will be justified in subsequent models.

Another problem with this interpretation is that it rests upon the assumption that all productions are tested in parallel. In Chapter 7 we will present an argument for "local seriality" in production systems. In such an interpretation, a production system, once activated, tests its productions in a sequence that is presumed to take time. In calibrating models operating under this assumption, estimates need to be made for the duration of the time to test a production.

In Fig. 3.12, the four digit number at the start of each line shows the total number of actions (a) and the total number of productions tested (p) at that point in the trace. The format is $a00p$. Thus after subitizing two dots $a = 10$ and $p = 10$, while after three dots $a = 12$ and $p = 12$. We can see from the trace that the incremental actions are a =VS=> and IVS. Let the time to do a single modify on VSTM be t_{VS}, and let the time to test a production be t_{PD}. Then the model slope is $2 \times t_{VS} + 2 \times t_{PD}$ per element. We will make one further assumption, which, like the others in this section, is (a) intuitively plausible, (b) apparently ad hoc, and (c) to be justified in subsequent sections. We assume that production testing time takes about twice as long as VSTM modification, that is, $t_{PD} = 2 \times t_{VS}$. Now when we equate model slope to our empirical subitizing slope, we get: $2 \times t_{VS} + 2 \times t_{PD} = 2 \times t_{VS} + 2 \times (2 \times t_{VS}) = 6 \times t_{VS} \sim 45$ msec. Thus, $t_{VS} \sim 7.5$ msec, and $t_{PD} \sim 15$ msec.

In summary, we now maintain the following view:

a. Production systems are *locally serial:* productions are considered serially, and their consideration takes time.
b. The time to test a production, t_{PD}, is approximately 15 msec.
c. Actions on VSTM take time, but are very rapid; t_{VS} is about 7.5 msec.

COUNTING: THEORETICAL AND EMPIRICAL BACKGROUND

The series of experiments reported earlier in this chapter provide information about the second of the three quantification operators: counting. Recall that when adult subjects quantified dots in the range $4 \leqslant n \leqslant 20$, their response latencies generated the 300- to 400-msec slopes shown in Table 3.1.

At least two strategies for counting can be adopted by subjects in this task:

1. counting by subitizing and adding: groups of items are subitized and marked and the result is added to the cumulative sum;
2. counting by enumeration (one-at-a-time counting): each item is fixated, marked, and the next name on an internal list of number names is accessed.

Our adult and child subjects report the use of both of these strategies on different occasions, sometimes mixing methods during a single trial. Beckwith and Restle (1966) also investigated quantification in the counting range. They presented their subjects with random patterns of identical items and instructions to "enumerate as quickly as possible." The latencies obtained yielded average slopes of 350 msec per item for adult subjects and random patterns in the range $n = (12, 15, 16, 18)$. These data are consistent with the average slope of 399 msec for $n = (10-20)$ obtained with adult subjects in Experiment 2. Although Beckwith and Restle (1966) concluded that their subjects divided the elements into clusters for enumeration and either computed a running sum or added all of the subtotals at the end, their subjects also may have used mixed methods. Since the counting reaction times are generated by an unknown mixture of two different processes, we can make only an approximate fit of model to data. Although it might be parsimonious to view counting by enumeration as a special case of subitizing and adding—with group size equal to one—we believe it to be quite a distinct quantification operator. In the next two sections we will describe first a model for subitizing and adding, and then a model for counting by enumeration, that is, for the counting operator. The major distrinction between these two models is the locus of the information that generates quantitative symbols. In the first model, information about discrete objects in VSTM is encoded and a quantitative symbol is placed in SSTM. There the symbol is modified, via addition rules, to produce the running sum. In the second model (enumeration), encoding of the information in VSTM results in the symbol for the object (rather than a quantitative symbol) being placed in SSTM where it evokes processes that revise the current quantitative symbol. The updating process is *not* addition, but simply the accessing of the next number name.

Subitizing and Adding

How does this combination function in information-processing terms? Figure 3.13 presents a flow chart depicting the temporal sequence of operations in terms of subprocesses without reference to the memory stores involved, and Fig. 3.14 shows the information flow in the system. The first subprocess is concerned with grouping the elements to be quantified. This is accomplished by appropriate control of the succession of areas of the display fixated. Beckwith and Restle's (1966) finding that patterns composed of clusters of elements which form "good" groups (in the Gestalt sense of the term) take less time to enumerate than random patterns is attributed to the fact that "good" groups provide a more clear-cut basis for determining the sequence of fixations and, thus, expedite the clustering process.

The next subprocess is subitizing. A fixated group gives rise via iconic memory to a representation in VSTM. This is processed by PS.SUB2 and the resulting quantitative symbol is placed in SSTM. There the next subprocess adds it to a quantitative symbol representing the running total of the groups subitized so far in quantifying the current target. A test is applied to discover if there are any more target elements in the display which have not yet been grouped. If there are additional elements, the current group is marked to prevent requantification, and the sequence of subprocesses is repeated. In the absence of additional

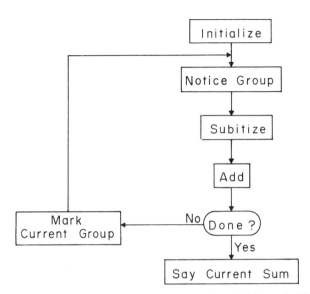

FIG. 3.13   Sequence of operations for counting via subitizing and adding.

elements quantification terminates and the current quantitative symbol in semantic STM becomes the final one. The inclusion of the "marking" subprocess represents an important distinction between the operation of PS.SUB2 in conjunction with addition and its independent operation. As already indicated, PS.SUB2 can function effectively within a single subitizing episode without attention-directing processes to ensure the avoidance of double processing.

We next consider the flow of information generated by these processes. In Fig. 3.14 we present another view of the process of counting via subitizing and adding: one that indicates the memory buffers involved. In Chapter 7 we will present the full model that utilizes these buffers; at this point we simply want to show the locus of information and activity during counting via subitizing and adding. Visual short-term memory and SSTM have already been briefly defined in the description of PS.SUB2.

The crude discrimination productions place a representation of the external elements in VSTM. There the subitizing productions encode the dots and place a single quantitative symbol for a subitized segment in SSTM. This in turn triggers the addition productions and addition takes place in SSTM.

PS.SUBADD

The model for counting via subitizing and adding has been described so far only in terms of two "black box" diagrams, one indicating the flow of control (Fig. 3.13) and the other showing the flow of information (Fig. 3.14). In this section we will describe a PSG model that will integrate both flows, and that will be

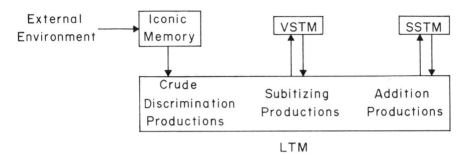

FIG. 3.14   Information flow in subitizing and adding.

consistent with the general system architecture and parameter estimates which we have adopted. Although PSG is a type of programming language and thus very general and flexible, it is also, as we have noted previously, a psychological theory of the human IPS. Any models constructed in PSG are constrained to the extent that they fit this general theory. Further constraints arise from the elaboration of the model and its relative timing assumptions that we have begun in this chapter. Finally, the empirical results from quantification studies form another constraint on the models we can construct. Obviously if the models cannot be mapped into the data, they are unacceptable.

PS.SUBADD, a model for counting via subitizing and adding, is shown in Fig. 3.15. As before, we will briefly describe the model and then expand the description as we work through traces of it operating on various stimulus configurations. Before commencing the description, it should be noted that in addition to its substantive relevance in the context of quantification, this model is important in another respect. It is the most extensive model of an "elementary" operation that we will deal with in this book. In subsequent chapters we will treat quantification as elementary with respect to higher level models, for example, conservation, but here we have an elaborate model of the process itself. One of the great powers of PSG is the ease with which such recursive elaboration can be effected, all within the same global system architecture.

Stimulus representation. PS.SUBADD functions by repeatedly noticing, quantifying, and marking groups of elements while maintaining cumulative sum. A display that was to be treated as two groups, one containing three dots and the other containing two, would be represented as:

VSTM: ((GRP (ELM DOT1)(ELM DOT2)(ELM DOT3))(GRP (ELM DOT4)(ELM DOT5)))

As in PS.SUB2, the system can directly detect groups, but it cannot determine the size of a group until it "unpacks" a group.

Main control. The system in Fig. 3.15 will be described from the bottom up.
The production that gets the system started is PDC1 (3900). It detects an active
count goal and fires: placing a symbol for 0 (QS 0) in SSTM, and activating
PS.SUBADD by "calling" it as a subroutine (PS PS.SUBADD). PS.SUBADD
(3300–3700) has four productions that control and coordinate the sequence of
subsystems utilized in subitizing and adding. PX1 detects two quantitative
symbols and activates a single pass through PSADD (PS.1 PSADD). (The PS.1
action makes one pass through a production system, firing either one or none of
its productions.) PX2 is the "termination" production. When it detects (in
addition to the active count goal) a quantitative symbol and the absence of any
groups in VSTM, it fires, satisfying the goal and "saying" the result.

```
00200              Addition subsystem
00300    ADD1:(ACTION (6 ===> 7)(5 ===> 6)(4 ===> 5)(3 ===> 4)(2 ===> 3)(1 ===> 2))
00400    ADD2:(ACTION (6 ===> 8)(5 ===> 7)(4 ===> 6)(3 ===> 5)(2 ===> 4))
00500    ADD3:(ACTION (6 ===> 9)(5 ===> 8)(4 ===> 7)(3 ===> 6))
00600
00700    PA0:((QS 0)(QS) --> (**))
00800    PA1:((QS 1)(QS) --> (**) HOLD ADD1 RELEASE)
00900    PA2:((QS 2)(QS) --> (**) HOLD ADD2 RELEASE)
01000    PA3:((QS 3)(QS) --> (**) HOLD ADD3 RELEASE)
01100    PSADD:(PA0 PA1 PA2 PA3)
01200
01300              Marking subsystem
01400    PDM:((SEE (XLM)) --> (XLM =VS=> SAW))
01500    PSM:(PDM)
01600
01700              Ungrouping (Group unpacking) subsystem
01800    PDUN:((SEE (NEW.GRP (XLM X))) --> (NEW.GRP (XLM X) =VS=> NEW.GRP)
01900          (IVS (XLM X)))
02000    PDUNX:((SEE (NEW.GRP)) --> (NEW.GRP =VS=> OLD.GRP))
02100    PSUN:(PDUN PDUNX)
02200
02300              Subitizer
02400    PDVS1:((SEE (XLM))(SEE (XLM)) ABS --> (QS 1))
02500    PDVS2:((SEE (XLM))(SEE (XLM)) (SEE (XLM)) ABS --> (QS 2))
02600    PDVS3:((SEE (XLM))(SEE (XLM)) (SEE (XLM)) (SEE (XLM)) ABS --> (QS 3))
02700    PSVS:(PDVS1 PDVS2 PDVS3)
02800
02900              Group detector
03000    PDVG:((SEE (GRP)) --> (GRP =VS=> NEW.GRP)(PS PSUN))
03100
03200              Control for counting via subitizing and adding
03300    PX1:((GOAL * COUNT)(QS)(QS) --> (PS.1 PSADD))
03400    PX2:((GOAL * COUNT)(QS X)(SEE (GRP)) ABS --> SAT (SAY X))
03500    PX3:((GOAL * COUNT)(SEE (OLD.GRP)) --> (PS PSM)(PD PDVG)(PS.1 PSVS))
03600    PX4:((GOAL * COUNT)(SEE (GRP)) --> (PD PDVG)(PS.1 PSVS))
03700    PS.SUBADD:(PX1 PX2 PX3 PX4)
03800
03900    PDC1:((GOAL * COUNT) --> (QS 0) (PS PS.SUBADD))
04000    PSCOUNT:(PDC1)
```

FIG. 3.15 PSG model for subitizing and adding: PS.SUBADD.

PX3 is the workhorse production. It fires when one group has been unpacked and quantified but there are other groups remaining in VSTM that are unaccounted for. This knowledge is represented somewhat indirectly. PX2 fails only if there *is* a group in VSTM (i.e., only when SEE(GRP) ABS is false), since at least one QS and the active count should always be present during quantification. Thus, by its location after PX2, PX3's condition is effectively SEE(GRP) *and* SEE(OLD.GRP). When PX3 fires it takes three actions. First it executes PSM, a one-production production system which marks all the elements in VSTM (see 1400–1500). These are the unpacked elements from the most recently quantified group. Then it tests a single production (PD PDVG) whose function is to unpack a group of elements so that they can be quantified (see 3000). Finally, PX3 fires a single pass through PSVS in order to quantify the elements that have just been unpacked. PSVS (2300–2700) is almost identical to the model in PS.SUB2, except that it does not need to modify goals, since it is under the control of a higher level process.

PX4, the last of the four main PSC productions to be tested, is the first to fire when PSC starts up. It fires when there are no old groups in VSTM, that is, on the first pass. Its actions are to unpack the group (PD PDVG) and to subitize it (PS.1 PSVS).

Addition.   Although addition is not a process of central importance to us at this point, we have explicitly included it in PS.SUBADD, rather than leave it as an unmodeled subprocess. The system is shown in Fig. 3.15 (lines 200–1100). It is functionally equivalent to a search through the "rows" of an addition table for x or y, whichever comes first. (Only a few entries are shown for clarity.) Suppose that the system has two quantitative symbols, say (QS 2) and (QS 4). Then PA0 tests for either one being 0, and fails; next, PA1 tests for either one being 1, and it too fails. Finally, PA2 detects the fact that one of them is (QS 2), and fires. PA2 has four actions. The first is to tag the symbol whose value led to the firing of PA2 (QS 2). The tagging in this case is simply to embed the symbol (∗∗), but any tag would suffice.

The other meaningful action in PA2 is ADD2 (we will discuss HOLD and RELEASE below), which is written as an "action chain" (line 400). This is a PSG convention that allows one to write a string of actions on a separate line—they are entirely equivalent to a list of actions on the right-hand side of a production. The function of ADD2 is to add 2 to the second of the two quantitative symbols in SSTM. Recall that (x ===> y) is a PSG action that looks for the symbol X in the second element in SSTM and replaces it with the symbol Y. Since the second SSTM element is of the form (QS n), where n is a number, one and only one of these actions will actually result in a substitution. In the example we are considering the second element in SSTM is (QS 4), and execution of ADD2 results in the action (4 ===> 6) being successfully completed. At the end of the firing of PSADD, the SSTM contents will have been changed from (QS 2)(QS 4) to ((QS 2))(QS 6). [The PSG accounting system treats each of the actions in ADD1, ADD2, and so on, as normal actions. Since on any pass only one of them actually makes a substitution, we have turned the accounting system off (HOLD) prior to firing these action chains, and then turned it back on (RELEASE).]

PSADD utilizes no extra SSTM capacity beyond the two quantitative symbols being added. Since the PA0, PA1, and so on, sequence always "catches" the smaller of the two symbols, its slope is a function of min(x, y) and is equal to t_{PD}, the time to test a production. In the previous section we estimated t_{PD} to be around 15 msec; thus, PSADD yields a slope within the ball park of the 20 msec per min(x, y) that Groen and Parkman (1972) reported.

A trace of PS.SUBADD.   Figure 3.16 shows a trace of PS.SUBADD operating on a display that gets encoded in VSTM as two groups of two elements each. The initial state of SSTM and VSTM is shown as 0000 (the numbers affixed to each dot in VSTM are never used by the system, they are included to allow the reader to follow the fate of individual elements in VSTM). The trace starts *after* PDC1 has fired (that is, at the beginning of PS.SUBADD). The first production to fire is PX4, which in turn fires PDVG and PSVS. PDVG sees a group in VSTM, marks it as a NEW.GRP, and proceeds to unpack it (PS PSUN). PSUN operates by repeatedly deleting the first element from NEW.GRP and placing it directly in VSTM: the operation is insert in visual STM, (IVS (XLM X)). The general logic is to take a list of items, such as (XX A B C D), and produce first (A) (XX B C D), then (B)(A)(XX C D), and so on, until finally we get (D)(C)(B)(A) (XX). In this case the XX is the tag NEW.GRP, and the A, B, C, and D are (ELM DOT1) (ELM DOT2), and so on. The effect of all of this unpacking can be seen in the contents of VSTM after 10013. The psychologically important function of PSUN is that it requires an amount of effort on VSTM that is directly proportional to the size of the group being unpacked. However, these actions on VSTM are still assumed to be extremely rapid, estimated as before to be around 7.5 msec each.

Thus, from 3006 to 9013, two elements are unpacked from the first group. Then, since PX4 fires (PS.1 PSVS) immediately after (PS PSUN), the two elements are subitized by PDVS2 (9013). This places a quantitative symbol in SSTM (the first modification of SSTM thus far), and PX1 fires next at 10014. The addition of 0 to anything is handled as a special case by PA0, (11015) and PS.SUBADD cycles again, this time firing PX3 (12018). The actions for PX3 are similar to PX4, but first it must mark the old elements in VSTM, so it fires PSM, which repeatedly marks all the accessible VSTM elements (13019 to 14020). The cycle of ungrouping, subitizing, and adding is repeated on the second group (16022 to 28034). Finally, PX2 fires, outputs the result, and the system stops. The final state is shown at 31036.

ps.subadd start!

0000. SSTM: ((GOAL * COUNT) (QS 0) NIL NIL)
       VSTM: ((GRP (ELM DOT1) (ELM DOT2)) (GRP (ELM DOT3) (ELM DOT4)))

0004. PX4: ((GOAL * COUNT) (SEE (GRP)) --> (PD PDVG) (PS.1 PSVS))
1005. PDVG: ((SEE (GRP)) --> (GRP =VS=> NEW.GRP) (PS PSUN))
3006. PDUN: ((SEE (NEW.GRP (XLM X))) --> (NEW.GRP (XLM X) =VS=> NEW.GRP) (IVS (XLM X)))
5007. PDUN: ((SEE (NEW.GRP (XLM X))) --> (NEW.GRP (XLM X) =VS=> NEW.GRP) (IVS (XLM X)))
7009. PDUNX: ((SEE (NEW.GRP)) --> (NEW.GRP =VS=> OLD.GRP))
9013. PDVS2: ((SEE (XLM)) (SEE (XLM)) (SEE (XLM)) ABS --> (QS 2))

10013. SSTM: ((QS 2) (GOAL * COUNT) (QS 0) NIL)
       VSTM: ((ELM DOT2) (ELM DOT1) (OLD.GRP) (GRP (ELM DOT3) (ELM DOT4)))

10014. PX1: ((GOAL * COUNT) (QS) (QS) --> (PS.1 PSADD))
11015. PA0: ((QS 0) (QS) --> (**))

12015. SSTM: (((QS 0)) (QS 2) (GOAL * COUNT) NIL)
       VSTM: ((ELM DOT2) (ELM DOT1) (OLD.GRP) (GRP (ELM DOT3) (ELM DOT4)))

12018. PX3: ((GOAL * COUNT) (SEE (OLD.GRP)) --> (PS PSM) (PD PDVG) (PS.1 PSVS))
13019. PDM: ((SEE (XLM)) --> (XLM =VS=> SAW))
14020. PDM: ((SEE (XLM)) --> (XLM =VS=> SAW))
16022. PDVG: ((SEE (GRP)) --> (GRP =VS=> NEW.GRP) (PS PSUN))
18023. PDUN: ((SEE (NEW.GRP (XLM X))) --> (NEW.GRP (XLM X) =VS=> NEW.GRP) (IVS (XLM X)))
20024. PDUN: ((SEE (NEW.GRP (XLM X))) --> (NEW.GRP (XLM X) =VS=> NEW.GRP) (IVS (XLM X)))
22026. PDUNX: ((SEE (NEW.GRP)) --> (NEW.GRP =VS=> OLD.GRP))
24030. PDVS2: ((SEE (XLM)) (SEE (XLM)) (SEE (XLM)) ABS --> (QS 2))

25030. SSTM: ((QS 2) (GOAL * COUNT) ((QS 0)) (QS 2))
       VSTM: ((ELM DOT4) (ELM DOT3) (SAW DOT2) (SAW DOT1) (OLD.GRP) (OLD.GRP))

25031. PX1: ((GOAL * COUNT) (QS) (QS) --> (PS.1 PSADD))
26034. PA2: ((QS 2) (QS) --> (**) HOLD ADD2 RELEASE)

28034. SSTM: (((QS 2)) (QS 4) (GOAL * COUNT) ((QS 0)))
       VSTM: ((ELM DOT4) (ELM DOT3) (SAW DOT2) (SAW DOT1) (OLD.GRP) (OLD.GRP))

28036. PX2: ((GOAL * COUNT) (QS X) (SEE (GRP)) ABS --> SAT (SAY X))

********** 4

31036. SSTM: ((GOAL + COUNT) (QS 4) ((QS 2)) ((QS 0)))
       VSTM: ((ELM DOT4) (ELM DOT3) (SAW DOT2) (SAW DOT1) (OLD.GRP) (OLD.GRP))

FIG. 3.16   Trace of PS.SUBADD on two groups of two elements each.

Calibration of PS.SUBADD.   In this section we will compare the number of steps taken by PS.SUBADD with the reaction time data from our experiments. We will deal with just three parameters: t_{PD} —time to test a production; t_{VS}— time to modify VSTM; and t_{ACT} —time for an action. For the first two, we already have estimates of 15 and 7.5 msec, respectively. The third, t_{ACT} , is an average over several different kinds of actions, including SSTM modifications and insertions, as well as the PS and PS.1 actions. However, we will assume all such actions are of equal duration.

In Fig. 3.17, a trace of PS.SUBADD on a single two-element group is shown, together with an expanded accounting system. The three columns on the left show the cumulative number of actions (AC), modifications on VSTM (VS), and productions tested (PD). The numbers in any row show the state of the system just *prior* to the firing of the satisfied production listed on that line. By repeatedly running PS.SUBADD on various stimulus configurations we can generate information on the totals for these three parameters.

The results of several such simulations are presented in Table 3.2. The upper part of the table summarizes the model's behavior under an encoding in which the largest group possible (that is, within subitizing range) is formed for each value of n. The bottom of the table shows the results of minimum group size (that is, for each value of n, there are n one-element groups). Notice that the second row in the table corresponds to the final count from Fig. 3.17.

We have previously estimated that $t_{PD} = 2t_{VS}$. Now we make one further order-of-magnitude estimate, that $t_{ACT} = 10t_{VS}$, that is, t_{ACT} = 75 msec. Using these weights, and letting t_{VS} be equal to one time unit, we get the final weighted sum shown in the column under Σ in Table 3.2. That is, for each of the counts under ACT, VS, and PD, Σ = 10 × ACT + VS + 2 × PD. The pure subitizing slope obtained by subtracting the times between two adjacent rows in Table 3.2 within the first group (e.g., 1 from 2, or 2 from 3) is, as before, 6 units, or 45 msec. The upper slope of this curve can be estimated by subtracting the totals for 3 from 3 + 3, or 2 from 3 + 2. This yields a difference of approximately 135 units and hence a slope of about 45 units per dot. Multiplying by the 7.5-msec estimate, we get an upper slope of approximately 338 msec, quite close to the 300-msec slope from our experimental studies.

```
AC VS PD
00 00 00  SSTM: ((GOAL * COUNT) NIL NIL NIL)
          VSTM: ((GRP (ELM DOT1) (ELM DOT2)))

00 00 01    PDC1: ((GOAL * COUNT) --> (QS 0) (PS PS.SUBADD))
02 00 05    PX4: ((GOAL * COUNT) (SEE (GRP)) --> (PD PDVG) (PS.1 PSVS))
03 00 06    PDVG: ((SEE (GRP)) --> (GRP =VS=> NEW.GRP) (PS PSUNG))
04 01 07    PDUNG: ((SEE (NEW.GRP (XLM X))) --> (NEW.GRP (XLM X) =VS=> NEW.GRP) (IVS (XLM X)))
04 03 08    PDUNG: ((SEE (NEW.GRP (XLM X))) --> (NEW.GRP (XLM X) =VS=> NEW.GRP) (IVS (XLM X)))
04 05 10    PDUNGX: ((SEE (NEW.GRP)) --> (NEW.GRP =VS=> OLD.GRP))
05 06 14    PDVS2: ((SEE (XLM)) (SEE (XLM)) (SEE (XLM)) ABS --> (QS 2))
06 06 15    PX1: ((GOAL * COUNT) (QS) (QS) --> (PS.1 PSADD))
07 06 16    PA0: ((QS 0) (QS) --> (**))
08 06 18    PX2: ((GOAL * COUNT) (QS X) (SEE (GRP)) ABS --> SAT (SAY X))


********** 2


11 06 22  SSTM: ((GOAL + COUNT) (QS 2) ((QS 0)) NIL)
          VSTM: ((ELM DOT2) (ELM DOT1) (OLD.GRP))
```

FIG. 3.17   Trace of PS.SUBADD on two elements in a single group.

TABLE 3.2
Model Effort for PS.SUBADD Under Different
Stimulus Encodings, and Weighted Total

	Group size				Model effort			
n	1st	2nd	3rd	4th	ACT	VS	PD	Σ^a
1	1				11	4	20	154
2	2				11	6	22	160
3	3				11	8	24	166
4	3	1			19	15	41	287
5	3	2			19	17	44	295
6	3	3			19	19	47	303
7	3	3	1		27	26	64	424
2	1	1			17	9	35	249
3	1	1	1		27	14	50	384
4	1	1	1	1	35	19	65	499

$^a\Sigma = 10 \times ACT + VS + 2 \times PD$

Figure 3.18 shows a plot of model time versus n, with the relative amounts of time contributed by ACT, PS, and PD, using our final estimates of $t_{VS} = 7.5$ msec, $t_{PD} = 15$ msec, and $t_{ACT} = 75$ msec.

Counting by Enumeration

In counting by enumeration, the system attends to individual dots and sequences through the number names. Counting thus requires two auxiliary structures in LTM: a finite ordered list of number names, together with processes for generating number names indefinitely and processes to ensure that each item is noticed only once. There may be several different forms of such processes for directing attention in the external environment ranging from motor routines that move or touch objects as they are noticed, to self-defined eye movement patterns.

More than half of the processing time per item appears to come from moving through the number–name list. Recall that when Beckwith and Restle (1966) gave explicit instructions to "enumerate as quickly as possible," they found average slopes of 350 msec per item (579 msec for children aged 7 to 9 years) in the range $n = 12, 15, 16, 18$. In a task requiring subjects to implicitly recite the alphabet from an initial letter to a final letter, Olshavsky and Gregg (1970) found a processing rate of 150 msec per item, which is similar to the rate of implicit recitation found by Landauer (1962). When subjects were required to scan a specified number of letters, the rate increased to 260 msec per item.

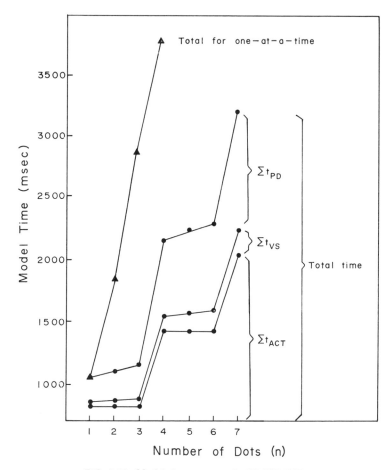

FIG. 3.18   Model time versus n for PS.SUBADD.

Figure 3.19 shows a flow chart for counting by enumeration. It is expressed in terms of subprocesses rather than as a production system, and there is no indication of the memory stores involved. The increase in latency with n is attributed to the "next," "mark," and "notice" subprocesses included in the loop. The subprocesses "mark" and "notice" are not well defined but are simply intended as a surrogate for any strategies, such as those mentioned above, which might be used to direct attention to each item being quantified once and only once and, also, to determine when counting is complete.

The counting production system.   In constructing PS.SUB2 it was asserted that the addition of a visual STM to the information-processing system was necessary to preserve consistency with the latency data and that the subtizing productions operate upon the contents of VSTM. The counting quantification

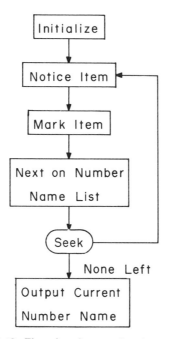

FIG. 3.19   Flow chart for counting via enumeration.

operator, in contrast, focuses upon SSTM rather than VSTM. It can be argued that its first construction and subsequent transmission via social learning from generation to generation was necessitated by the limits imposed by the capacity and decay characteristics of VSTM which render the extension of subitizing to the quantification of large collections impossible.

In the case of PS.COUNT, VSTM is not processed by quantifying productions, but by a single parameterized discrimination production system. The target to be quantified not only plays a part in satisfying the conditions for the activation of PS.COUNT, but determines the value of the parameterized discrimination production system. The more detailed the definition of the target the more elaborate the discrimination production system which will scan VSTM. If a target is detected, a semantic element representing it is placed in SSTM by the discrimination production system. The important distinction between this form of quantification and subitizing—adding with a group size of 1 is that now the symbol entering SSTM is not a quantitative symbol, but rather a token for the target object. Thus, it has yet to be "quantified."

When counting is under way, the arrival in SSTM of a target element activates the quantification productions proper, which in this case operate upon SSTM rather than VSTM. Their function is to update the member of the number sequence currently present in SSTM as the quantitative symbol derived from the ongoing counting episode. The arrival of an initial semantic element results in the number 1 being placed in SSTM; the subsequent arrival of another semantic element leads to the replacement of the number 1 by the number 2, and so on. As the number is updated the semantic element is marked to ensure that erroneous updating does not occur.

It is evident that the sequential detection of targets free from double-processing errors is essential to the successful functioning of PS.COUNT. This objective is in part achieved by the addition to the parameterized discrimination production system of productions which mark target objects in VSTM as they are detected and instigate the placing of semantic elements in SSTM. Sequential detection and avoidance of double processing are also greatly facilitated by the fact that PS.COUNT is not fixation bound and shifts in fixation from feature to feature of the problem space are possible during a single counting episode. This provides the basis for productions which take their input from VSTM and give rise to externally observable motor movements. Their function is to regulate the information entering the visual encoding channel so that the process of detecting target objects in VSTM is simplified. The moving or touching of features of the display are obvious examples of such motor movements. Less obvious but serving the same purpose is the visual "touching" of features via the regular patterns of eye movement that characteristically accompany counting.

Figure 3.20 summarizes the information flow in PS.COUNT. How compatible is it with the 300-msec slope obtained in the adult latency data? If moving or touching features of the problem space results in only a single object (at a time) being admitted via iconic memory to visual STM, each unit increase in n, the number of target objects, entails an additional operation of every one of the processing steps indicated in Fig. 3.19. The only aspects of counting performance included in the intercept are the initial activation of PS.COUNT and the decoding and externalization of the final result. With the random collections of dots used as stimuli in our experiments, moving or touching individual features was not possible. It also appeared likely that the adult subjects were encompassing areas of the collection rather than individual dots within each fixation and that the regular patterns of eye movement were fulfilling the function of ensuring that the same area was not fixated twice during the counting episode.

If dots are admitted to VSTM in groups, the crude discrimination productions and attention-directing productions operating on the external environment only contribute to an increase in latency on each occasion that a new group reaches VSTM. The target-detection and the number-generating production systems operating on SSTM make the major contribution to increasing latency, since they recur with each unit increase in the number of target objects. This relative apportionment of the latency is consistent with the data obtained by Olshavsky and Gregg (1970) which has already been mentioned. The rate of 150 msec per item on implicit alphabet recitation appears to be a reasonable indication of the rate of number generation since for $6 < n < 10$ the numbers are presumably obtained from a list.

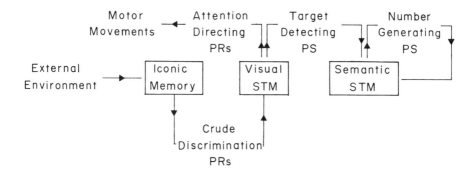

PS:COUNT

FIG. 3.20 Information flow for counting via enumeration.

If 150 msec is accepted as an estimate of the increase in latency with n attributable to the number-generating production system, then another 150 msec remains to cover the operation of the target-detecting production system, the crude discrimination productions, and the attention-directing productions. This evaluation appears to be compatible with the processing rates of productions operating on visual STM presented in the discussion of subitizing and with the smaller increases in latency attributed to the productions triggered by a new group rather than a new target object.

The explanatory weight assigned to the distinction between group- and target-object triggered productions is consistent with the results from our experiment with child subjects. It will be recalled that a slope of 1049 msec (corresponding to 300 msec for adults) was obtained with random dot collections in which $3 < n < 8$. A partial explanation of the much longer latency in the children's performance is suggested by the distinction between group- and target-object triggered productions. Many of the children, in contrast to the adults, made head movements which apparently were operationally equivalent to directing attention to single dots in the display by finger pointing or touching. As indicated above, if only a single object at a time is admitted via iconic memory to visual STM, each unit increase in the number of target objects requires an additional operation of not only the target-detecting and number-generating production systems, but also the crude-discrimination and attention-directing productions. This would result in greater increases in latency with n than the adult approach based on fixations of areas of the collection rather than individual dots. Although both the children and adults used a mixture of the two forms of counting, it is likely that the adult slopes reflect a high percentage of subitizing and adding trials, while the children's data are almost entirely generated by "pure" enumeration.

PS.COUNT

The PSG model for PS.COUNT is shown in Fig. 3.21, and runs on two- and three-element displays are listed in Fig. 3.22a and b. The version of the model shown in Fig. 3.21 assumes that the COUNT goal is active until the end of the quantification episode: for clarity, no explicit goals have been included. Also, only productions to access number names from 0 thru 4 have been included, but the form of a full system should be evident.

This description will focus entirely upon the trace in Fig. 3.22. The number printed in the left-most column has the same format as in our previous models: *aaopp*—where *aa* is the total action count and *pp* is the total production count. First look at Fig. 3.22a. The first two lines show the initial states of VSTM and SSTM. VSTM contains two DOTs. The initial contents of SSTM consist solely of a response element, with value zero (QS 0). The first production to fire is PDV1. It detects an unmarked element in VSTM and marks it with the tag SAW. The state of VSTM after PDV1 fires is shown after 2004. In addition, PDV1 puts a symbol for the matched element into SSTM (functionally, it transfers it from VSTM to SSTM). The state of SSTM after PDV1 fires is also shown at 2004. PDV1 does three things: it notices an element in VSTM, it marks it in VSTM so that it will not notice it again, and it puts a token for that element in SSTM. PDV1 is the only production in PS.COUNT that uses VSTM; all the others process the contents of SSTM exclusively.

Next, one of the next-number-name productions (PDC.01) increments the response symbol. The cycle of ELM detection and incrementing of the QS is repeated on the next element (4005–6011).

```
00300  ;COUNTING BY ENUMERATION
00400
00500  XLM:(CLASS ELM XDOT)
00600  X:(VAR)
00700
00800  PDC.01:((XLM) (QS 0) --> (COUNTED **)( 0 ===> 1))
00900  PDC.12:((XLM) (QS 1) --> (COUNTED **)( 1 ===> 2))
01000  PDC.23:((XLM)(QS 2) --> (COUNTED **)( 2 ===> 3))
01100  PDC.34.((XLM)(QS 3) --> (COUNTED **)(3 ===> 4))
01200  PDV1:((SEE (XLM X)) --> (XLM =VS=> SAW)(XLM X))
01300  PDC1:((QS X) -->(QS ==> SAID) (SAY X))
01400
01500  PSCOUNT:(PDC.01 PDC.12 PDC.23 PDC.34 PDV1 PDC1)
01600  STMI:((QS 0) NIL NIL NIL)
01700  VSTMI:((ELM DOT 1)(ELM DOT 2))
```

FIG. 3.21 PS.COUNT.

```
0000.  SSTM: ((QS 0) NIL NIL NIL)
       VSTM: ((ELM DOT 1) (ELM DOT 2))
0004.    TRUE: PDV 1: ((SEE (XLM X)) --> (XLM =VS=> SAW) (XLM X))
2004.  SSTM: ((ELM DOT 1) (QS 0) NIL NIL)
       VSTM: ((SAW DOT 1) (ELM DOT 2))
2005.    TRUE: PDC.01: ((XLM) (QS 0) --> (COUNTED **) (0 ===> 1))
4005.  SSTM: ((COUNTED (ELM DOT 1)) (QS 1) NIL NIL)
4009.    TRUE: PDV 1: ((SEE (XLM X)) --> (XLM =VS=> SAW) (XLM X))          (a)
6009.  SSTM: ((ELM DOT 2) (COUNTED (ELM DOT 1)) (QS 1) NIL)
       VSTM: ((SAW DOT 1) (SAW DOT 2))
6011.    TRUE: PDC.12: ((XLM) (QS 1) --> (COUNTED **) (1 ===> 2))
8011.  SSTM: ((COUNTED (ELM DOT 2)) (QS 2) (COUNTED (ELM DOT 1)) NIL)
8016.    TRUE: PDC 1: ((QS X) --> (QS ==> SAID) (SAY X))

********** 2

10016.  SSTM: ((SAID 2) (COUNTED (ELM DOT 2)) (COUNTED (ELM DOT 1)) NIL)
        VSTM: ((SAW DOT 1) (SAW DOT 2))

--------------------------------------------------------------------------------
0000.  SSTM: ((QS 0))
       VSTM: ((ELM DOT 1) (ELM DOT 2) (ELM DOT 3))
0004.    TRUE: PDV 1: ((SEE (XLM X)) --> (XLM =VS=> SAW) (XLM X))
2004.  SSTM: ((ELM DOT 1) (QS 0) NIL NIL)
       VSTM: ((SAW DOT 1) (ELM DOT 2) (ELM DOT 3))
2005.    TRUE: PDC.01: ((XLM) (QS 0) --> (COUNTED **) (0 ===> 1))
4005.  SSTM: ((COUNTED (ELM DOT 1)) (QS 1) NIL NIL)
4009.    TRUE: PDV 1: ((SEE (XLM X)) --> (XLM =VS=> SAW) (XLM X))          (b)
6009.  SSTM: ((ELM DOT 2) (COUNTED (ELM DOT 1)) (QS 1) NIL)
       VSTM: ((SAW DOT 1) (SAW DOT 2) (ELM DOT 3))
6011.    TRUE: PDC.12: ((XLM) (QS 1) --> (COUNTED **) (1 ===> 2))
8011.  SSTM: ((COUNTED (ELM DOT 2)) (QS 2) (COUNTED (ELM DOT 1)) NIL)
8015.    TRUE: PDV 1: ((SEE (XLM X)) --> (XLM =VS=> SAW) (XLM X))
10015.  SSTM: ((ELM DOT 3) (COUNTED (ELM DOT 2)) (QS 2) (COUNTED (ELM DOT 1)))
        VSTM: ((SAW DOT 1) (SAW DOT 2) (SAW DOT 3))
10018.    TRUE: PDC.23: ((XLM) (QS 2) --> (COUNTED **) (2 ===> 3))
12018.  SSTM: ((COUNTED (ELM DOT 3)) (QS 3) (COUNTED (ELM DOT 2)) (COUNTED (ELM DOT 1)))
12023.    TRUE: PDC 1: ((QS X) --> (QS ==> SAID) (SAY X))

********** 3

14023.  SSTM: ((SAID 3) (COUNTED (ELM DOT 3)) (COUNTED (ELM DOT 2)) (COUNTED (ELM DOT 1)))
        VSTM: ((SAW DOT 1) (SAW DOT 2) (SAW DOT 3))
```

FIG. 3.22   Trace of PS.COUNT on (a) two elements, and (b) 3 elements.

When everything in VSTM has been marked, the only production that can fire is PDC1, which finally "says" the result (8016). The final state of SSTM and VSTM is shown at 10016.

Figure 3.22b shows PS.COUNT running on a three-element display. The system functions exactly as before, up to 8011, when the third element is detected. After it has been accounted for, the final count is 14023. The totals for quantifying 2 dots are: actions = 8, VSTM actions = 2, and PDs = 16. For 3 dots we get: actions = 11, VSTM actions = 3, and PDs = 23. The increment per dot for each is thus Δ_{ACT} = 3, Δ_{VSTM} = 1, and Δ_{PD} = 7. Using our previous estimates for t_{ACT} = 75 msec, t_{VS} = 7.5 msec, and t_{PD} = 15, we get an estimated slope for counting by enumeration of 3 X (75) + 7 X (15) + 7.5 = 337.5 msec. This is well within the 300–350-msec slope obtained in the experimental work.

ESTIMATION

In view of the lack of clarity about the nature of the ongoing processing which is the typical subjective accompaniment to estimation as represented in the third of our quantification examples, it is hardly surprising that there is as yet no PS.EST, a running production system constituting a sufficient theory of estimation. In lieu of PS.EST, we will only attempt to characterize at the metaphorical level the type of estimation quantification operator which would be consistent with the theories of subitizing and counting already presented in detail in PS.SUB2 and PS.COUNT.

The necessity of the existence of a quantification operator other than subitizing and counting is clear since they only deal with discontinuous quantity. If PS.SUB2 or PS.COUNT is applied first to an elephant and then to a mouse, the quantitative symbols which are generated are identical. Quantitative symbols must also be produced in situations involving large numbers of discontinuous elements and/or brief exposure durations where neither PS.SUB2 nor PS.COUNT can operate effectively. The importance of the estimation quantification operator arises from its contribution to repairing the deficiencies of subitizing and counting.

The type of estimation quantification operator which would be consistent with PS.SUB2 and PS.COUNT can be illustrated in a discussion of the quantification of continuous quantity. The function of measurement is to divide continuous quantities into discontinuous sections and, thus, render them amenable to quantification. The process of division into discontinuous units is relatively free from error since it involves the repeated application of a standard unit to a continuous quantity by a "hands on," concrete method exemplified by the use of a ruler to determine length or a balance to determine weight. The standard units employed do not vary in size within or between quantification episodes.

The relationship of estimation to measurement becomes clear if we consider possible variations in the measurement process in the context of a specific example. A popular method of introducing children to the techniques involved in measuring area is to present them with a square of 100 cm^2 and a square of 1 cm^2, and invite them to discover how often the smaller square can be laid on the larger one without covering the same area twice. This technique has all of the characteristics outlined above and is tantamount to the use of a two-dimensional ruler.

As a first variation let us assume that a smaller square is still provided, but that its area is unknown. It is still possible to determine how many iterations are required to cover the larger square, but this quantitative symbol can no longer be used to derive the appropriate quantitative symbol from the standard scale for area measurement. The outcome of measurement is consequently rendered local in its frame of reference, and this can only be extended as the same unidentified standard is applied to the other squares. Since the application of the standard involves a concrete method, and the unit does not vary in size within or between quantification episodes, this measurement technique is still relatively free of error.

In the second variation a smaller square is not provided. The subject has to "imagine" a standard unit and carry out the process of iteration without a concrete version of it to aid him. As a consequence, this technique not only produces quantitative symbols which are local in their frame of reference, but it is also prone to error, since variations in the size of the "imagined" standard unit are highly likely to occur both within and between quantification episodes.

This second variation of the measurement process employed in the squares task provides a specific example of the basic characteristics of the estimation quantification operator. Its operation is predicated on the assumption that the system has the capacity to generate *size analog symbols* (SASs) which can be simplistically viewed as internal representations of the space occupied by continuous or discontinuous quantities in the external environment. No attempt will be made to explain the physiological basis of SASs or the locus and manner of their generation. Direct comparison of SASs is the means by which the system copes with the problem of divining the quantitative difference between an elephant and a mouse.

In addition to their function in such direct comparisons, SASs constitute the standard units available to the system for use in the iterative estimation process employing an imagined standard. Although the system always has the ability to generate new SASs, it is probable that once a fund of SASs (derived from interaction with the environment during development) is available in LTM, the system uses these iteratively in quantification in preference to generating new single SASs corresponding to environmental features. The SASs available as standards vary widely between systems since they are based on the idiosyncratic experience of each system. Some people estimate length in terms of football fields, others in terms of cars. In addition, within any single system many possible standards exist in LTM for use in processing each class of quantity such as length, number, and volume. The requirements of the particular task situation determine which of the range of standards is employed.

In adults some of the standard SASs stored in LTM may be linked to one or other of the standard measurement scales. This comes about as a result of situations in which the operation of the estimation quantification operator overlaps with the use of conventional measurement techniques. Suppose that we possess a SAS representing the length of our current car; while reading the handbook we note that the measured length is 18 feet. Subsequently, estimates of length derived by iteration of the car SASs as a standard can be expressed in terms linked to the standard length measurement scale. They are, thus, no longer local in their frame of reference but are still subject to a relatively high degree of error due to variations in the imagined standard within and between quantification episodes.

Application of estimation to discontinuous quantities also results in the linking of SASs to quantitative symbols with general reference. A group of spectators occupying a small section of a football field is quantified by means of PS.COUNT or PS.SUBADD. The resulting number is linked to the outcome of applying estimation to the same group. The outcome in this case would probably be two SASs, one representing the total space occupied by the group and the other the density of occupation of the space. Repeated application of these twin SASs to the remainder of the crowd viewing the game would produce an estimate of the total number of spectators. These linked standards could also be employed on any future occasion when estimates of the size of crowds are required.

The repeated applicaton of imagined standards during estimation has been mentioned on several occasions. We will end our discussion by offering a few speculative remarks on the nature of this process. It appears plausible that it might have much in common with the mode of operation of PS.COUNT. Each SAS can be regarded as a discrimination production system processing VSTM. The discrimination production system applies the SAS iteratively to the continuous or discontinuous features of the current contents of VSTM which constitute the target to be quantified. As each application takes place a semantic element is placed in SSTM. This enables productions processing SSTM to update a quantitative symbol representing the number of successful iterations. If the SAS being employed is already linked with a standard measurement scale or number, the productions update the current scale value or number in SSTM.

It is clear that the proposed estimation process cannot function effectively unless the discrimination production systems include productions which ensure that double processing of sections of the contents of VSTM does not occur. This may be achieved, as in the case of PS.COUNT, by productions which either mark sections as they are processed or give rise to regular patterns of eye movement which simplify the administration of target sections in VSTM by regulating the information entering the visual encoding channel.

DEVELOPMENT OF THE QUANTIFICATION OPERATORS

The general topic of transition and the development of quantification operators in particular will be discussed at length in the final chapter. At the present juncture we will only consider aspects of the development of the quantification operators which will be required as background to the accounts of class inclusion, conservation, and transitivity that follow in successive chapters.

Flavell (1971) has argued that the concept of developmental primacy is ill-defined without simultaneous consideration of relative starting points, growth rates, and points of "functional maturity." In adults the subitizing quantification operator (Q_s), the counting quantification operator (Q_c), and the estimation quantification operator (Q_e) are fully developed and utilized under appropriate conditions. They are, consequently, related by what Flavell (1972) terms "addition": once available, all three "continue to be used for the remainder of one's cognitive career [p. 287]." It is our contention that the development of Q_c and Q_e as quantification operators depends upon the prior emergence of Q_s. The operators are, thus, also related by "mediation." Flavell (1972) describes the mediation of item x_2 by item x_1 as follows: "The acquisition of x_1 could be described as constituting some sort of developmental route or path to x_2, as providing an occasion or opportunity for the emergence of x_2, as facilitating the genesis of x_2 ... [p. 312]."

The assertion of the developmental primacy of Q_s is based on the fact that a quantification operator such as PS.SUB2 can be constructed by the system as a result of its interaction with the environment without any acquisition of socially transmitted technology. The process of construction will be fully described in the final chapter. As a result, Q_s is the first of the three quantification operators to produce consistent outcomes and comprises the basis of the system's conception of quantity. Q_c and Q_e develop concurrently with Q_s, but it takes longer before they begin to produce consistent outcomes. Q_c requires a socially transmitted technology including verbal labels, noticing orders, and place keeping. None of these processes is required by PS.SUB. In the early stages of development Q_e is the source of much inconsistency, since the generation of more than one SAS in the quantification of a single environmental feature is frequently required before a consistent outcome is obtained. Such multiple generation is the outcome of a protracted developmental process.

Thus, we postulate the onset of Q_s prior to the onset of Q_c, and a growth period during which the upper range of Q_s increases from $n = 1$ or 2 to $n = 3$ or 4, while the range of Q_c is extended indefinitely. A hypothetical plot of maximum numerical range (n) against age, as Fig. 3.23 indicates, yields a curve for Q_s that starts at the origin (birth) and asymptotically approaches the upper limit, and a curve for Q_c that starts during the second year and increases, perhaps positively accelerated, indefinitely. The two curves cross in the region of $n = 2-3$ and age 2 to 3 years.

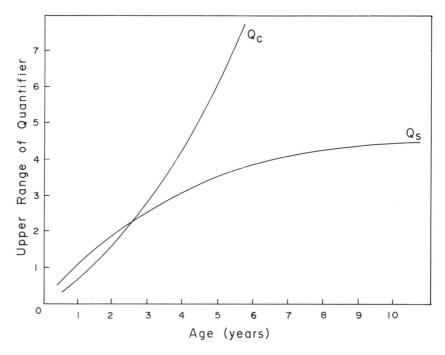

FIG. 3.23   Hypothetical plot of development of Q_s and Q_c.

A number of important developmental consequences stem from the primacy of Q_s and its position as the basis of the system's conception of quantity. The system uses Q_s in preference to Q_c and Q_e whenever this is possible. This is clearly demonstrated by the twin latency slopes obtained in our quantification experiments with adults and with 5-year-old children.

In our view, Q_s also plays an essential part in determining the transition of Q_c from a mechanical, socially transmitted process to the status of an indicator of quantitative information. How do number labels reached at the termination of counting episodes acquire semantic significance and convey information about the quantitative aspect of the environment? The answer to this question lies in the application of Q_c to situations within the range of Q_s. As the same collections are quantified by Q_s and processed by Q_c, the status of an indicator of quantitative information is acquired by Q_c. This transition is probably facilitated by the attachment of number labels to the subitizing productions in PS.SUB and the detection by the system of the resulting correspondences between the outcomes derived from PS.SUB and PS.COUNT.

The primacy of Q_s is equally important in the development of Q_e. SASs acquire semantic significance as indicators of quantitative information as a result of the application of Q_e to discontinuous collections which are also quantified by Q_s or by Q_c if, as occurs in some cases, the development of Q_c is proceeding faster than that of Q_e. The inconsistency of the outcomes produced by Q_e in comparison with those obtained when Q_s or Q_c is applied to the same situations plays an important part in initiating the generation of multiple SASs in the quantification of a single environmental feature. The crucial importance of this innovation in the operation of Q_e will become apparent in the discussion of conservation (Chapter 5).

As already indicated, our operational definition of Q_s is based upon reaction times for verbal responses. Thus, it is difficult to obtain the direct empirical evidence from very young children which is necessary to confirm or refute the developmental relationships between Q_s, Q_c, and Q_e that we have postulated. The results obtained in the experiment with five-year-old children are consistent with our proposals, but data from younger subjects are required to put them to the acid test.

Gelman (1972a), in a comprehensive review of empirical investigations of early number concepts, has reached diametrically opposed conclusions on the developmental relationship of subitizing and counting. For our present concern, the most relevant evidence cited by Gelman in support of her standpoint is derived from a study by Beckmann (1924) and is reproduced in Table 3.3. Beckmann classified children as counters if they were observed to count before giving an answer and if they said that they counted when asked how they knew an answer. He classified as subitizers those who responded rapidly without giving indications of counting and who, when asked how they knew an answer, said things like, "It looks like two," or "I can see it's two." On this basis Gelman (1972a) asserts that "counting is the preeminent mechanism used by young children to estimate numbers of all sizes, with the possible exception of 1 and 2. . . . The ability to subitize small numbers also appears in preschool children. But, . . . it appears to develop *after* children have learned to estimate a number by counting [p. 128]." Since they are derived from 4- to 6-year-old children, Beckmann's data, like the results of our experiment with 5-year-olds, are inconclusive about the relationship between subitizing and counting. It should be mentioned,

●

●

●

FIG. 3.24   A configuration likely to be subitized (see page 31).

however, that there is nothing in his data which is inconsistent with our account of the development of Q_s and Q_c. This includes the results concerned with the number 2 that are inconsistent with Gelman's view and which she suggests may indicate a possible exception to the primacy of counting.

Any arguments founded on data such as Beckmann's must be tempered with caution on methodological grounds. Since no attempt was made to control or measure the exposure times of the collections being quantified, it appears probable that both under- and overestimation of the frequency of subitizing occurred. Underestimation would arise from occasions when Q_s and Q_c were applied to the same collections. Overestimation of subitizing, as defined by us in terms of response time, is indicated by the finding that 60% of the 6-year-olds subitize when $n = 6$. Recall that our adult studies revealed an upper limit for Q_s that was never as high as 6.

Recent studies by Schaeffer, Eggleston, and Scott (1974) further support our position. Referring to subitizing as "pattern recognition of small numbers," they report that in a group of 13 children (mean age 3 years, 8 months), 12 could correctly recognize 2 items, 7 could recognize 3 items, and 6 could recognize an array of 4 items. In the "recognition" task, the children were shown the stimulus and asked "how many?" The children were explicitly instructed not to count or point, but just to say how many items there were. However, when this same

TABLE 3.3

Percentage of Children in Beckmann's Study Who Counted or
Subitized When Estimating Numbers[a]

		Age of children				
Number	Process	4–0 (48)[b]	4–6 (26)	5–0 (27)	5–6 (20)	6–0 (24)
2	Count	25	17	11	4	2
	Subitize	75	83	89	96	98
3	Count	71	33	35	21	5
	Subitize	29	67	66	79	95
4	Count	80	80	71	52	17
	Subitize	20	20	29	48	83
5	Count	100	88	76	61	33
	Subitize	–	12	24	39	67
6	Count	100	96	90	64	41
	Subitize	–	4	10	36	59

[a] From Beckmann (1924, Table 8, p. 28), reproduced as Table IV in Gelman (1972b).
[b] Number in brackets indicates the size of each age group.

group of 13 children was asked to count the arrays, only one of them could correctly count the 2-, 3-, and 4-item arrays.

In concluding this discussion two further points will be mentioned which seem to be consistent with the developmental primacy of Q_s rather than Q_c. The first is derived from phylogenesis. The evidence for the existence of a quantification capability in lower organisms such as birds (Koehler, 1949) is more easily reconciled with the developmental primacy in humans of a quantification operator such as Q_s which does not depend on socially transmitted technology.

The second argument anticipates the content of Chapter 5 since it is concerned with the emergence of conservation. It will be presented at this point, although its full force will not be apparent until an account of the development of conservation has been offered. If Q_c is developmentally prior to Q_s and makes the developmental running, then we would expect that conservation rules would be derived and applied, in particular in situations where $n > 3$, much earlier than appears to be the case. Beckmann's data, for example, suggest that Q_c should be capable of detecting consistent sequences by quantifying collections before and after transformations at numerical levels well above 5, while Q_s is still functioning at the 3 level. There is, however, no evidence that the detection of consistent sequences leads to the derivation of the conservation rules by Q_c and their subsequent application to the operations of Q_s. On the contrary, the data suggest that the appearance of the conservation rules and the numerical limit to their applicability generally keep pace with the gradual buildup of the numerical range of Q_s.

RELATIVE MAGNITUDE DETERMINATION

Earlier in this chapter we pointed out that in many tasks the child is required to make quantitative comparisons between two or more collections. Thus, quantification operators are required to generate quantitative symbols for each of the

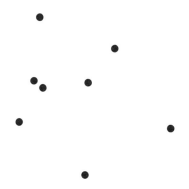

FIG. 3.25   A configuration likely to be counted (see page 31).

collections to permit the comparisons to be made. Having discussed the nature of the quantification operators at considerable length, we must now turn to the processes involved in relative magnitude determination. Recall that in Chapter 2 we described a program for quantitative comparison as an example of a production system. Although the program contained specific rules for the control of the overall flow, it did not throw any light on the comparison process per se, since the operator RELATE, which determines the relationship between two quantitative symbols, was unspecified, and the system asked for the result of the relational operator via a terminal call. Thus, in this section we focus upon the process whereby the relative magnitude of two internal quantitative symbols is determined.

We will begin by presenting a formal description of the principal processes involved in quantitative comparison.

Let

$x,y \equiv$ internal symbols representing collections of material;

$x_i \equiv$ quantitative symbol for collection x produced by operator Q_i; (e.g., x_s if produced by Q_s; x_e if produced by Q_e).

$=, >, < \equiv$ relations of "same," "greater than," and "less than," respectively, between two quantitative symbols;

$\overset{Q}{=}, \overset{Q}{>}, \overset{Q}{<} \equiv$ relations of equal, more, and less, respectively, quantity between two symbols for collections.

Then the three main productions which govern quantitative comparison in adults are:

$$(x_i = y_i) \dashrightarrow (x \overset{Q}{=} y) \tag{3.11}$$

$$(x_i < y_i) \dashrightarrow (x \overset{Q}{<} y) \tag{3.12}$$

$$(x_i > y_i) \dashrightarrow (x \overset{Q}{>} y). \tag{3.13}$$

These productions provide a link between two types of knowledge that we view as distinct. One type of knowledge concerns relations among quantitative symbols; for example, that the internal representation for "3" is to be considered "less than" the representation for "5." The other type of knowledge concerns the quantitative relations among entities in the environment; for example, that there are more red balls than blue balls. If you count collection x and find that it has three items, and then count collection y and find that it has five items, you would draw the obvious conclusion that there are more y things than x things. However, this conclusion is drawn through an inferential step, and it is precisely this class of inferences that these three productions explicitly represent. For adults, such a distinction seems trivial, but for children it is an important cognitive acquisition. Schaeffer, Eggleston, and Scott (1974) found that young children who could correctly count a collection of objects (i.e., could coordinate number names with exhaustive and nonredundant enumeration) did not seem to realize that they had produced a quantitative symbol. Furthermore, young children who could correctly count, say, four items and then five items, still did not know that the collection of five things was more than the collection of four.

Thus, the function of each of these productions is to take as input from SSTM one of three symbols representing the outcome of comparing two quantitative symbols generated by the application of a quantification operator to two collections and to place the appropriate quantitative relational attribute symbol in SSTM. The addition of a quantitative relational attribute symbol to SSTM represents an increase in the system's knowledge of the extensive properties of the collections being compared. It indicates that a fact such as, for example, "collection x is equal in quantity to collection y" is now a feature of the current knowledge state of the system. The three production rules can be viewed as explicit statements that the quantitative symbols generated by the three quantification operators are what Wallach (1969) terms "indicator properties." These are "perceptible properties, sameness of which indicates equality and difference inequality [p. 207]."

The relational attribute symbols placed in SSTM are the same regardless of which quantification operator produces the symbols involved in the comparison of quantitative symbols. In adults, the quantitative symbols compared are generally numbers, since PS.COUNT generates numbers and PS.SUB does like-

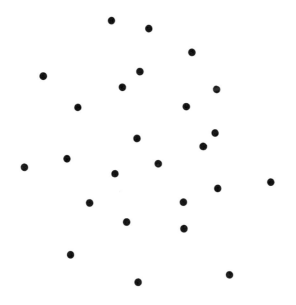

FIG. 3.26   A configuration likely to be estimated (see page 31).

wise due to the number labels attached to the subitizing productions. As indicated above, estimation also produces numbers in cases where the standard SASs being employed are linked to numerical values as a result of previous experience. Where numbers are the quantitative symbols, the same productions carry out the comparison of the symbols generated by all three quantification operators.

The number comparison productions distinguish the three relationships between the symbols with reference to their relative positions in the number sequence. Thus,

$=$ $\equiv$ both symbols occupy the same position in the number sequence;

$<$ $\equiv n_1$ occurs earlier in the number sequence than n_2;

$>$ $\equiv n_1$ occurs later in the number sequence than n_2.

It appears unlikely that adults distinguish these basic relationships by running through the number sequence until one of the numbers being compared is detected and then deducing which relationship applies. Such a process can be short-circuited by using productions which represent the outcomes of previous comparisons. These enable the relationship between specific pairs of symbols to be produced directly without further processing. Another relatively economical approach, particularly if large numbers are being compared, is to employ productions which determine relative positions in the number sequence by comparing the number of digits in the numbers.

Although the quantitative symbols compared by adults are generally numbers, the number-comparing productions are not the only quantitative comparison productions required. As indicated in the discussion of estimation, the system retains into adulthood the capability of generating SASs. This necessitates the existence of productions which directly compare pairs of SASs and distinguish the three relationships between them. Moving from the outcome of these comparisons to the appropriate quantitative relational attributes is more complex than in the case of numbers, since frequently multiple SASs are generated for each of the collections being quantified. This aspect of the operation of Q_e will be discussed further in Chapter 5.

The Development of Relative Magnitude Determination Processes

Earlier in this chapter arguments were adduced in support of the developmental primacy of Q_s and the view that PS.SUB is the first quantification operator to provide consistent outcomes. Consequently, the quantitative symbols placed in SSTM by Q_s provide the basis for the first quantitative comparisons. As the subitizing productions have not yet been associated with number labels, Q_s does not place numbers in SSTM. The symbols involved in the quantitative comparison are two lists of tokens. Each list is placed in SSTM as a result of the successful operation of a subitizing production and contains a token for each of the positive discrimination productions on the condition side of the successful subitizing production.

The comparison process is carried out by productions which move through the contents of the two lists in parallel establishing whether both lists have a token in each location. These list-processing productions are considered to be among the child's innate repertoire of productions. The composition of this innate repertoire will be discussed at considerable length in the final chapters. The list-comparison productions yield one of three distinct outcomes as they complete the token-for-token comparison of the two lists (L1 and L2):

L1 has a token remaining and L2 does not.
L1 does not have a token remaining and L2 has.
Neither L1 nor L2 has a token remaining.

These three results constitute the initial semantic basis for the concepts of "more," "less," and "equal."

In general, it appears that the ability to cope with all three relations is not attained simultaneously. Equality and inequality seem to develop sequentially, although the experimental evidence on their order of appearance is inconclusive (Beilin, 1968). Within the inequality relation there is some indication that "more" is coped with successfully before "less" (Donaldson & Wales, 1970). The latter sequence seems eminently plausible since the "less" relationship is presumably derived as the result of an additional processing step. In terms of the example above the system first derives the relationship in terms of the list with a token remaining and then "restates" it in terms of the list without a token.

Detection of the three distinct outcomes of comparing subitizing quantitative symbols antedates the appearance of the three main productions linking the results of quantitative symbol comparisons to quantitative relational attributes. The three productions emerge as the outcome of a two-step developmental process. As Q_c and Q_e develop they generate quantitative symbols which are placed in SSTM. These symbols are, at first, different for each of the three quantification operators and as a result, three distinct processes for comparing pairs of symbols emerge. The second step in the developmental process is very important. This is the recognition by the system of the equivalence of the outcomes obtained from each of the three comparison processes. In line with the account of the development of the quanitification operators offered above, we hypothesize that recognition results from the application of two of the quantification operators to the same collections. When Q_c, for example, has begun to yield consistent outcomes, it first acquires the status of an indicator of quantitative information as the same collections are quantified by Q_s and processed by Q_c. As already indicated, this process is facilitated by the attachment of number labels to the subitizing productions. Subsequently, continuation of double processing leads to the detection of the equivalence of the outcomes of the Q_c quantitative comparison process and the "more," "less," and "equal" results obtained via Q_s. In informal terms, the establishment of this equivalence constitutes a broadening of the semantic basis of the concepts of "more," "less," and "equal." In formal terms, it is marked by the emergence of the three basic productions linking the results of comparison of pairs of quantitative symbols to relational attribute symbols. The relational attribute symbols are thus the same for both quantification operators. The process of detecting equivalence may be assisted by the application of both quantification operators to situations in which a collection is quantified, transformed, and requantified. The quantitative comparison, consequently, is a test of the effect of the transformation. The saliency of situations involving transformations of this type is indicated by evidence (Donaldson & Wales, 1970) that when children are confronted with two collections and are asked which is more, they initially select the collection which they have seen "made more" (i.e., it has undergone an addition transformation), rather than the collection with the greater quantity.

ONE—ONE CORRESPONDENCE

Before concluding this chapter devoted to quantification processes, we must consider how the establishing of one—one correspondence relates to the account of quantification which we have offered. The placing of two collections in one—one correspondence, as illustrated at the top of Fig. 3.27, has gained prominence in research on number concepts since it is the first step in the classic Piagetian test of equivalence conservation. It has also become a familiar feature in introductory mathematics since the set theoretic approach to the inculcation of natural number concepts places considerable emphasis on this type of activity.

We have chosen to consider one—one correspondence after a discussion of the processes involved in relative magnitude determination, since we view it as a specific quantitative comparison technique which emerges *subsequent* to the relative magnitude (RM) processes described in the previous section.[6] Our account of the development of RM concluded at the point at which the three main productions linking the results of quantitative symbol comparisons to quantitative relational attributes have emerged and their area of application extends to the operations of all three quantification operators. The results of quantitative symbol comparisons are obtained by applying a quantification operator first to one collection, then to the other, and submitting the resulting

---

[6] Note the distinction we are making between RM and one—one comparison. One—one comparison is a high level strategy for determining the relative quantity of two *external* collections. RM is a simple, internal, low-level process for determining the relative magnitude of two *internal* symbols. The logic of RM is essentially an internal one—one comparison of the components of quantitative symbols (for example, tokens and lists).

quantitative symbols to comparison productions. This procedure is sufficient, but not ideal, in terms of processing economy when the collections being compared comprise regularly arranged discontinuous elements. In such situations one–one correspondence emerges as a more economical comparison technique. Only a single pass across the collections is required and the results are directly obtained without the generation and comparison of quantitative symbols. These comparison results provide an additional source of acceptable input to the three main productions. The importance of processing economy in determining the course of development will be discussed in the final chapter. One of the specific examples to be described is concerned with class-inclusion performance, and the effects of the pursuit of processing economy are very similar to those which give rise to the one–one correspondence quantitative comparison technique.

The viewpoint we adopt toward one–one correspondence may appear difficult to reconcile with the results of experiments in which 2- to 4-year-old children have successfully dealt with the quantitative comparison of collections arranged in one–one correspondence as the initial step in trials aimed at determining their grasp of the conservation principle. Such data would appear to be consistent with the early appearance of one–one correspondence as an independent development, rather than its derivation as a more economical version of already existing comparison processes based on the quantification operators. This issue can be resolved by consideration of examples of the one–one correspondence situations employed in these experiments. The successful quantitative comparisons made by young children when Mehler and Bever (1967) confronted them with the type of situation illustrated in Fig. 3.27 can be just as plausibly attributed to the application of Q_e as to one–one correspondence. The equality judgments arise from the comparison of SASs generated by the quantification of the respective lengths or densities of the two rows.

A similar explanation can be offered for young children's success in coping with the rather different type of one–one correspondence situation employed by Bryant (1974) which is also illustrated in Fig. 3.27. In all three situations, there are 20 dots in the upper row and 19 in the lower. In situation A, when asked which of the pair has more dots, children make the correct choice more than half the time. In situation B they make the wrong choice more than half the time, and in situation C they choose correctly and incorrectly with equal frequency. The large number of dots renders Q_s and Q_c inappropriate. If applied to length in $A1$, or density in $A2$, Q_e would produce the correct result.

The saliency of the density of such rows and the consequent activation of Q_e are supported by Bryant's results for situation C. The children were almost evenly divided between those who maintained that the top row contained more counters and those who considered the bottom row represented the greater quantity. This is consistent with the situation which would be reflected by Q_e, namely that both the upper and lower rows are "more dense" in part. For situation B, Q_e is applied to length, yielding a consistent, but incorrect result.

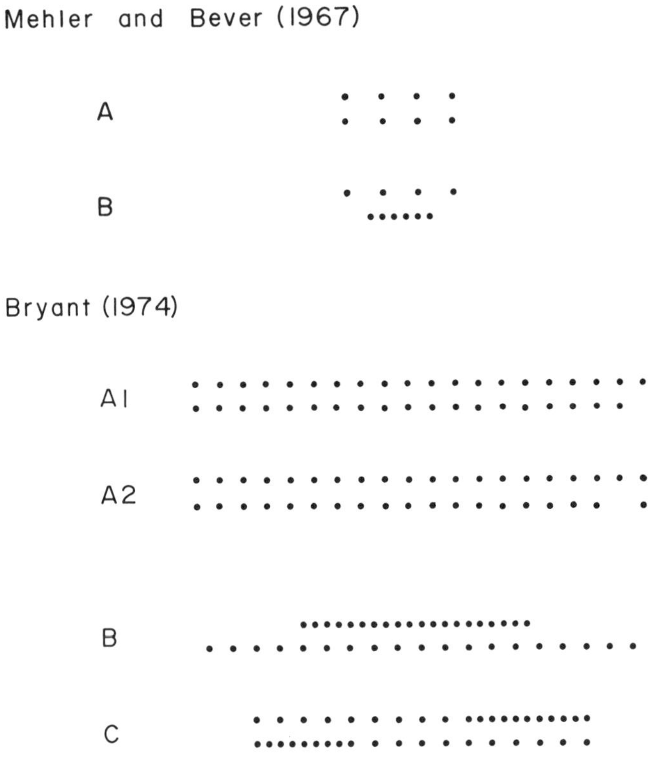

FIG. 3.27 Conservation of quantity stimuli. (From Mehler & Bever, 1967; Bryant, 1974.)

The arguments in support of our view of one–one correspondence are not limited to offering alternative interpretations of opposed data. Experimental results exist which are compatible with our position and apparently inconsistent with arguments for the early, independent emergence of one–one correspondence as a technique for quantification comparison. Smedslund (1964) maintains that a partial explanation of the persistent and "illogical" absence of conservation in young children is that, despite appearances to the contrary, the initial "equality" of the two collections arranged in one–one correspondence is not accepted at the beginning of the test. Renwick (1963) quotes examples of young children's responses which indicate that the establishing of one–one correspondence is not at first regarded as giving valid information about the relative number of objects in two collections. In her view, it is only when the act of pairing becomes connected with the operation of counting that its numerical significance is appreciated and it is accepted as a valid alternative to counting as a source of comparative numerical information.

Evidence derived from a large-scale experimental study is provided by Brainerd (1973). His subjects were 180 Canadian children aged 5 to 7 years. Among other tests, the children were given six items designed to tax their ability to make quantitative judgments on the basis of one–one correspondence. They were asked to look very closely at the two rows and to figure out whether or not they contained the same number of dots. To insure that the six pairs of classes could be quantified only by correspondence, two restrictions were imposed. First, the children were told that they should not count the dots. Second, the two classes always were arranged in such a manner that perceptual cues could not be used: when the rows contained the same number of dots, they were of unequal length; when they did not contain the same number of dots either they were of equal length or the row containing fewer dots was the longer of the two. Typical examples of the situations employed are presented in Fig. 3.28.

Brainerd's procedure, viewed in our terms, should have ensured that the subjects did not employ Q_c. The numerical level of the rows was also beyond the range of Q_s. The adoption of a layout in which rows containing the same number of dots were of unequal length should have ruled out the possibility of correct quantitative equality judgments reached by applying Q_e. Size analog symbols generated on the basis of the length or density of the rows would result in erroneous judgments of inequality. Unfortunately, the same cannot be said of the layout when the rows contained unequal numbers. Having the rows of equal length, or having the row with fewer dots the longer of the two prevents correct inequality judgments from being produced by the application of Q_e to the *length* of the rows. But these expedients do not rule out this possibility if Q_e is applied to the *density* of the two rows. Consequently, in the remainder of our

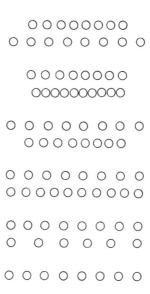

FIG. 3.28 Conservation of quantity stimuli. (From Brainerd, 1973.)

discussion we will only consider the data obtained from the items with equal numbers of dots in the rows.

The results obtained by Brainerd indicate that only 15 of the 180 children could cope successfully with the trials in which the two rows contained an equal number of dots. This outcome in a situation in which convincing efforts were made to prevent the application of the quantification operators affords strong support to the view that one–one correspondence makes a relatively late appearance in development and depends upon the prior existence of quantitative comparison processes based on the quantification operators.

QUANTIFICATION PROCESSES AND THE STRUCTURE
AND ORGANIZATION OF THE IPS

The major implications for the structure and organization of the information-processing system arise from our treatment of subitizing. It will be recalled that the decision to add a visual encoding channel to the system was taken to enable the productions in PS.SUB2 to receive input from a visual STM. The hypothesized sequence of processing of information in the visual encoding channel commences when visual stimulation registering on the sense organs gives rise to a representation in an unselective, iconic memory. Visual encoding productions which are only capable of making crude distinctions process the contents of iconic memory and transfer parts of the representation to VSTM. Further visual encoding productions, of which the subitizing productions are particular examples, process the contents of visual STM and transfer the results of this procedure to SSTM. These amendments to the information-processing system arising from our treatment of quantification processes and additional modifications which will be suggested in the following discussions of class inclusion, conservation, and transitivity will be integrated in the general account of the system to be presented in Chapter 7.

4
Class Inclusion

In Chapter 2 we described a production system, PS.QC1, which constitutes a model of how quantitative comparisons are accomplished. A trace was presented of the sequence of actions arising when a subclass comparison question "Are there more reds or blues?" was input to the system. This is a perfectly straightforward question and poses no problems for PS.QC1. A much more interesting situation arises when the question requires a quantitative comparison between a superclass and a subclass. This is the characteristic feature of the class-inclusion (CI) task which Piaget (1952) regards as capturing the essence of concrete operational functioning. It originated in his study of the concept of number and was systematically investigated by Inhelder and Piaget (1964).

The Genevan view of both the task and its interpretation is presented in the following passage from Piaget and Inhelder (1969):

> If, for example, in a group B of 12 flowers within which there is a subgroup A of six primroses, you ask the child to show first the flowers B and next the primroses A, he responds correctly, because he can designate the whole B and the part A. However, if you ask him, "Are there more flowers or more primroses?" he is unable to respond according to the inclusion $A < B$ because if he thinks of the part A, the whole B ceases to be conserved as a unit, and the part A is henceforth comparable only to its complementary A'. He may reply, therefore, "the same," or, if there are a clear majority of primroses in the set, he may say that there are more primroses. The understanding of the relative sizes of an included class to the entire class is achieved at about eight and marks the achievement of a genuine operatory classification [p. 103].*

Empirical results obtained by presenting children with both subclass comparisons and CI tasks afford examples of striking changes in performance with development.

In this chapter we will briefly summarize the empirical and theoretical background for the CI task. Then we will describe a cycle of model building and

*From *The Psychology of The Child* by Jean Piaget and Barbel Inhelder, Translated from the French by Helen Wever, © 1969 by Basic Books, Inc., Publishers, New York.

empirical investigation that results in two final models: one for CI failure (PS.QC2) and one for CI success (PS.QC3).

EMPIRICAL STUDIES

A considerable number of empirical studies on variants of the CI task have been conducted in the past decade (e.g., Ahr & Youniss, 1970; Blair-Hood, 1962; Kofsky, 1966; Kohnstamm, 1963, 1968; Smedslund, 1964; Wohlwill, 1968). Although some investigators have chosen to use CI as a standard measure of cognitive development (e.g., Jennings, 1969; McGhee, 1971), this may be somewhat premature, for, as we will show, the results of these studies exhibit the degree of variation and inconsistency that is characteristic of investigations of concrete operations. This has prompted attempts to produce both methodological refinements (Smedslund, 1964, 1966a, b) and theoretical revisions (Flavell, 1971; Flavell & Wohlwill, 1969; Wallace, 1972b).

Several of these studies have been summarized and evaluated elsewhere (Klahr & Wallace, 1972). Their essential features are shown in Table 4.1, and the results of the experiments are presented in Fig. 4.1.

CAUSES OF FAILURE

The explanations offered for failure on the CI task can be broadly divided into two categories: processing failures and encoding failures. The former arise when

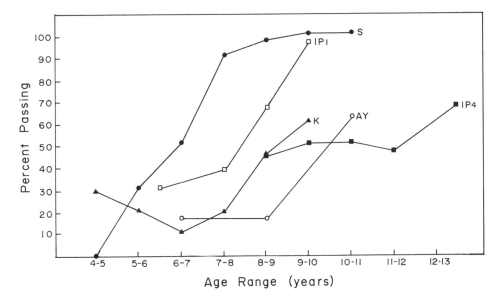

FIG. 4.1 Results of four studies of class inclusion. S—Smedslund (1964); IP1, IP4—Inhelder and Piaget (1964); K—Kofsky (1966); AY—Ahr and Youniss (1970).

TABLE 4.1
Summary of Class-Inclusion Experiments[a]

---

1. Inhelder and Piaget (1964) (IP1, IP2)
   a. Items: pictures of flowers mixed with pictures of other objects.
   b. Distribution: 4 yellow primulas (A), 8 primulas (B), 16 flowers (C), 20 objects (D).
   c. Subclass ratios: IP1 A/A' = 4/4; IP2 B/B' = 8/8.
   d. Question form: IP1 = more B or more A?; IP2: more C or more B?
   e. Mode: pictorial, some reference to external world (e.g., flowers in the woods).
   f. 50% age: IP1, 7–8 years; IP2, 7–8 years.

2. Inhelder and Piaget (1964) (IP3, IP4)
   a. Items: pictures of animals partitioned by boxes.
   b. Distribution: 3–4 ducks (A), 6–9 birds (B), 11–14 animals (C).
   c. Subclass ratios: IP3 A/A' = 3/3 to 4/5; IP4 B/B' = 3/5 to 5/5.
   d. Question form: IP3: more B or more A?; IP4: more C or more B?
   e. Mode: pictorial, some *in extenso* references.
   f. 50% age: IP3, 9 years; IP4, 9 years.

3. Smedslund (1964) (S)
   a. Items: geometrical "two-dimensional" objects (pieces of linoleum).
   b. Distribution: 10 red round pieces (A), 13 red pieces (B).
   c. Subclass ratios: A/A' 10/3.
   d. Question form: more red ones or more round ones?
   e. Mode: objects actually present, but covered immediately prior to question. Then uncovered and question repeated.
   f. 50% age: 6 years.
   g. Subjects: 160, upper middle class, university town, public school, Boulder, Colorado.

4. Kofsky (1963, 1966) (K)
   a. Items: small wooden blocks (2" x 2" x 1").
   b. Distribution: 3 red triangles, 2 blue triangles, 4 blue squares.
   c. Subclass ratios: for K1, A/A' = 3/2; for K2, A/A' = 4/2.
   d. Question form:
      K1: "More triangles or more reds?" or "More reds or more triangles?"
      K2: "More blues or more squares?" or "More squares or more blues?"
      K3: "More blues or more triangles?"
   e. Mode: objects actually present.
   f. 50% age: 8–9 years (scoring: correct only if K1 and K2 correct).
   g. Subjects: 122, above average intelligence, nursery and elementary school, Rochester, New York.

(continued)

TABLE 4.1 (*continued*)

---

5. Wohlwill (1968), Experiment 3
   a. Items: pictures of common items.
   b. Distribution: 12 different collections, ranging from drums and guitars to ball players and cowboys. Three conditions:
      A. Identity within and segregation between subsets.
      B. Similarity within and intermingling between subsets.
      C. As in B, plus two extraneous objects.
   c. Subclass ratios: from 6/2 to 5/3.
   d. Question form: more A or more B (or more B or more A).
   e. Mode: pictorial mode, stimuli present. Verbal mode: entire set generated verbally, e.g., "Suppose I had six jackets and two hats, would I have more jackets or more things to wear?"
   f. 50% age: not reached in this group.
   g. Subjects: 54, lower middle-class public school, Worcester, Massachusetts.

6. Ahr and Youniss (1970), Experiment 1 (AY)
   a. Items: paper cutouts of cats and dogs, and red flowers and yellow flowers.
   b. Distribution: 8 objects, presented in horizontal row with subclasses integrated.
   c. Subclass ratios: systematic experimental variation, from 8/0 (8 cats, no dogs) to 4/4 (4 cats, 4 dogs).
   d. Question form: systematic experimental variation:
      more A or more B; fewer A or fewer B.
   e. Mode: pictorial, objects always present, no *in extenso* references.
   f. 50% age: 10 years.
   g. Subjects: 60, grades 1, 3, 5 middle-class parochial school, Washington, D.C.

---

[a]Parenthetical codes (IP1, S, K, etc.) correspond to graphs in Fig. 4.1. We use Piaget's notation in which A is the subclass in the CI question, B is the superclass composed of A and A′.

the child is unable to make the appropriate subclass comparison; the latter result from a misinterpretation of the CI instructions.

As indicated earlier, Inhelder and Piaget (1964) suggest a processing failure:

> When answering "Are there more of the As or of the Bs?" he cannot compare the As with Bs, and he compares them with the As, precisely because he cannot handle class-inclusion. . . . He cannot think simultaneously of the part and the whole . . . [p. 101].

The explanation offered by Wohlwill (1968) and Ahr and Youniss (1970) is based upon a misinterpretation hypothesis. Wohlwill (1968) summarizes his findings thus:

... the perception of two contrasting subclasses, unbalanced as to number, creates a strong tendency to translate a class inclusion question into a subclass comparison question. This tendency can be counteracted to some extent by procedures designed to weaken the set (counting the subclass and the superordinate class . . . , including extraneous objects . . .). It is presumably at its weakest when the items are presented in purely verbal form . . . [p. 462].

The experiments by Ahr and Youniss (1970) demonstrate that the greater the numerical imbalance between subclasses, the greater was the tendency to make the erroneous subclass comparison.

It is not clear what the connection is between any of these reasons for failure and the effects of procedural variations. Procedural variations can be classified as changes in either the verbal instructions or in the physical stimuli. The verbal instructions can be varied in many ways to facilitate the appropriate comparison. Wohlwill (1968) notes that "even to an adult there appears something slightly tricky about such questions as 'Are there more pears or more fruit?' " The difficulty seems to follow from two interpretive steps: (a) The *or* is applied not to the two relational statements implied, "[more pears (than fruit)] or [more fruit (than pears)] ," but instead to the two classes, "[pears] or [fruit] ." (b) The *or* is interpreted exclusively rather than inclusively because that is its overwhelmingly common usage.

It is easy for one familiar with the CI task to forget the initial confusing impact of the conjunction of these two interpretations. In a different form, the power of the exclusive interpretation of *or* becomes apparent (e.g., "Are there pears or fruit on the table?"), and the tricky nature of the CI question can easily take on a not-so-subtle pejorative tone (e.g., "In the APA, are there more psychologists or more clinicians?"; "In the department, are there more people or more students?").

Several variations in the wording of the question are apparent: "More *A* or more *B*?; more *A* than *B* or more *B* than *A*?; which is more, *A* or *B*?"; substituting "less" for "more," and so forth. Similarly, one can imagine many stimulus variations, some of which have already been found to be influential: familiarity of objects or class name, subclass ratios, number of objects, similarity of objects, objects present, objects present but out of view, objects absent but enumerated, objects absent and *in extenso,* and so on. The problem that one faces in generating these variations is that their effects must ultimately be interpreted, but the interpretation cannot be made upon the basis of any existing theory. Current theories are stated at a level of generality that makes impossible specific predictions about the effects of the procedural variations listed previously.

The significant effect of different combinations of these variations is clear. Figure 4.1 shows the extremely wide range of performance on the CI task that is generated by the studies summarized in Table 4.1. Consider, for example, Smedslund's study. His results indicate children reach the 50% mark on CI almost three years before the age reported by Kofsky (1966) and almost four years before that reported by Ahr and Youniss (1970). Yet a priori Smedslund's (1964) procedure would seem to be more difficult than the others because he used geometrical forms rather than objects having a natural semantic hierarchy (for example, people and men), and his objects were not visible at the time the CI question was posed. We say "seem to be more difficult" because until we have a detailed model of the class-inclusion process, we must rely upon our intuition for predictions about the effect of procedural variation.

As we noted at the end of Chapter 2, the interaction of semantic and formal class-inclusion factors makes it difficult to interpret many of these results. A specific example of the complexity of this issue is provided by Markman (1973). She showed that if the class name cannot be applied to the subclass (as in the case of family versus children), then subjects make fewer errors than in the conventional case where the class name can be applied to the subclass (for example, animals versus dogs).

In summary, then, we have various theoretical accounts on one hand, and the complex set of results obtained from the experimental studies on the other. A gap exists between the hypothetical structures and processes which form the basis of the theory and the level of performance as represented by the experimental data. Because they are stated in such general terms, it remains open to question whether the theories are sufficient to account for the complex and varied behavior they purportedly explain. A much more detailed account of the functioning of specific processes is necessary before these uncertainties can be dispelled.

PROCESS MODELS FOR CLASS-INCLUSION SUCCESS AND FAILURE

Our first steps in the information-processing analysis of class inclusion (Klahr & Wallace, 1972) resulted in the construction of four models of quantification. Two of these represented alternative models of the developmental state underlying CI failure, while the other two were alternative explanations of CI success. All four models were founded on the basic quantitative comparison production system PS.QC1, but they included different specifications of the way the display was quantified. At the time these models were proposed, they were not specified at the detailed level of those in Chapter 3. Rather they consisted of the aggregate components indicated in Fig. 4.2. However, this level of functional analysis will suffice to show how the inadequacies of all of these initial models can be systematically revealed through further formal and empirical analysis.

First, we will describe the four quantification operators shown in Fig. 4.2. Recall that in PS.QC1 (Fig. 2.1), P11 says that if the goal is quantification of some value X, then the system should apply some (unspecified) quantification operator, producing a quantitative symbol for value X. Figure 4.2 shows four

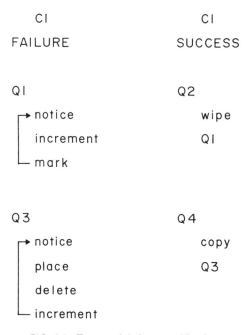

FIG. 4.2   Four models for quantification.

possible quantification schemes. The first of these (Q1) consists of a sequential progression of noticing the objects on a list, incrementing a quantitative symbol, and marking the objects as they are processed to avoid double processing. The other quantification operator (Q3) involves the decomposition of the list, internally representing the test collection, into two sublists by sequentially noticing objects, moving them to a new list, and incrementing a quantitative symbol. The major distinction between Q1 and Q3 is that Q1 marks the objects noticed but otherwise leaves the initial list intact while the latter destroys the initial list by removing the objects noticed from it.

With either Q1 or Q3 as a quantification operator, PS.QC1 can cope with a quantitative comparison involving disjoint subsets, for example, "Are there more reds or more blues?" It is, however, inadequate to succeed on a CI task, since both Q1 and Q3 make it impossible for the second application of the quantification operator to deal with an intact internal representation of the test collection. PS.QC1, utilizing either Q1 or Q3, constitutes a sufficient model of unsuccessful performance on CI since the requisite double processing of objects that are, for example, both blue and square will fail if either quantification operator is used.

Alternative information-processing theories of successful CI performance can be produced by modifying Q1 and Q3 in the manner indicated in Fig. 4.2. Q2 differs from Q1 in that it includes a process (wipe) which removes marks from the objects in an internal representation of a collection before the quantification of each value commences. Double processing of objects is possible and, consequently, success can be attained on CI tasks. Q4, unlike Q3, first creates a copy of the entire internal list and then carries out its destructive quantification on the copy. The original internal representation remains intact and this enables the double processing required for CI success to take place.

EMPIRICAL TESTS OF THE FOUR STATE THEORIES

When these quantification operators are included in PS.QC1, we have four *state theories* for CI performance. PS.QC1, using either Q1 or Q3, represents the state in which children fail CI but pass subclass comparison. When Q2 or Q4 is used with PS.QC1, we have a state theory of CI success. The implied transitions from failure to success are from Q1 to Q2 or from Q3 to Q4. In this section we will describe some small-scale empirical tests of predictions that follow from these models. The results will demonstrate that PS.QC1 functioning with any of these quantifiers is inadequate to explain children's performance.

All four theories involve the assumption that the child possesses an internal representation of the test collection. This must be a complete intensive representation to permit the processing of individual objects and, in information-processing terms, would take the form of a list structure in which each object is represented by a sublist. Since it appeared to be highly improbable that such a representation could be maintained continuously in STM throughout the performance of a class-inclusion task, it was assumed that it must be stored in LTM. This assumption permits the prediction that the latency from the presentation of the test collection and the accompanying question to the child's response should be consistent with the prevailing estimates of LTM fixation time. If 5 sec per chunk is accepted as a fixation time estimate, a latency greater than 5 sec would be predicted for class-inclusion performance, since the child must not only set up an internal representation in LTM but must also carry out a quantitative comparison. A latency of about 5 sec assumes that the complete intensive representation of the test collection is transferred from STM to LTM as a single chunk. It can be argued that a collection composed of two homogeneous subsets is more likely to be processed as two chunks. Acceptance of this suggestion would lead to a prediction of a class-inclusion latency greater than 10 sec.

Experiment I. Subjects and Procedure

These latency predictions were tested in an experiment in which 17 children aged between 5 years, 6 months and 6 years each underwent four formal class-inclusion problems in which shape and color defined the superset—subset relations. To ensure comprehension of the questions the children were first required to demonstrate in a matching task that they could discriminate and appropriately label the shapes and colors to be used in the class-inclusion situations. Their understanding of the term "more" was also checked by administering three items in which two rows of blocks, identical in shape and color but unequal in number, were presented and the question "Is there more in this row (pointing) or more in this row?" posed.

All of the class-inclusion items were alike in involving a major subset of 7 objects and a minor subset of 6 objects, thus yielding a 13-object superset. The method adopted was to present the test collections with the two subsets mixed rather than separate. It was hoped that this would reduce any likelihood of the children encoding the task as a subclass comparison.

Results of Experiment I.   Under the conditions outlined, the average response latency obtained from the 68 class-inclusion trials was 3.6 sec. Since it might be argued that this figure is depressed by low latencies on trials where the children generated a response by guessing rather than by quantitative comparison, the average was recalculated with individual latencies less than one second being excluded. This procedure yielded an average response latency of 4.1 sec, which is still inconsistent with the predictions founded on the assumption that the child constructs a complete intensive representation of the test collection in LTM. The latency data appear to be more consistent with a process largely taking place in STM such as the version of the counting quantification operator, Q_c, described in Chapter 3. Q_c, it will be recalled, involves sequentially noticing internal representations of objects stored in semantic STM and transferring a succession of numerical labels from LTM to semantic STM.

The importance accorded by the Q3 and Q4 models to the creation of a copy of the internal representation of the test collection before commencing quantification gives rise to an eminently testable prediction. Children who fail CI should succeed on a task consisting of an externalized version of the internal situation produced by the quantification operator Q4 and, thus, requiring no double processing of objects. A situation satisfying these criteria was used by Piaget (1952) but no clear-cut results are reported. With a view to testing this prediction a small-scale experimental study was carried out.

Experiment II. Subjects and Procedure

The subjects for the experiment were 16 children (8 boys and 8 girls) aged between 6 years and 6 years, three months. All had initially demonstrated that they could discriminate and appropriately label the shapes and colors to be used in the test situations and that they understood the term "more." They had then failed on three class-inclusion items of the standard type with the subsets separated. All three trials involved eight objects which were distributed 7:1, 6:2, and 5:3 between the major and minor subsets on successive trials. The class-inclusion items were followed by six trials in which the child was confronted with two identical collections of objects arranged in parallel rows. On three of the trials the supersets were defined by color and the subsets by shape while this relationship was reversed on the other three trials. As in the class-inclusion items, all of the collections consisted of eight objects. The trials were evenly divided between a 7:1, 6:2, and 5:3 numerical ratio between the subsets. The scored question on each trial was of the type, "Are there more triangles here (pointing to the bottom row) or more reds there (pointing to the top row)?" In half of the questions the value defining the superset was mentioned first while in the remainder the value defining the major subset was mentioned first.

Results of Experiment II. As Table 4.2 indicates, none of the subjects was successful on all six trials. Overall the children gave fail responses on 58 of the 96 trials. Their behavioral and verbal protocols gave a clear indication of the strategy being followed on 45 of the 58 unsuccessful trials. On 32 of these trials the children treated the two identical collections as a single array. When quantification of the two values was attempted, combining the two collections had the effect of transforming the task into a class-inclusion item which the children duly failed. In the remaining 13 unsuccessful trials, the children ignored one of the identical collections throughout. Once again, when quantification of the two values was attempted this resulted in the subject setting himself a class-inclusion problem and failure followed.

The preponderance of fail responses weakens the plausibility of explanations of class-inclusion performance which, like the Q3 and Q4 state theories, hinge on the creation of a copy of the internal representation of the test collection. More specifically, the type of strategies underlying the vast majority of the fail responses suggests that the possession of a copy of the test collection may be more of a hindrance than a help. Both of the strategies described above can be interpreted on an informational overload basis. Confronted with two collections comprising four subsets, some of the children simplify the situation by aggregating all identical objects and, thus, reducing the subset total from four to two. Others achieve the goal of simplification by interpreting the presence of two identical collections as indicative of the redundancy of one of them. By ignoring one collection the subset total is, once again, reduced from four to two.

Several empirical predictions arise from the difficulty pinpointed by Hayes (1972) in the functioning of the state theories of class-inclusion failure. The point is relevant to both theories but since Hayes' discussion specifically mentions the marking operation, we will deal with it entirely in the context of the Q1 state theory. In terms of the Q1 theory, if the value defining the superset is quantified first, all of the objects in the internal representation of the test collection have been marked at the conclusion of the first application of the quantification operator. There are accordingly no unmarked objects left when the attempt is made to produce a quantitative symbol for the value defining the major subset. This represents a serious limitation on the applicability of the Q1 state theory since it is only sufficient when the major subset value is quantified

TABLE 4.2
Distribution of Subjects' Scores in Experiment II

Number of correct responses	0	1	2	3	4	5	6
Number of subjects	4	3	1	2	3	3	0

first. A possible solution to the difficulty would be to modify Q1 so that failure to find any unmarked objects after quantifying the superset would result in the production of a zero quantitative symbol for the major subset value. If the equal probability of attempting to quantify the superset or subset values first is accepted, this modification would lead to the empirical prediction that on 50% of class-inclusion trials the correct response would be produced for the wrong reason. The results of the experimental studies reviewed earlier in the present chapter are clearly inconsistent with this prediction. The level of success of children failing on class inclusion typically falls well below that of chance.

An alternative solution would involve an addition to the quantitative comparison production system PS.QC1 rather than a modification of Q1. PS.QC1 does not include procedures for dealing with failed goals. If such productions were added, the generation of a failed goal symbol would occur when the attempt to obtain a quantitative symbol for the major subset value fails. This would lead to the reactivation of the goal of quantitative comparison and a second attempt would be made to attain it. Since a straight repetition of the previous sequence of events would lead to the same impasse, it is assumed that in the second attempt the goal of quantifying the major subset value would be established first.

With the suggested additions, PS.QC1 would be sufficient to account for failure both on trials when the major subset value or the superset value is quantified first. This theory of failure on class inclusion gives rise to an empirically verifiable prediction concerning response latencies. If one accepted the equiprobability of attempting to quantify the superset or major subset values first, then the response latencies of children failing class inclusion on a series of items involving the same numerical ratio between the subsets would yield a bimodal distribution. Since they involve a return to the quantitative comparison goal preparatory to a second attempt to derive the quantitative symbols, trials on which the superset is quantified first should yield significantly longer latencies than those in which the major subset is processed first and, consequently, no failed goal symbol is generated. In terms of PS.QC1, trials on which the superset is quantified first would require approximately twice as many actions as those in which the major subset is processed first. Experimental data relevant to the testing of this prediction are already available in the shape of the latencies distribution curve obtained from the four class-inclusion trials in Experiment I referred to earlier. These data are inconsistent with the prediction. The latencies on the trials in which the children gave fail responses do not conform to a biomodal distribution.

The above discussion makes it abundantly clear that modifications in the functioning of Q1, Q2, Q3, and Q4, or additions to the production system PS.QC1 itself, are not sufficient to save our initial state theories of class-inclusion performance. New state theories of failure and success on class inclusion must be constructed which take into account empirical evaluation of the intial theories. These new state theories should avoid depending on a complete, intensive, internal representation of the test collection, as characterized PS.QC1. This might be achieved by emphasizing the role of STM and increasing the extent to which the state theories are stimulus bound, that is, the extent to which they make use of the test collection itself as an external memory. The fate of the empirical predictions derived from Q3 and Q4 indicates that a process which copies an internal representation of the test collection should not be allowed in the new state theories. Finally, to attain plausibility, a new state theory of failure on class inclusion must satisfactorily resolve the difficulty highlighted by Hayes (1972).

REVISED STATE THEORIES

Revised state theories of class-inclusion failure, PS.QC2, and of successful class-inclusion performance, PS.QC3, have been devised in accordance with the criteria previously stated. Production systems in the form of running computer programs in PSG constitute the fully explicit statements of these theories. Before a detailed account of PS.QC2 and PS.QC3 is provided, we will present a description of their main features. Particular emphasis will be placed on the features which represent attempts to avoid the weaknesses of PS.QC1.

The methods adopted in PS.QC2 and PS.QC3 of avoiding dependence on an internal representation of the test collection in LTM are consistent with the suggestions made above in increasing the emphasis on STM and on the use of the test display. The main STM implications have already been described in Chapter 3 since they constitute essential features of the mode of operation of PS.SUB and PS.COUNT. They involve abandonment of the single STM hypothesis in favor of the visual encoding channel comprising iconic memory and visual STM from which semantic STM derives its input.

When PS.QC2 or PS.QC3 is functioning with an active goal of quantifying the first value in the class-inclusion task, it is assumed that PS.SUB or PS.COUNT processes the contents of visual STM with the first value as the target being quantified. As any marking required by the quantification operators occurs in visual STM, its effect is of short duration and it in no way constitutes an impediment when the second value in the class-inclusion task succeeds the first as the target to be quantified. Both quantification episodes take place without any necessity for the construction of a representation of the test collection in LTM.

The state theory of failure on class inclusion, PS.QC2, also embodies a fundamental modification aimed at ensuring sufficiency while avoiding the weaknesses Hayes (1972) detected in PS.QC1. As in the case of the introduction of the visual encoding channel, this modification entails substantial additions to the general structure and organization of the IPS within the Newell and Simon (1972) framework. We assume that *attentional grain* plays an important part in governing the operation of the productions processing visual STM during the quantification episodes. The concept of attentional grain hinges on the nature of the targets provided in SSTM for the productions which process VSTM. We hypothesize that these targets belong to one of two types. The first is defined in terms of global objects. Targets are regarded as defining entire objects, for example, "red *and* square," "blue *and* circle." Values are not viewed in isolation but as features of a description of a global object. Where the information defining the target in SSTM is couched in terms of the value of a single attribute, for example, "red," the effect of *global object attentional grain* is to define the target in terms of all of the values of the first "red" object processed—"red *and* triangle *and* big." Global object attentional grain results in the values of each object being viewed operationally as a single, composite value. As a consequence, a single processing visit to an object exhausts its informational potential during a problem-solving episode. Figure 4.3a illustrates the situation produced by the conjunction of global object attentional grain and a single value target. The entire object is marked as having been processed after a single visit with the target "red."

The second type of target is defined in terms of attributes rather than global objects. The information defining the target in SSTM is viewed in terms of distinct values. If it comprises the value of a single attribute, such as "red," each object processed is examined purely in terms of the color attribute and the

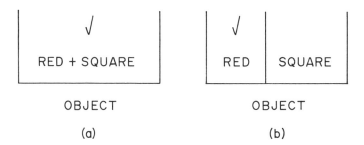

FIG. 4.3 Two kinds of attentional grain. (a) global object; (b) dimensional.

informational potential of other attributes remains unaffected. Thus, it is possible with *dimensional attentional grain* to make repeated processing visits to the same object during a problem-solving episode if the problem is concerned with more than a single attribute dimension. Figure 4.3b illustrates the situation produced when dimensional attentional grain is operative. Only the color attribute of the object is marked and a subsequent visit to process the shape attribute is possible.

An example of the effect of differences in attentional grain is provided by the performance of 5-year-olds on series completion tasks of the type presented in Table 4.3 (Klahr & Wallace, 1970a). The problem is presented and the child is asked "What comes next?" Some 5-year-olds exhibit global object attentional grain by failing to process each attribute of the presented series independently. Each color-orientation combination is treated as a distinct, global object. A single pass across the series with this strategy produces success on the first problem where both attributes have a period of two, but failure on the second problem where orientation has a period of two but color has a period of three. In contrast, adoption of dimensional attentional grain by other 5-year-olds leads to two passes across the series in which the color and orientation attributes are considered separately. This leads to success on both problems.

In discussing the development of one–one correspondence as a technique of quantitative comparison, we assumed that the cognitive system emphasizes processing economy as represented in the avoidance of redundant or unnecessary processing. Attentional grain is consistent with this emphasis. Until informational feedback indicates its inappropriateness, a developing PS such as PS.QC2 functions on the assumption that environmental input can be effectively dealt with if each object is processed once in a problem-solving episode. It is not that the system is incapable of repeated processing of individual objects within an episode, but simply that, as this may involve unnecessary processing, it is not resorted to in the first instance. If it proves to be necessary, global object attentional grain is abandoned in favor of dimensional attentional grain which permits multiple-processing visits to individual objects during a problem-solving episode.

We hypothesize that in a child who fails CI tasks the quantitative-comparison production system, PS.QC2, is still in a state of its development in which, when confronted with discontinuous material, it calls upon the productions processing visual STM to function for it and for any other production system which PS.QC2 uses, in a global object-oriented fashion. The effect of this on the overall operation of PS.QC2 will be described in some detail. This aspect of the functioning of PS.QC2 and PS.QC3 involves another substantial addition to the structure and organization of the underlying cognitive system, namely the introduction of an auditory encoding channel. This channel will not be discussed in detail at the present juncture but, analogous to the visual encoding channel, it is presumed that auditory stimulation produces a representation in echoic memory, an unselective memory store. Segments of acoustic input are encoded

TABLE 4.3
Color Orientation Problems

No.			Problem			Solution
1	BL[a]	YD	BL	YD	BL	YD
2	YD	GL	BD	YL	GD	BL

[a]Color: *B*lue, *Y*ellow, *G*reen. Orientation: *D*own, *L*eft.

and transferred from echoic memory to an auditory STM and, after a further encoding process, to semantic STM. There is a considerable amount of interaction between the auditory storage and processing chain and the channel processing visual information.

It is assumed that the global object orientation is established as soon as the interaction between the verbal and visual encoding of the CI task and the current production system context reaches the point at which PS.QC2 is activated in a discontinuous material mode. This occurs when the initial utterance of the word "more" has activated PS.QC2 and its preliminary sampling of the external problem space via the production's processing visual STM has established that discontinuous material is to be processed. As a consequence, the remainder of the encoding of the question is dominated by a global object orientation. This results in the encoding of target objects rather than target values for quantitative comparison. For example, consider a typical CI collection of two red squares and one red triangle. The class-inclusion question "Are there more reds or more squares?" results in the encoding of "red not square" and "square not red" as target objects for quantitative comparison. Each of the values mentioned in the question is regarded as an indicator of a group of discrete whole objects. The implication of this is that the groups will be nonoverlapping. Thus, it is *psychologically* equivalent to establishing the two logical targets (*A* not *B*) and (*B* not *A*). These target objects govern the subsequent operations of the productions processing visual STM when operating in the service of the quantification operators. They operate on objects which, as wholes, match the target objects. In the case of the "red not square" target object, the red triangle matches the prescription perfectly. No perfect matches to the "square not red" target object are discovered. This produces conflict and, accordingly, they operate on the "square-red" objects which, as wholes, come closest to matching the prescription. The relaxation of the target criteria to permit the acceptance of a partial match is an attempt to end the conflict without abandoning the global object attentional grain. The importance of conflict resolution in the functioning of the cognitive system will be considered in Chapter 7.

The cooccurrence in development of failure on CI tasks and the ability to establish the type of target objects proposed are supported by evidence from a recent Japanese study (Hatano & Kuhara, 1972) which suggests that children between 5 years, 3 months and 6 years, 2 months who fail CI tasks are capable of dealing with (*A* not *B*) relations. Only 4 of the 13 subjects could cope successfully with formal CI when, for example, the test question "Are there more circles or green figures?" was posed with reference to a collection of two green squares, six green circles, and three yellow triangles. In contrast, 12 of the 13 subjects succeeded on an item in which two blue squares, four blue circles, and three white squares were presented and followed by the question "Are there any nonwhite squares?" Before being scored as having passed the item, each subject who responded "Yes" was requested to "Please point out the nonwhite squares."

Regardless of the order in which the target objects are quantified, PS.QC2 results in the comparison of the two subsets and the production of the classic erroreous conclusion that there are more objects having the value determining the major subset. The inclusion of the concept of global object attentional grain in PS.QC2 renders it impossible for the superset to be quantified. Coupled with the abandonment of any type of marking which permanently prevents reprocessing of objects, this provides a sufficient state theory of failure on class inclusion.

If PS.QC2 is to satisfy the formal criterion of developmental tractability, it must be amenable to modification that gives rise to a sufficient state theory of successful class-inclusion performance. It is certainly amenable, since alteration of the attentional grain with which PS.QC2 functions is sufficient to produce success on class inclusion. The state theory of successful performance, PS.QC3, differs from PS.QC2 in that it calls upon the productions processing visual STM, and any other production systems which PS.QC3 uses, to function in a dimension-oriented fashion rather than with a global object orientation. The first evidence of this in the operation of PS.QC3 is that target values are encoded for quantitative comparison rather than target objects. In the above examples "red" and "square" are encoded as target values. Consequently, the productions processing visual STM quantify, or admit to semantic STM for quantification, objects possessing the target values. This results in the comparison of quantitative symbols derived by processing the objects possessing the value determining the superset, "red," and those exhibiting the value determining the major subset, "square." These results in turn give rise to the correct response that there is more of a superset value, "red."

The models we are proposing for CI failure and success do not map simply on to any of the previously suggested causes of failure. Rather, they represent a complex interplay among verbal encoding, visual encoding, and the concept of attentional grain. Before presenting the production system models for PS.QC2 and PS.QC3, we will summarize their essential features with respect to the CI task.

TABLE 4.4
Summary of Encodings for CI Failure Model (PS.QC2)

	Order A	Order B
Initial input	(MORE) (RED) (SQUARE)	(MORE) (SQUARE) (RED)
Verbal encoding	(RED NOT-SQUARE) (SQUARE NOT-RED)	(SQUARE NOT-RED) (RED NOT-SQUARE)
Iconic encoding of stimuli	(OB RED SQUARE) (OB RED SQUARE) (OB RED TRIANGLE)	
Encoding in VSTM	(OB RED SQUARE) (OB RED SQUARE) (OB RED NOT- SQUARE)	
First quantification	Target: (RED NOT-SQUARE) find 1, produce QS	Target: (SQUARE NOT-RED) fail, relax to (SQUARE) find 2, produce QS
Second quantification	Target: (SQUARE NOT-RED) fail, relax to (SQUARE) find 2, produce QS	Target: (RED NOT-SQUARE) find 1, produce QS
Result	REDS = 1 SQUARES = 2	SQUARES = 2 REDS = 1

The functioning of PS.QC2 on a display of two red squares and one red triangle is summarized in Table 4.4. Both possible orders of attention to the values "red" and "square" are shown, but we will describe just one of them. The verbal input is initially represented in STM as (MORE), (RED), and (SQUARE). A verbal encoding production (PDV1, to be described below), functioning at the level of global attentional grain, constructs from this raw input two target values: (RED NOT-SQUARE) and (SQUARE NOT-RED). These targets in turn control the stimulus encoding. What is initially

(OB RED SQUARE) (OB RED SQUARE) (OB RED TRIANGLE),

becomes, in VSTM

(OB RED SQUARE) (OB RED SQUARE) (OB RED NOT-SQUARE).

During the first quantification pass, the target, (RED NOT-SQUARE), is successfully matched against the corresponding OB in VSTM, producing a quantitative symbol indicating one target object. On the second quantification pass, the target (SQUARE NOT-RED) does not match anything in VSTM, and the target

TABLE 4.5
Summary of Encodings for CI Success Model (PS.QC3)

Initial input	(MORE) (RED) (SQUARE)
Verbal encoding	(RED) (SQUARE)
Iconic encoding	(OB RED SQUARE) (OB RED SQUARE) (OB RED TRIANGLE)
Encoding in VSTM	(OB RED) (OB SQUARE) (OB RED) (OB SQUARE) (OB RED) (OB TRIANGLE)
First	Target:
quantification	(RED)
	find 3, produce QS
Second	Target:
quantification	(SQUARE)
	find 2, produce QS
Result	REDS = 3
	SQUARES = 2

is relaxed to simply (SQUARE). The two (OB RED SQUARE) elements in VSTM match this target, and a quantitative symbol for two squares is generated. Finally, the system compares its two quantitative symbols and concludes (erroneously) that there are more squares than reds. The right-hand side of Table 4.4 shows that the same result occurs when the target order is reversed.

The corresponding summary for the model of CI success (PS.QC3) is shown in Table 4.5. Since both orders are equivalent, only one is shown. PS.QC3 functions with dimensional attentional grain. Thus, both the verbal encoding and the stimulus encoding take place at the dimensional level throughout. The representation in VSTM is simply a collection of individual occurrences of each value in question. This produces the straightforward quantification results shown in Table 4.5.

A PROGRAM FOR PS.QC2

In this section, we will follow the general format, used in previous chapters, for describing models written as production systems. First we will indicate a few features of the model (Fig. 4.4), and then we will describe a trace of it on a class-inclusion problem (Fig. 4.5).

PS.QC2 is an extension and improvement of PS.QC1 (shown in Fig. 2.1). There are some minor syntactic changes that relate to implementation issues; they will not be discussed in any detail here. One major psychologically relevant extension is the replacement of an operator call for quantification with an actual quantification production system. The old P11 (line 3400 in Fig. 2.1) has been modified (line 5300, Fig. 4.4) to introduce a goal of counting, and the counting production system based upon PS.COUNT (Fig. 3.21) has been included directly in the model (1900 to 3000, Fig. 4.4). Another important feature of PS.QC2 is the elaboration of the verbal encoding scheme. The word MORE still generates the goal (* GOAL MORE) as before (P3), but the old verbal encoder PDV0 has been changed to PDV1, which generates the disjunctive global object orientation described in the previous section. The general control structure (P1 to P11) remains essentially the same as in PS.QC1.

The trace of PS.QC2 is shown in Fig. 4.5. The few changes in convention from the traces in previous chapters will be mentioned as they are encountered.

```
00200  PS.QC2   Model for CI failure
01900           Counting by enumeration
02200  PDC.01:((NEW X0) (QS 0) --> (COUNTED **)( 0 ===> 1))
02300  PDC.12:((NEW X0) (QS 1) --> (COUNTED **)( 1 ===> 2))
02400  PDC.23:((NEW X0)(QS 2) --> (COUNTED **)( 2 ===> 3))
02500  PDC.34:((NEW X0)(QS 3) --> (COUNTED **)(3 ===> 4))
02600  PDVS1:((GOAL * COUNT X0)(SEE (OB X0)) --> (OB =VS=> SAW)(NEW X0))
02700  PDC1:((GOAL * COUNT X0)(QS 0) --> RELAX.TARGET)
02800  PDC2:((GOAL * COUNT X0) (QS X1) --> SAT (QS ===> QS X0))
02900
03000  PSCOUNT:(PDC.01 PDC.12 PDC.23 PDC.34 PDVS1 PDC1 PDC2)
03100
03200           Goal Manipulation
03300  PA:((* GOAL) (* GOAL) --> (* ===> %))
03400  PZ:((* GOAL) ABS (% GOAL) --> (% ==> *))
03500
03600           Verbal Encoding
03700  PDV1:((MORE) (WVAL1) (WVAL2) --> (X0 ===> OLD X0)(X1 ====> OLD X1)
03800                               (VALUE(WVAL1 NOT-WVAL2))
03900                               (VALUE(WVAL2 NOT-WVAL1)))
04000
04100           Main produtions
04200  P1:((+ GOAL MORE) (X0 REL X1 ) --> (OLD **)(SAY X0)(SAY REL)(SAY X1))
04300  P3:((MORE) --> (MORE ==> * GOAL MORE))
04400  P4:((* GOAL MORE) --> (* GOAL COMPARE))
04500  P5:((+ GOAL COMPARE) (% GOAL MORE) --> (% ===> +))
04600  P7:((QS) (QS) (* GOAL COMPARE) -->
04700     (QS ==> OLD QS)(QS ===> OLD QS) RELATE)
04800  P6:((* GOAL COMPARE) (X0 REL) --> (* ==> +))
04900
05000  P9:((* GOAL COMPARE) (VALUE X0) --> (VALUE ===> OLD VAL)
05100    (* GOAL QUANTIFY X0))
05200  P10:((* GOAL QUANTIFY X0) (QS X0) --> (* ==> +))
05300  P11:((* GOAL QUANTIFY X0) --> (GOAL * COUNT X0)(QS 0)(PS PSCOUNT) )
05900
06000  PSEXEC:(PA PDV1 P1 P3 P4 P5 P7 P6 P9 P10 P11 PZ)
```

FIG. 4.4   PSG model for PS.QC2: CI failure.

0. SSTM: ((* GOAL MORE) (VALUE (RED NOT.SQUARE)) (VALUE (SQUARE NOT.RED)) ....

    P4: ((* GOAL MORE) --> (* GOAL COMPARE))
    PA: ((* GOAL) (* GOAL) --> (* ===> %))
    P9: ((* GOAL COMPARE) (VALUE X0) --> (VALUE ===> OLD VAL) (* GOAL QUANTIFY X0))
    PA: ((* GOAL) (* GOAL) --> (* ===> %))

5. SSTM: ((* GOAL QUANTIFY (RED NOT.SQUARE)) (% GOAL COMPARE) (OLD VAL (RED NOT.SQUARE))
          (% GOAL MORE) (VALUE (SQUARE NOT.RED) ....

    P11: ((* GOAL QUANTIFY X0) --> (GOAL * COUNT X0) (QS 0) (PS PSCOUNT))

7. VSTM: ((OB (RED SQUARE))(OB (RED SQUARE))(OB (RED NOT.SQUARE)))

    PDVS1: ((GOAL * COUNT X0) (SEE (OB X0)) --> (OB =VS=> SAW) (NEW X0))

9. VSTM: ((OB (RED SQUARE))(OB (RED SQUARE))(SAW (RED NOT.SQUARE)))

    PDC.01: ((NEW X0) (QS 0) --> (COUNTED **) (0 ===> 1))
    PDC2: ((GOAL * COUNT X0) (QS X1) --> SAT (QS ===> QS X0))

15. SSTM: ((GOAL + COUNT (RED NOT.SQUARE)) (QS (RED NOT.SQUARE) 1) (COUNTED (NEW (RED NOT.SQUARE)))
           (* GOAL QUANTIFY (RED NOT.SQUARE)) ....

    P10: ((* GOAL QUANTIFY X0) (QS X0) --> (* ==> +))

16. SSTM: ((+ GOAL QUANTIFY (RED NOT.SQUARE)) (QS (RED NOT.SQUARE) 1) (GOAL + COUNT (RED NOT.SQUARE))
           (COUNTED (NEW (RED NOT.SQUARE))) (% GOAL COMPARE) (OLD VAL (RED NOT.SQUARE))
           (% GOAL MORE) (VALUE (SQUARE NOT.RED)) (OLD SQUARE) (OLD RED) NIL NIL NIL NIL)
     VSTM: ((OB (RED SQUARE))(OB (RED SQUARE))(SAW (RED NOT.SQUARE)))

    PZ: ((* GOAL) ABS (% GOAL) --> (% ==> *))
    P9: ((* GOAL COMPARE) (VALUE X0) --> (VALUE ===> OLD VAL) (* GOAL QUANTIFY X0))
    PA: ((* GOAL) (* GOAL) --> (* ===> %))

20. SSTM: ((* GOAL QUANTIFY (SQUARE NOT.RED)) (% GOAL COMPARE) (OLD VAL (SQUARE NOT.RED))
           (+ GOAL QUANTIFY (RED NOT.SQUARE)) (QS (RED NOT.SQUARE) 1) (GOAL + COUNT (RED NOT.SQUARE))
           (COUNTED (NEW (RED NOT.SQUARE))) (OLD VAL (RED NOT.SQUARE)) (% GOAL MORE) (OLD SQUARE)
           (OLD RED) NIL NIL NIL)

    P11: ((* GOAL QUANTIFY X0) --> (GOAL * COUNT X0) (QS 0) (PS PSCOUNT))
    PDC1: ((GOAL * COUNT X0) (QS 0) --> RELAX.TARGET)

24. SSTM: ((GOAL * COUNT (SQUARE)) (QS 0) (* GOAL QUANTIFY (SQUARE)) (% GOAL COMPARE)
           (OLD VAL (SQUARE NOT.RED)) (+ GOAL QUANTIFY (RED NOT.SQUARE)) (QS (RED NOT.SQUARE) 1) ....

     VSTM: ((OB (SQUARE)) (OB (SQUARE)) (SAW (RED NOT.SQUARE)))

    PDVS1: ((GOAL * COUNT X0) (SEE (OB X0)) --> (OB =VS=> SAW) (NEW X0))
    PDC.01: ((NEW X0) (QS 0) --> (COUNTED **) (0 ===> 1))
    PDVS1: ((GOAL * COUNT X0) (SEE (OB X0)) --> (OB =VS=> SAW) (NEW X0))
    PDC.12: ((NEW X0) (QS 1) --> (COUNTED **) (1 ===> 2))
    PDC2: ((GOAL * COUNT X0) (QS X1) --> SAT (QS ===> QS X0))

35. SSTM: ((GOAL + COUNT (SQUARE)) (QS (SQUARE) 2) (COUNTED (NEW (SQUARE))) (COUNTED (NEW (SQUARE)))
           (* GOAL QUANTIFY (SQUARE)) (% GOAL COMPARE) (OLD VAL (SQUARE NOT.RED))
           (+ GOAL QUANTIFY (RED NOT.SQUARE)) (QS (RED NOT.SQUARE) 1),.........

FIG. 4.5

VSTM: ((SAW (SQUARE)) (SAW (SQUARE)) (SAW (RED NOT.SQUARE)))

```
P10: ((* GOAL QUANTIFY X0) (QS X0) --> (* ==> +))
PZ: ((* GOAL) ABS (% GOAL) --> (% ==> *))
P7: ((QS) (QS) (* GOAL COMPARE) --> (QS ==> OLD QS) (QS ===> OLD QS) RELATE)
P6: ((* GOAL COMPARE) (X0 REL) --> (* ==> +))
P5: ((+ GOAL COMPARE) (% GOAL MORE) --> (% ===> +))
P1: ((+ GOAL MORE) (X0 REL X1) --> (OLD **) (SAY X0) (SAY REL) (SAY X1))
```

********** SQUARE

********** MORE.THAN

********** RED

46. SSTM: ((OLD (+ GOAL MORE)) (SQUARE MORE.THAN RED) (+ GOAL COMPARE) (OLD QS (SQUARE) 2)
      (OLD QS (RED NOT.SQUARE) 1) (+ GOAL QUANTIFY (SQUARE)) (GOAL + COUNT (SQUARE))
      (COUNTED (NEW (SQUARE))) (COUNTED (NEW (SQUARE))) (OLD VAL (SQUARE NOT.RED))
      (+ GOAL QUANTIFY (RED NOT.SQUARE)) (GOAL + COUNT (RED NOT.SQUARE))
      (COUNTED (NEW (RED NOT.SQUARE))) (OLD VAL (RED NOT.SQUARE)))

FIG. 4.5 (contd.)   Trace of PS.QC2: CI failure.

Throughout the ensuing description, line numbers (e.g., "6000") refer to the model in Fig. 4.4 and action counts (e.g., "15.") refer to the trace in Fig. 4.5.

Figure 4.5 starts with the state of SSTM after the verbal encoder has created the MORE goal and the two global object targets. (For ease of reading, only the first few elements in SSTM are shown in most of this trace. Occasionally, the entire contents are listed.) The productions that next fire, in sequence, are P4, PA, P9, and PA again, producing the situation shown at (5.). At this point, SSTM contains the goal of quantifying RED NOT-SQUARE things, and P11 fires next, generating a COUNT goal, and activating PS.COUNT.

The PS.COUNT used by PS.QC2 is almost identical to the model described in Chapter 3. The items from VSTM are individually noticed, marked, and admitted to SSTM by PDVS1. In PS.QC2, the production PDVS1 is our first example of the use of a parameterized encoding production: the target value in the goal is used to control the search of VSTM. When P11 activates PS.COUNT, PDVS1 is the first production to fire, at (7.), since the (RED NOT-SQUARE) in the COUNT goal is used by SEE, which in turn finds (OB (RED NOT-SQUARE)).

Then PS.COUNT goes through its cycle of incrementing and marking (as COUNTED) the target object, finally producing the quantitative symbol and satisfied count goal shown at (15.). Then P10 fires, producing the SSTM situation shown at (16.). The full SSTM and VSTM contents are shown here to summarize the first quantification episode.

Now the model prepares to quantify the second target, firing PZ, P9, PA, and after (20.), P11, which produces a goal of counting the (SQUARE NOT-RED) items. PS.COUNT cannot find any such objects, and PDC1 fires, indicating that the target must be relaxed. The effects of this relaxation are shown at (24.): both the target object in the SSTM goals and the consideration of objects in VSTM have relaxed from (SQUARE NOT-RED) to simply (SQUARE).

Now PS.COUNT can find the objects it seeks, and the counting sequence PDVS1, PDC.01, PDVS1, PDC.12, PDC2 produces the satisifed goal and quantitative symbol shown at (35.).

From this point on, PS.QC2 functions essentially the same as PS.QC1, finally producing the erroneous result that there are more squares than reds.

A PROGRAM FOR PS.QC3

The PSG model for successful performance on CI, PS.QC3, is almost identical to PS.QC2. There are only two differences, both of which relate to implementation of a dimensional, rather than global object, orientation:

1. The verbal encoding production, PDVS1, now creates targets consisting of single values.

2. The effect of attentional grain upon the VSTM is simulated by encoding the stimulus as a set of distinct values.

Both of these changes are shown at the start of the trace for PS.QC3 (Fig. 4.6). The trace is also almost identical to Fig. 4.5. (Since PS.QC3 is so similar to PS.QC2, we do not show a separate figure for the model. Only this trace is shown.) The differences occur after (9.) and (24.) when the counting goal is satisfied immediately, without any necessary relaxation.

The careful reader will have noticed several features of all of these quantitative comparison models (PS.QC1, PS.QC2, and PS.QC3) that would seem to limit their claim to reasonable generality. For example, only the word "MORE" will trigger PDV1 and P3, so that other forms of the CI question cannot be posed. Another problem, in this case an apparent superfluity, is the cascading of the goals for MORE and COMPARE. P4 generates COMPARE, given MORE, and P5 satisifes MORE, given that COMPARE is satisfied. A similar direct link between QUANTIFY and COUNT occurs in P11. Rather than attempt to justify these features at this point, we will simply draw attention to them. Subsequently, in Chapter 5, they will all be treated by construction of a more general model in which the current models up through PS.QC3 will be seen as special cases.

DEVELOPMENTAL TRANSITION FROM PS.QC2 TO PS.QC3

The successful construction of two sufficient state theories immediately raises the problem of explaining the transition from state to state. In terms of the system as a whole, the transition from PS.QC2 to PS.QC3 is to be attributed to the discovery by the system that effective quantitative comparison demands a production system functioning at the finer level of detail represented by the dimensional orientation. How is this discovery made? The only substantive evidence relevant to this question emanates from training studies in which an attempt has been made to inculcate successful CI performance (Kohnstamm, 1968). The most effective procedure appears to be one in which children who initially fail CI are repeatedly instructed to count the superset, count the major subset, and then have the CI question put with feedback on the accuracy of their response.

The success of this approach would be explained in terms of our state theories as follows. Children whose performance improves as a result of this type of training are in a developmental state in which PS.COUNT, when activated directly by verbal instructions, engages in dimension-oriented processing. Quantitative comparison, in contrast, takes place via PS.QC2 and is conducted at the global object-processing level. The initial instructions to count lead to two passes through PS.COUNT on a dimensional basis, both culminating in knowledge that successful results have been obtained. The CI question which follows activated PS.QC2 produces global object-oriented processing and ends in informational feedback that an inaccurate response has been produced. Repetition of this sequence, which places dimension-oriented processing followed by success in juxtaposition to global object-oriented processing followed by failure, appears to maximize the likelihood of a decision that a change in the attentional grain of PS.QC2 is required. This line of argument is supported by the detailed protocols of the instructional sessions provided by Kohnstamm (1963). The informational feedback following erroneous CI responses was frequently of a type which emphasized the dimensional as opposed to the global object aspect of the test collection. A child who, when confronted with a collection of three red squares and two red circles, only quantified the two red circles would, for example, be asked by the experimenter "Aren't these (the red squares) red too?"

The information-processing account of the transition from failure to success on CI offered above fares reasonably well when assessed on the formal criterion of generality. As noted above, change of attentional grain from a global object to a dimensional orientation constitutes a plausible explanation of transition from failure to success in children's performance on two-dimensional series completion problems (Klahr & Wallace, 1970a). As will be suggested in the next chapter, it also constitutes an essential feature of a sufficient theory of the acquisition of conservation of continuous quantity (Klahr & Wallace, 1973).

CLASS-INCLUSION PERFORMANCE AND THE STRUCTURE AND ORGANIZATION OF THE IPS

The sufficient theories of preoperational and concrete operational CI performance have both structural and organizational implications for the information-processing system. On the structural side, they necessitate the addition of an auditory encoding channel comprising an echoic memory, an auditory STM,

0. SSTM: ((MORE) (RED) (SQUARE) ....
    VSTM: ((OB (RED)) (OB (SQUARE)) (OB (RED)) (OB (SQUARE)) (OB (RED)) (OB (TRIANGLE)))

    PDV1: ((MORE) (WVAL1) (WVAL2) --> (X0 ===> OLD X0) (X1 ====> OLD X1) (VALUE (WVAL1)) (VALUE (WVAL2)))

4. SSTM: ((VALUE (SQUARE)) (VALUE (RED)) (MORE) ....

    P3: ((MORE) --> (MORE ==> * GOAL MORE))

5. SSTM: ((* GOAL MORE) (VALUE (SQUARE)) (VALUE (RED)) ....

    P4: ((* GOAL MORE) --> (* GOAL COMPARE))
    PA: ((* GOAL) (* GOAL) --> (* ===> %))
    P9: ((* GOAL COMPARE) (VALUE X0) --> (VALUE ===> OLD VAL) (* GOAL QUANTIFY X0))

9. SSTM: ((* GOAL QUANTIFY (SQUARE)) (* GOAL COMPARE) (OLD VAL (SQUARE)) (% GOAL MORE) ....

    PA: ((* GOAL) (* GOAL) --> (* ===> %))
    P11: ((* GOAL QUANTIFY X0) --> (GOAL * COUNT X0) (QS 0) (PS PSCOUNT))
        PDVS1: ((GOAL * COUNT X0) (SEE (OB X0)) --> (OB =VS=> SAW) (NEW X0))
        PDC.01: ((NEW X0) (QS 0) --> (COUNTED **) (0 ===> 1))
        PDVS1: ((GOAL * COUNT X0) (SEE (OB X0)) --> (OB =VS=> SAW) (NEW X0))
        PDC.12: ((NEW X0) (QS 1) --> (COUNTED **) (1 ===> 2))
        PDC2: ((GOAL * COUNT X0) (QS X1) --> SAT (QS ===> QS X0))

24. SSTM: ((GOAL + COUNT (SQUARE)) (QS (SQUARE) 2) (COUNTED (NEW (SQUARE))) (COUNTED (NEW (SQUARE)))
        (* GOAL QUANTIFY (SQUARE)) (% GOAL COMPARE) (OLD VAL (SQUARE)) (% GOAL MORE) (VALUE (RED))
        (OLD RED) (OLD SQUARE) NIL NIL NIL)

    P10: ((* GOAL QUANTIFY X0) (QS X0) --> (* ==> +))
    PZ: ((* GOAL) ABS (% GOAL) --> (% ==> *))
    P9: ((* GOAL COMPARE) (VALUE X0) --> (VALUE ===> OLD VAL) (* GOAL QUANTIFY X0))
    PA: ((* GOAL) (* GOAL) --> (* ===> %))
    P11: ((* GOAL QUANTIFY X0) --> (GOAL * COUNT X0) (QS 0) (PS PSCOUNT))
        PDVS1: ((GOAL * COUNT X0) (SEE (OB X0)) --> (OB =VS=> SAW) (NEW X0))
        PDC.01: ((NEW X0) (QS 0) --> (COUNTED **) (0 ===> 1))
        PDVS1: ((GOAL * COUNT X0) (SEE (OB X0)) --> (OB =VS=> SAW) (NEW X0))
        PDC.12: ((NEW X0) (QS 1) --> (COUNTED **) (1 ===> 2))
        PDVS1: ((GOAL * COUNT X0) (SEE (OB X0)) --> (OB =VS=> SAW) (NEW X0))
        PDC.23: ((NEW X0) (QS 2) --> (COUNTED **) (2 ===> 3))
        PDC2: ((GOAL * COUNT X0) (QS X1) --> SAT (QS ===> QS X0))

47. SSTM: ((GOAL + COUNT (RED)) (QS (RED) 3) (COUNTED (NEW (RED))) (COUNTED (NEW (RED)))
        (COUNTED (NEW (RED))) (* GOAL QUANTIFY (RED)) (% GOAL COMPARE) (OLD VAL (RED))
        (+ GOAL QUANTIFY (SQUARE)) (QS (SQUARE) 2) (GOAL + COUNT (SQUARE)) (COUNTED (NEW (SQUARE)))
        (COUNTED (NEW (SQUARE))) (OLD VAL (SQUARE)))

    P10: ((* GOAL QUANTIFY X0) (QS X0) --> (* ==> +))
    PZ: ((* GOAL) ABS (% GOAL) --> (% ==> *))

49. SSTM: ((* GOAL COMPARE) (+ GOAL QUANTIFY (RED)) (QS (RED) 3) (GOAL + COUNT (RED)) (COUNTED (NEW (RED))
        (COUNTED (NEW (RED))) (COUNTED (NEW (RED))) (OLD VAL (RED)) (+ GOAL QUANTIFY (SQUARE))
        (QS (SQUARE) 2) (GOAL + COUNT (SQUARE)) (COUNTED (NEW (SQUARE))) (COUNTED (NEW (SQUARE)))
        (OLD VAL (SQUARE)))
    VSTM: ((SAW (RED)) (SAW (SQUARE)) (SAW (RED)) (SAW (SQUARE)) (SAW (RED)) (OB (TRIANGLE)))

    P7: ((QS) (QS) (* GOAL COMPARE) --> (QS ==> OLD QS) (QS ===> OLD QS) RELATE)
52. ACTION- (RED MORE.THAN SQUARE)
    P6: ((* GOAL COMPARE) (X0 REL) --> (* ==> +))

FIG. 4.6

54. SSTM: ((% GOAL MORE) (+ GOAL COMPARE) (RED MORE.THAN SQUARE).........
      P5: ((+ GOAL COMPARE) (% GOAL MORE) --> (% ===> +))
      P1: ((+ GOAL MORE) (X0 REL X1) --> (OLD **) (SAY X0) (SAY REL) (SAY X1))

********** RED

********** MORE.THAN

********** SQUARE

59. SSTM: ((OLD (+ GOAL MORE)) (RED MORE.THAN SQUARE) (+ GOAL COMPARE) (OLD QS (RED) 3)
              (OLD QS (SQUARE) 2) (+ GOAL QUANTIFY (RED)) (GOAL + COUNT (RED)) (COUNTED (NEW (RED)))
              (COUNTED (NEW (RED))) (COUNTED (NEW (RED))) (OLD VAL (RED)) (+ GOAL QUANTIFY (SQUARE))
              (GOAL + COUNT (SQUARE)) (COUNTED (NEW (SQUARE))))

FIG. 4.6 (contd.)   Trace of PS.QC3:CI success.

and a semantic STM (which is also in the visual encoding channel.) The structural modifications must permit easy interaction between the auditory and visual information-processing channels.

The new organizational feature is of a fundamental nature. It is presumed that the avoidance of redundant or unnecessary processing is a basic systemic principle. The concept of attentional grain, which constitutes the core of our account of the development of successful CI performance, is based on this principle, as is our view of one–one correspondence. This processing economy principle will be assigned an increasing amount of explanatory weight in the discussions of conservation and transitivity that follow. To be consistent with our proposals as to how the transition from PS.QC2 to PS.QC3 occurs, the system must be capable of comparing the outcomes of processing episodes and detecting when a relaxation of the global-object attentional grain (a manifestation of the processing economy principle) is likely to increase the effectiveness of the system's interaction with the environment.

5

Conservation of Quantity

The classic version of the Piagetian test for conservation of quantity starts with the presentation of two distinct collections of equal amounts of material (for example, two rows of beads, two vessels of liquid, or two lumps of clay). First the child is encouraged to establish their quantitative equality (for example, "Is there as much to drink in this one as in that one?" or "Is it fair to give this bunch to you and that bunch to me?"). Then he observes one of the collections undergo a transformation that changes some of its perceptual features while maintaining its quantity (for example, stretching, compressing, pouring into a vessel of different dimensions). Finally, the child is asked to judge the relative quantity of the two collections after the transformation. To be classified as "having conservation" the child must be able to assert the continuing quantitative equality of the two collections without resorting to a requantification and comparison after the transformation; that is, his response must be based not upon another direct observation, but rather upon recognition of the "logical necessity" for initially equal amounts to remain equal under "mere" perceptual transformations.

The problem for students of cognitive development has been stated by Wallach (1969):

> Much as conservation is later taken entirely for granted, Piaget . . . and others . . . have shown clearly that until the age of six or seven children believe that quantities do change under such transformations. What happens at that point? How do these children come, like us, to consider it an absurdity even to ask whether amounts might change with different containers or arrangements? [p. 191]

This chapter is organized as follows: first, we present a theory of concrete operational performance on tasks involving conservation of discontinuous quantities such as collections of beads. Next, we consider the developmental course of the system from the preoperational to the concrete operational level of performance with discontinuous quantity; then we describe the extension of this capability to conservation of continuous quantities such as lumps of plasticene or jars of water. In both sections the theories which will be advanced are predicated on the account of the three quantification operators and their developmental interrelationship presented in Chapter 3. The systems of rules that underlie conservation performance are then incorporated into a PSG model for quantitative comparison and conservation.

CONSERVATION OF DISCONTINUOUS QUANTITY

Before commencing the description of our theory of concrete operational performance, it is necessary to define the symbols which will be employed. A few of them should already be familiar to the reader since they were used in the account of quantification processes in Chapter 3.

Let

$x, y \equiv$ internal symbols representing collections of materials;

$x', y' \equiv$ representations for collections of material after any transformation;

$Q_i \equiv$ any quantification operator i, i = s, c, e, where s = subitizing, c = counting, e = estimation;

$x_i \equiv$ quantitative symbol for collection x produced by operator Q_i;

$T_\pm \equiv$ addition and subtraction transformation;

$T_p \equiv$ perceptual transformation (the class of all $T_\pm$ and the class of all T_p are mutually exclusive);

$=, >, < \equiv$ relations of "same," "greater than," and "less than," respectively, between two quantitative symbols;

$\overset{Q}{=}, \overset{Q}{>}, \overset{Q}{<} \equiv$ relations of equal, more and less quantity, respectively, between two symbols for collections.

There are two kinds of dynamics for which we need additional notation:

i. $T(x) \to x'$ internal representation for the application of a transformation to an external collection.

ii. $Q_i(x) \to x_i$ denotes the application of a quantification operator i to a collection: it produces a quantitative symbol.

The first prerequisite for concrete operational performance on tasks requiring conservation of discontinuous quantity is the existence of the three main quantitative comparison productions described in Chapter 3 and their application to the operations of all three quantification operators:

$$(x_i = y_i) --> (x \overset{Q}{=} y) \qquad (5.1)$$

$$(x_i < y_i) --> (x \overset{Q}{<} y) \qquad (5.2)$$

$$(x_i > y_i) --> (x \overset{Q}{>} y) \qquad (5.3)$$

Recall that the function of each of these productions is to take as input from semantic STM one of three symbols representing the outcome of comparing two quantitative symbols generated by the application of a quantification operator to two collections and to place the appropriate quantitative relational attribute symbol in semantic STM.

In addition to the classic conservation test involving two collections of equal amounts of material, there is a major variant in which only a single collection is used. For example, Elkind and Schoenfeld (1972) describe an experiment in which the child was simply presented with "one quantity (five pennies, ..., etc.) and was asked to look at it carefully. Then the appearance of quantity was changed (the five pennies were spread out). After the transformation was performed, the child was asked whether there were more, less, or the same number of pennies as before [p. 531]." No initial comparison exists in such a test, and the posttransformation judgment is based upon the relative quantity in the initial and final forms of the collection. In the discussion that follows, we will use Elkind's (1967) terminology and refer to the two-collection task as *equivalence conservation* (EC) and the one-collection task as *identity conservation* (IC).

Equivalence Conservation

For successful performance on EC, the system requires three further productions in addition to the three quantitative comparison productions.

$$(x \overset{Q}{=} y) (T_p(y) \to y') --> (x \overset{Q}{=} y') \qquad (5.4)$$

$$(x \overset{Q}{=} y) (T_+(y) \to y') --> (x \overset{Q}{<} y') \qquad (5.5)$$

$$(x \overset{Q}{=} y) (T_-(y) \to y') --> (x \overset{Q}{>} y') \qquad (5.6)$$

All three productions test for the initial quantitative equality of collections x and y. Their conditions also test for occurrence of a transformation of one of the collections y to y'. In Production (5.4) the transformation is a perceptual one and the action side places the symbol $(x \overset{Q}{=} y')$ in semantic STM indicating that the collections x and y' are of equal quantity. Productions (5.5) and (5.6) are concerned with addition and subtraction transformations and place symbols in semantic STM, respectively, indicating that x is less or greater in quantity than

y'. In all three cases a symbol representing the final quantitative relationship between the two collections appears in semantic STM without any requantification and quantitative comparison after the transformation.

The sequences of processing steps underlying successful EC performance can be represented as follows:

1. Two collections are quantified:

$$Q_i(x) \rightarrow x_i; Q_i(y) \rightarrow y_i.$$

2. Their quantitative equality is established. This requires the application of a production that says, in effect, if the quantitative symbols for two collections are the same, then those collections are of the same quantity. Production (5.1) fulfills this prescription:

$$(x_i = y_i) \dashrightarrow (x \overset{Q}{=} y).$$

3. Collection y undergoes a perceptual transformation:

$$T_p(y) \rightarrow (y').$$

4. The relative amount of the two collections is determined by applying conservation Production (5.4):

$$(x \overset{Q}{=} y)\,(T_p(y) \rightarrow y') \dashrightarrow (x \overset{Q}{=} y').$$

This production, it will be recalled, states that if you know that collections x and y were of equal quantity, and that y underwent a perceptual transformation which changed it to y', then you also know that collections x and y' are of equal quantity. Since the two elements that appear as conditions in this production have been previously entered into semantic STM, the condition is satisfied. Thus, the action is taken: the symbol $(x \overset{Q}{=} y')$, representing the fact that x is equal in quantity to y', is added to semantic STM.

Indentity Conservation

Concrete operational performance on IC also requires three productions in addition to the quantitative comparison productions. The nature of the IC test situation requires that these differ from the EC productions.

$$(T_p(x) \rightarrow x') \dashrightarrow (x' \overset{Q}{=} x) \tag{5.7}$$

$$(T_+(x) \rightarrow x') \dashrightarrow (x' \overset{Q}{>} x) \tag{5.8}$$

$$(T_-(x) \rightarrow x') \dashrightarrow (x' \overset{Q}{<} x) \tag{5.9}$$

Each of the productions comprises one condition concerned with the occurrence of a transformation of a single collection x to x'. In Production (5.7) the transformation is perceptual and the action places $(x' \overset{Q}{=} x)$ in semantic STM, indicating that the transformed and original collections are equal in quantity. If the addition and subtraction transformations tested for by the condition sides of Productions (5.8) and (5.9) have occurred, symbols indicating that x' is greater or less than x in quantity are placed in semantic STM. In the case of IC any direct quantitative comparison of x and x' after a transformation would only be possible if a quantitative symbol generated by applying a quantification operator to x prior to the transformation was still present in semantic STM. Productions (5.7), (5.8), and (5.9) obviate the necessity for any prior quantification of x and retention of a quantitative symbol.

The sequence of processing steps involved in successful IC performance, like the IC productions, is simpler than the EC counterpart. It can be represented as follows:

1. Collection x undergoes a perceptual transformation:

$$T_p(x) \rightarrow (x').$$

2. Apply IC production

$$(T_p(x) \rightarrow x') --> (x' \overset{Q}{=} x). \tag{5.7}$$

Then $(x' \overset{Q}{=} x)$ is added to semantic STM.

Having formally defined concrete operational performance on EC and IC of discontinuous quantity, we will now turn to the development of conservation of discontinuous quantity and the manner in which this capability is extended to cover continuous quantities.

DEVELOPMENT OF CONSERVATION OF QUANTITY

A developmental theory of conservation must account for the emergence and coordination of the productions outlined in the previous section. It must describe the process whereby addition and subtraction transformations acquire a special status with regard to quantity, since the development of discriminations between quantity-changing transformations, T_+ and T_-, and quantity-preserving transformations, T_p, is central to the concept of quantity conservation. It must also indicate how a system that has reliable means of both quantification and discriminating between the effects of transformations on quantity develops the crucial conservation inference: if nothing is added or subtracted, equal quantities remain equal.

In this section, we will offer an account of conservation based upon the emergence of Q_s, Q_c, and Q_e as reliable quantifiers. Consistent with the emphasis placed on the developmental primacy of Q_s in Chapter 3, we will argue that Q_s first enables the system to develop conservation productions for IC with discontinuous quantity. From this development stem extensions to EC of discontinuous and continuous quantity, to conservation of inequality as well as equality within Q_s, and to the corresponding aspects of the operations of Q_c and Q_e.

Identity Conservation and Q_s

With the passage of time, the system observes many different transformations applied to collections comprising a few elements either as a result of its own actions or those of an external agent. These situations are encoded and stored in LTM in the form of (initial state)–(transformation)–(final state) sequences. In some cases the representation of the initial and final states includes the outcome of applying Q_s, Q_c, or Q_e to specific collections.

At first, none of the quanitification operators is sufficiently reliable to provide a basis for the discrimination of quantity-preserving transformations from quantity-modifying transformations. The emergence of Q_s as the first reliable indicator of quantity makes this initial differentiation possible. The many naturally occurring forms of the identity conservation paradigm provide the necessary experience for this learning. On innumerable occasions (for example, handling blocks, dolls, or cookies) the child quantifies a small collection via Q_s, observes a transformation, quantifies the resultant collection, and compares the two quantitative symbols. Some transformations consistently yield the result that $x_s = x'_s$. Others yield $x_s > x'_s$, and still others $x_s < x'_s$. These *specific consistent sequences* derived from particular repeated sequences of events are stored in LTM and subsequently are classified into three distinct types of *common consistent sequence* on the basis of the results of this quantitative comparison:

$$(x_s) \cdots (T_p(x) \to x') \cdots (x'_s) \cdots (x'_s = x_s)$$
$$(x_s) \cdots (T_+(x) \to x') \cdots (x'_s) \cdots (x'_s > x_s)$$
$$(x_s) \cdots (T_-(x) \to x') \cdots (x'_s) \cdots (x'_s < x_s)$$

What were initially discriminable but arbitrarily labeled transformations become classified according to the relation they produce between the initial and final quantitative symbols, x_s and x'_s. Thus, certain transformations (e.g., rotations, compressions) are classified as those for which Q_s consistently yields the same result after the transformation as before. Other transformations are associated with the consistent production of either greater (e.g., transfer from parent's hand to collection) or lesser quantities (e.g., placing one or more of the elements of a collection in the mouth and swallowing).

This three-way classification defines the transformations. When a transformation is observed, its class, denoted by the relation it produces between the intitial and resultant quantitative symbols, x_s and x'_s, is determined. Thus the transformations themselves become known to the system as either quantity-preserving (T_p) or as quantity-changing $(T_\pm)$.

The next phase in the development of IC is attributed to the operation of the basic systemic principle (introduced at the conclusion of Chapter 4) of avoiding redundant or unnecessary processing. It is assumed that the common consistent sequences are used to predict the effect of the transformations on the relationship between x_s and x'_s and the predictions are verified by quantifying x' and carrying out the final quantitative comparison. Success in this predictive phase results in confirmation that the quantification of x' and the subsequent quantitative comparison constitute unnecessary processing and may be omitted. As a consequence, three production rules are constructed which subsequently govern the system's operations in situations where IC transformations are applied to collections within the range of Q_s:

$$(x_s)(T_p(x) \rightarrow x') - -> (x'_s = x_s)$$
$$(x_s)(T_+(x) \rightarrow x') - -> (x'_s > x_s)$$
$$(x_s)(T_-(x) \rightarrow x') - -> (x'_s < x_s)$$

Evidence for the utilization of conservation rules with small collections. Our account of the development of IC thus far rests heavily upon the assertion that, even for small collections of objects within the subitizing range, the system attempts to eliminate the final requantification and quantitative comparison by developing a reliable predictor of the outcome. In this section, we will present some evidence that supports this view. Until recently, investigations of number conservation within the subitizing range have been eschewed because they allegedly permit employment of a primitive perceptually based requantification of the transformed collection. Since this requantification obviates the need for a conservation rule, it has been argued, collections of three or four elements cannot be used to study the development of conservation.

The validity of this line of argument can be questioned on two grounds. The account of Q_s presented in Chapter 3 is not consistent with the view that small collections are quantified on a primitive, largely perceptual basis. Such a perceptual viewpoint is reminiscent of the early "immediate apprehension" studies that lead to the discovery of subitizing.

The increasing number of studies of conservation performance in preschool children has as yet yielded very little evidence derived from situations within the numerical range of Q_s. In addition, most of the relevant studies are concerned with EC rather than IC. We will, however, consider them at this point. The best known study is that of Mehler and Bever (1967) which has already been referred to in our discussion of one—one correspondence in Chapter 3. They administered what they described as a test of conservation of discontinuous quantity to 200 children ranging in age from 2 years, 4 months to 4 years, 7 months and concluded on the basis of the results that children of 2 years, 6 months and 4 years, 6 months show more conservation than children of 4 years, 2 months. The pre- and posttransformation situations which they used are presented in Fig. 5.1.

In view of the notorious methodological difficulties involved in gathering data from subjects in the 2- to 4-year-old range, it is hardly surprising that the validity of Mehler and Bever's experimental results has been questioned. Studies by Achenbach (1969), Beilin (1968), Piaget (1968), and Rothenberg and Courtney (1968) have failed to replicate their findings, while Bever, Mehler, and Epstein (1968) and Calhoun (1971) have obtained results broadly confirmatory of the outcome of the original investigation.

Apart from the confused situation arising from the results of the replication studies, there are serious questions about the relevance of Mehler and Bever's findings to resolving the issue of the initial appearance of the conservation production rules in the functioning of Q_s. As Fig. 5.1 indicates, the initial situation involves establishing quantitative equivalence between two rows of four counters. The results of our experiment with 5-year-olds, however, suggest that three is the upper limit of the range of operation of Q_s in the age range studied by Mehler and Bever. The effect of the complex transformation combining T_p with T_+ is to place the final situation even more clearly beyond the range of Q_s.

Beilin (1968) presented a group of 3- to 5-year-old children with an EC task employing two collections. As in Mehler and Bever's experiment, each of the collections comprised four objects and there must therefore be doubts surrounding the operation of Q_s in the situation. The average score across all ages was 14% correct. A similar group of children were presented with a task involving only the terminal configurations in the original EC task. If children's responses were based only upon direct requantification of the transformed collections, then no significant differences would be predicted between performance in the two groups. However, the second group, those that judged only final configurations, were correct on 37% of the trials. Thus, it appears that children in this age range are attempting to use rules that involve both initial conditions and transformations, although their rules are not yet correct. Additional support for this view, plus evidence that the rules are initially limited in the range of objects and transformations to which they apply, is provided by Curcio, Robbins, and Ela (1971). They found that in a group of 167 preschoolers, 52 passed EC when their fingers were used as the items to be conserved, but only 13 passed when objects were used.

FIG. 5.1 Conservation displays.

The most relevant evidence on the operation of the conservation rules in the functioning of Q_s is provided in a study by Gelman (1972a) in which the experimental task taps IC in the 2 to 3 numerical range. Her subjects, who were aged 3 years, 6 months, were initially taught a game in which one row of three (or two) mice was arbitrarily designated the winner and a second row of two (or three) mice the loser. The children were not informed by the experimenter that number was the dimension of the situation determining which row was the winner. After they had learned to consistently select the winner on one of the arbitrary bases, the winning row was *covertly* submitted to T_+ or T_- (by the addition or subtraction of a mouse), or T_p (by shortening or lengthening the row). The game continued as before and the children were asked to select the winning row. Their responses to the "magical" transformations indicated a clear distinction between $T_\pm$ and T_p. Covert addition or subtraction of a mouse resulted in surprise, evidenced by search for the missing mouse or assertions that one had been added. There were frequent comments that there was now one less or one more mouse. Perceptual transformation of the winning array, in contrast, elicited substantially less comment from the children. Gelman (1972a) interprets these results as evidence that very young children "possess an adequate concept of basic cardinal numerosity and a logic that treats number as invariant under irrelevant transformations. When the numbers are small . . . children spontaneously focus upon the numerosity of a set. . . . in explaining changes in numerosity they appeal to addition and subtraction operations [pp. 87–88]." Gelman then replicated the common finding that children in this age range fail to conserve. She asks "why 3- and 4-year olds, who possess number invariance rules, fail to 'conserve' [p. 88]." The answer can only be obtained, she argues, when we realize that "the conservation test evaluates more than one thing." Among them are "logical capacity, the control of attention, correct semantics, and estimation skills (in our terms, *quantification operators*) [p. 89]."

Note that Gelman's "magic" task involved an appreciation of IC, not EC, the conservation task she used in her control experiment. It is quite consistent with our view that the children could possess IC Productions (5.7), (5.8), and (5.9), based upon Q_s, but not EC Productions (5.4), (5.5), and (5.6). Evidence for just such a situation comes from Elkind and Schoenfeld's (1972) finding that 4-year-old children do significantly better on IC tasks than they do on EC tasks, whereas 6-year-olds show no such differential performance across the two kinds of task.

An alternative explanation of the discrepancy between the outcome of the magic and conservation tasks is related to Gelman's notion of shifts in attention (Gelman, 1969). It is likely that the magic task taps Q_s, while conservation activates Q_e. The initial one-to-one correspondence in the conservation task could easily focus attention on length and density attributes, and thus activate Q_e. Furthermore, as Gelman notes, the *observed* T_p in the conservation task—

absent from the magic task—could also focus attention upon length and density, and hence activate Q_e.

Our account of the initial discrimination of $T_\pm$ from T_p assigns a major role to the development and utilization of Q_s. This seems plausible in the context of children's everyday experience. As Bunt (1951) has observed, in the course of play experiences and daily activities, there is ample opportunity for children to employ Q_s to detect the consistent effects of addition, subtraction, and perceptual transformations on small quantities of discrete items such as the other members of his family, toys, shoes, cutlery, and so on. With the development of Q_c and Q_e, this experience is gradually extended from small numbers of objects to larger and larger collections, progressing over time through the range usually studied in investigations labeled as conservation of discontinuous quantity, of number, and of continuous quantity.

As indicated at the outset of this section, in order to account for the development of conservation rules covering this extended range, we must add to the current capabilities of our developing system. The additions must include:

1. The ability to perform successfully on the equivalence conservation task.

2. The ability to conserve inequality as well as equality. Initial inequalities are, of course, impossible in the IC situation, but they are a regular feature of the child's experience in two-collection transformational situations.

3. The ability to conserve when comparisons are based upon the output of quantification operators other than Q_s.

4. The ability to coordinate pairs of quantitative symbols, as in conservation tasks involving the height and width of liquids in containers.

We will treat the development of each of these capacities in the order listed above, although we assume that they develop more or less concurrently once the components of identity conservation have developed. The only aspect of "stage" that we maintain is that the development of Q_s and the consequent discrimination of $T_\pm$ from T_p *start* before the onset of any of the other capacities.

Equivalence Conservation and Q_s

Consider the development of EC, assuming for the moment that Q_s is the only reliable indicator of quantity and that $T_\pm$ and T_p are differentiated. The general process of development is the same as that described in the development of IC. Systematic quantitative regularities among small collections of discrete objects are noticed and stored by the system in LTM as specific consistent sequences. These particular aspects of environmental regularity are attended to by the system because they are among the few quantitative things that the system *can* notice at this stage of its development. Thus, for example, it notices that whenever two collections (within the Q_s range) are initially equal and T_p is performed on one of them, they remain equal. Similar regularities are generated by observation and storage of the effects of T_+ and T_- on initially equal collections. As in the case of IC situations, these specific consistent sequences give rise to three common consistent sequences in LTM:

$$(x_s = y_s) \cdots (T_p(y) \to y') \cdots (y_s') \cdots (x_s = y_s')$$
$$(x_s = y_s) \cdots (T_+(y) \to y') \cdots (y_s') \cdots (x_s < y_s')$$
$$(x_s = y_s) \cdots (T_-(y) \to y') \cdots (y_s') \cdots (x_s > y_s')$$

The processing-economy systemic principle results in the application of the prediction and verification processes to the common consistent sequences. This leads to the construction of three production rules which thereafter govern the operation of the system in situations where collections within the range of Q_s undergo EC transformations. As in the case of the IC production rules, the EC rules obviate the necessity for quantifying the transformed collection and carrying out the final quantitative comparison:

$$(x_s = y_s)(T_p(y) \to y') --> (x_s = y_s')$$
$$(x_s = y_s)(T_+(y) \to y') --> (x_s < y_s')$$
$$(x_s = y_s)(T_-(y) \to y') --> (x_s > y_s')$$

There is some evidence from a training study (Wallace, 1972 a, p. 81) that the construction of the production rule governing the outcome of T_p is developmentally prior to that of the rules concerned with the effects of T_+ and T_-.

The EC production rules are clearly individually more complex than the IC rules since they require an additional element in the condition and must distinguish three quantities (x_s, y_s, y_s') rather than two (x_s, x_s'). Furthermore, the extension of EC rules to inequivalence rules, which will be discussed below, has no corresponding situation in IC, so that the compass of the two groups of rules is also unequal. However, there is no assumption of a developmental sequence for EC and IC. Both develop concurrently once $T_\pm$ and T_p have been differentiated, and this differentiation is based upon regularities that occur in both paradigms. Evidence for the co-occurrence of IC and EC over a variety of materials has been reported by Moynahan and Glick (1972) and Northman and Gruen (1970).

It is not assumed that EC operates by first applying a corresponding IC rule and then utilizing a transitive inference of the form

$$(x_s = y_s) (y_s = y_s') --> (x_s = y_s').$$

There is no necessity for the prior existence of transitivity rules since equivalence conservation is based upon empirical regularities. In the next chapter, which will be devoted to transitivity, we shall set forth the converse argument that "having" transitivity, as usually empirically determined, depends upon first "having" equivalence conservation.

In addition to the specific consistent sequences giving rise to the three common consistent sequences underlying equivalence conservation, the system also encounters the additional six forms of empirical results generated by each of the three transformations acting upon the two possible kinds of initial inequalities:

$$(x_s > y_s) \cdots (T_p(y) \to y') \cdots (y'_s) \cdots (x_s > y'_s)$$

$$(x_s > y_s) \cdots (T_+(y) \to y') \cdots (y'_s) \cdots (x_s > y'_s) \quad \text{or} \quad (x_s = y'_s) \quad \text{or} \quad (x_s < y'_s)$$

$$(x_s > y_s) \cdots (T_-(y) \to y') \cdots (y'_s) \cdots (x_s > y'_s)$$

$$(x_s < y_s) \cdots (T_p(y) \to y') \cdots (y'_s) \cdots (x_s < y'_s)$$

$$(x_s < y_s) \cdots (T_+(y) \to y') \cdots (y'_s) \cdots (x_s < y'_s)$$

$$(x_s < y_s) \cdots (T_-(y) \to y') \cdots (y'_s) \cdots (x_s < y'_s) \quad \text{or} \quad (x_s = y'_s) \quad \text{or} \quad (x_s > y'_s)$$

Two of the six do not give rise to consistent sequences. When T_+ is applied to the lesser of two collections, or T_- to the greater, the result can be any of the three relations. The ambiguity arises from the lack of a metric upon T_+ and T_-, so that the *amount* of the transformation is not utilized in encoding the environmental regularities.

Since these two situations do not provide any consistent sequences, they do not give rise to production rules. Thus, only four additional production rules develop from the empirical regularities involving initial inequalities:

$$(x_s > y_s)(T_p(y) \to y') \dashrightarrow (x_s > y'_s)$$

$$(x_s > y_s)(T_-(y) \to y') \dashrightarrow (x_s > y'_s)$$

$$(x_s < y_s)(T_p(y) \to y') \dashrightarrow (x_s < y'_s)$$

$$(x_s < y_s)(T_+(y) \to y') \dashrightarrow (x_s < y'_s)$$

Let us briefly summarize our account to this point. We have argued that the first operator to provide a basis for reliable quantitative comparisons is Q_s, and that its early stabilization facilitates the discrimination of T_p, T_+, and T_-. These, in turn, facilitate the observation of the empirical regularities that underlie the formation of the production rules for EC and IC. In the course of the development of the production rules governing the operation of Q_s, the other two quantification operators are also developing, and it is to that development and its relation to the IC and EC rules derived via Q_s that we now turn.

Generalization of Conservation Rules to Q_c

Thus far, all of the conservation production rules have been expressed in terms of the results of comparisons of quantitative symbols derived by applying Q_s. How might the IC, EC, and initial inequalities rules generalize to the operations of Q_c? The system would have to recognize the appropriate correspondences between quantitative comparison outcomes derived via Q_c and those obtained from Q_s. In Chapter 3, we hypothesized that application of two quantification operators to the same collections played an important part in the emergence of such correspondences. In addition, we suggested that equivalence detection is facilitated when comparisons arise from the quantification, transformation, and requantification of a collection; that is, when they are tests of the effect of the same transformation. Thus, the generalization of conservation production rules and the detection of correspondences between quantitative comparison outcomes may proceed concurrently: it is not necessary for the occurrence of rules to be dependent on the prior achievement correspondences. If the system's interaction with the environment has already resulted in the detection of correspondences between Q_s and Q_c quantitative comparison outcomes, then generalization of the production rules to Q_c is greatly facilitated.

Completion of the processes of establishing correspondences and of generalization of EC and IC rules is marked by the construction of Production Rules (5.1) to (5.9), which were described in the first section of this chapter. These comprise the three main quantitative comparison productions, the three EC rules, and the three IC rules stated in terms of quantitative relational attribute symbols. Their appearance does not represent attainment of the level of concrete operations across the complete range of conservation tasks, since the area of application of the quantitative relational attribute symbols is confined to Q_s and Q_c, and does not yet extend to Q_e. Completion of the correspondence and generalization processes would also result in the appearance of four production rules concerned with situations involving initial inequalities. These are restatements, in terms of quantitative relational attribute symbols, of the four rules derived via Q_s which were described above.

$$(x \overset{Q}{>} y)\,(\mathsf{T}_p(y) \to y') \dashrightarrow (x \overset{Q}{>} y') \qquad (5.10)$$

$$(x \overset{Q}{>} y)\,(\mathsf{T}_-(y) \to y') \dashrightarrow (x \overset{Q}{>} y') \qquad (5.11)$$

$$(x \overset{Q}{<} y)\,(\mathsf{T}_p(y) \to y') \dashrightarrow (x \overset{Q}{<} y') \qquad (5.12)$$

$$(x \overset{Q}{<} y)\,(\mathsf{T}_+(y) \to y') \dashrightarrow (x \overset{Q}{<} y') \qquad (5.13)$$

Having described the end result of the generalization of the conservation rules to Q_c and the relationship of this process to the establishment of correspondences between quantitative comparison outcomes, we will now consider how generalization of the rules from Q_s to Q_c proceeds. There are three possible sequences of events. These will be discussed in terms of IC, but the points made apply *mutatis mutandis* to EC and to situations involving initial inequalities.

As indicated above, the generalization process will be facilitated if the correspondence between Q_s and Q_c quantitative comparison outcomes has already been established. The effects of the prior establishment of correspondence will be indicated throughout our discussion by expressing quantitative comparison outcomes in terms of both quantitative symbols derived from individual quantification operators [e.g., $(x_s = y_s)$] and quantitative relational attribute symbols [e.g., $(x \overset{Q}{=} y)$].

The first possible sequence of events would involve the construction of rules by the system initially independent of the rules derived from Q_s. Specific consistent sequences in the operations of Q_c would be detected and stored in LTM. These would give rise to common consistent sequences and, subsequently, by the process of prediction and verification described above, rules would be derived. The scope of these rules would be confined to Q_c. Generalization would involve application of both quantification operators to the same situations, and detection by the system of the correspondence between Q_s and Q_c rules such as

$$(x_s)\,(T_p(x) \to x') \,-\!\!-\!\!> (x_s = x_s') \quad \text{or} \quad (x \overset{Q}{=} x')$$

$$(x_c)\,(T_p(x) \to x') \,-\!\!-\!\!> (x_c = x_c') \quad \text{or} \quad (x \overset{Q}{=} x')$$

and the consequent construction of the rule [see Production Rule (5.7)]:

$$(T_p(x) \to x') \,-\!\!-\!\!> (x \overset{Q}{=} x').$$

Compelling empirical evidence arguing against acceptance of this sequence as the actual train of events has already been reviewed in our discussion in Chapter 3 of the developmental relationship of Q_s and Q_c. If conservation rules governing the operations of Q_c were derived entirely independently of Q_s, then there would be evidence of their successful application, in particular in situations where, for the transformed collection, $n > 4$, much earlier in development than appears to be the case.

The second possible sequence of events represents the opposite extreme. It is based on the assumption that generalization of conservation rules derived from Q_s to the operations of Q_c occurs piecemeal as specific consistent sequences are detected in the functioning of Q_c. To illustrate the process involved we will add two symbols to our notation.

Let

    $a \equiv$ internal symbol representing a *specific* collection of material (that is, not variables like x, y, or z defined above);

    $a' \equiv$ representation of specific collection of material after any transformation;

    $a_i \equiv$ quantitative symbol derived by submitting specific collection, a, to quantification operator, i.

When specific consistent sequences such as

$$a_c \cdots (T_p(a) \to a') \cdots a'_c \cdots (a_c = a'_c) \quad \text{or} \quad (a \overset{Q}{=} a')$$

are derived from situations to which Q_s can also be applied, the system attempts to assimilate the sequence to the Q_s conservation rule

$$(x_s)(T_p(x) \to x') --> (x_s = x'_s) \quad \text{or} \quad (x \overset{Q}{=} x')$$

comprising the transformation that features in the sequence. Assimilation of Q_c specific consistent sequences to Q_s conservation rules would be facilitated by prior detection of the correspondence between Q_s and Q_c quantitative comparison outcomes. As already indicated, this may be brought about by the attachment of number labels to the subitizing productions in PS.SUB. This permits the same process of quantitative comparison to be applied to the quantitative symbols generated by Q_s and Q_c.

Piecemeal generalization of Q_s conservation rules to Q_c specific consistent sequences continues as the numerical range of Q_s increases in the course of development. Continuation of generalization of the rules to the operations of Q_c beyond the upper limit of Q_s poses no problem. The specific consistent sequences all involve collections of discrete elements. Consequently, the initial situations do not differ qualitatively from those in the Q_s range, while the transformations are identical—$T_\pm$: addition or subtraction of at least one discrete element, and T_p: any nondestructive transformation other than $T_\pm$.

There is, at present, a lack of empirical evidence on which a judgment can be based regarding the relative merits of this second possible sequence of events and the third contender. When generalization of the conservation rules to Q_e is discussed below, it will, however, be argued on formal grounds that the third possible sequence of events is the only one which could occur in the development of Q_e as well as Q_c.

The third alternative is predicated on the view that generalization of conservation rules from Q_s to Q_c occurs when specific consistent sequences, detected in the operations of Q_c on situations to which Q_s can also be applied, have given rise to the construction of common consistent sequences such as

$$(x_c) \cdots (T_p(x) \to x') \cdots (x'_c) \cdots (x_c = x'_c) \quad \text{or} \quad (x \overset{Q}{=} x').$$

This sequence of events avoids the prediction and verification phase necessary in the first alternative for the construction of Q_c rules independent of the functioning of Q_s. As in the case of the second alternative, generalization of Q_s conservation rules to Q_c common consistent sequences proceeds as the numerical range of Q_s increases and ultimately continues beyond the upper limit of Q_s.

Generalization of Conservation Rules to Q_e

Many of the judgmental situations encountered by the child deal with materials that are either beyond the range of Q_c or Q_s or are continuous. In such cases, only Q_e is appropriate. Q_e's wide scope, however, has associated with it a marked increase in processing complexity.

Although the overall course of the generalization of conservation rules is the same when the quantitative symbols are generated by Q_e as by Q_c, the use of Q_e introduces two difficulties. One is that the diversity of phenomena that must be represented as transformations is increased compared to the transformations upon small collections of discontinuous quantity. The other is that for the first time the system must quantify two dimensions of each quantity under consideration and the results of these double quantifications must be properly coordinated before any regularities can be detected and give rise to specific consistent sequences.

Inadequacy of unidimensional quantification. Initial attempts to quantify via Q_e lead to inconsistent results, because, as Halford (1970) has indicated, the quantitative symbols generated for comparison are based upon only one dimension of the situation.

Consider the classic nonconservation responses obtained with the Piagetian EC task using discontinuous materials. Some of the children carry out a terminal comparison of quantitative symbols derived from the lengths of the two collections being compared. Others compare symbols representing the density or distance between the elements of the collections. The early appearance of such unidimensional quantification by Q_e is attested to by Descoeudres (1922). In a task requiring the construction of a row of objects equal in quantity to a row already constructed by the experimenter, the younger children pay less attention to the number to be reproduced than to the space to be occupied by the row of elements. O'Bryan and Boersma (1971) have also provided evidence consistent with unidimensional quantification in nonconservers. The results of their study of eye movements indicate a steadily decreasing centration effect as one proceeds from children who are clearly nonconservers to those in a transitional state, and finally, to children who reveal logically justified conservation.

The developmental primacy of unidimensional quantification is consistent with the general systemic principle of processing economy as evidenced in the strategy of processing each element in a situation only once in a problem-solving episode unless feedback indicates that this is inappropriate. In neither IC nor EC situations are there the requisite regularities between transformations and terminal judgment comparisons based upon unidimensional quantification. Any transformation can result in all three relations on a single dimension, depending upon the change in the unattended dimension.

Two-dimensional estimation. Piaget's (1957) illustration of equilibration provides an account of the transition to two-dimensional quantification in the
context of a task requiring equivalence conservation of continuous quantity. He
attributes the shift to three factors which produce an oscillation of attention
between the dimensions of height and width and ultimately lead to the inclusion
of both. First of all, attention tends to be directed to the dimension on which
there is the greatest difference between the quantities of liquid. Since this
dimension varies from trial to trial, switching of attention between the dimensions is encouraged. Second, the generality of this tendency is evidenced by the
widely reported empirical finding that, in a two-alternative situation, repeated
responding to one of the alternatives increases the probability of an eventual
response to the other. A final factor involved in the switch to a two-dimensional
basis is the child's dissatisfaction with the inconsistency of the outcome of his
unidimensional judgments.

Our explanation of the shift of Q_e to a two-dimensional mode lacks the
probabilistic arguments addressed by Piaget, but it has a certain affinity with his
emphasis on the child's dislike of inconsistency. In accordance with the principle
of processing economy, the system determines the applicability to Q_e of the Q_s
conservation rules. Independent of the processing-economy principle, there is
striking empirical evidence that the preservation of consistency and agreement
between the judgmental outcomes of the quantification operators constitutes an
important goal. Intriguing examples of the expedients to which children will
resort to obtain consistency between the outcomes of Q_e and Q_c have been
provided by Inhelder and Sinclair (1969). Six-year-old children were asked to
use matches to construct a straight line equal in length to a zigzag line constructed by the experimenter. The subjects at first applied Q_e to one dimension
of the situation and were satisfied if the ends of the two lines coincided. When
encouraged to apply the numerical operations which they had already acquired
to the situation, however, the children readily recognized that equivalence of
length entailed having the same number of matches in both lines and began to
count to ensure that this criterion was satisfied. This led to conflict between the
outcomes of Q_e and Q_c, since it was not possible to construct a straight line with
the same number of matches as the experimenter's zig-zag line without violating
the constraint that the ends of the two lines coincide. Before the end-matching
approach was abandoned and the conflict resolved by applying Q_e to two
dimensions of the situation, some amusing compromise solutions were tried out.
Some of the subjects, for example, broke one of the matches in their row in two,
thus creating a line with the same number of elements as the experimenter's
without destroying the correspondence of the ends.

Attempts to apply the conservation rules to Q_e and to preserve agreement
between its outcomes and those of the other quantification operators are
doomed to failure due to its unidimensional basis. Failure to detect consistent

sequences in the functioning of Q_e constitutes the negative feedback required to indicate the inappropriateness in this aspect of the system's activity of the strategy of processing each element only once in a problem-solving episode. In its search for empirical regularities, therefore, the system widens the basis of its search and begins to attend to both dimensions, and consistent relationships between transformations and terminal judgments begin to emerge. Table 5.1 represents the initial form of these regularities. The table shows the nine possible relational outcomes resulting from the transformation of initially equal collections. For example, the first line indicates that final equality on both dimensions is only produced by T_p. The second line indicates that equality on one dimension and a relatively smaller amount of the transformed collection on the other is only produced by T_-, and so on. The table represents both EC (initially $x = y$ on both dimensions, and the final test is on x and y') and IC (final test is on x and x').

Two types of outcomes are equivocal with respect to the class of transformation that can produce them. Both of the outcomes that have simultaneous and opposite changes in two dimensions can be produced by T_p, T_+ or T_- (see lines 5 and 9 in Table 5.1). The other outcomes are uniquely associated with one of the three classes of transformations. Thus, the system has two classification tasks facing it if the Q_s conservation rules are to be generalized to the operations of Q_e. First it must classify the types of transformation with respect to their effect upon quantity, and then it must resolve the ambiguity of the transformations that produce compensatory changes in two dimensions.

The necessity of the successful completion of these two classification tasks before the Q_s conservation rules can be applied to Q_e becomes evident if the second of the three accounts of generalization discussed in connection with Q_c is considered in the context of Q_e. On this basis, generalization of conservation rules derived from Q_s to the operations of Q_e would occur piecemeal as specific consistent sequences are detected in the functioning of Q_e. Such an attempt by the system to fit the Q_s rules to Q_e as soon as bidimensional quantification produces consistent relationships between transformations and terminal judgments (and before the two classification tasks have been completed) would be fruitless.

The reason for this assertion can best be illustrated by considering the outcome of attempting to fit Q_s conservation rules to some of the specific consistent sequences which would arise from the regularities listed in Table 5.1. Lines 1, 5, and 9 of Table 5.1 are partly represented in the following specific consistent sequences, where

$a1_e$, $a2_e$ ≡ quantitative symbols generated by applying Q_e to dimensions 1 and 2 of a specific collection of material, a.

For perceptual transformations that leave both dimensions under consideration

TABLE 5.1

Initial Regularities for Identity and Equivalence
Conservation Based upon Two-Dimensional
Quantification via Q^a

| | | Relation between x_e and x'_e or x_e and y'_e | |
| | | on | on |
Line	Transformation	Dimension 1	Dimension 2
1	T_p	=	=
2	T_-	=	>
3	T_+	=	<
4	T_-	>	=
5	T_+, T_-, T_p	>	<
6	T_-	>	>
7	T_+	<	<
8	T_+	<	=
9	T_+, T_-, T_p	<	>

^{a} From Klahr and Wallace (1973, Table 1).

unchanged, (such as translation):

$$(a1_e)(a2_e) \cdots (T_p(a) \to a') \cdots (a'1_e)(a'2_e) \cdots (a1_e = a'1_e)(a2_e = a'2_e).$$
(5.14)

For perceptual transformations that change both dimensions:

$$(a1_e)(a2_e) \cdots (T_p(a) \to a') \cdots (a'1_e)(a'2_e) \cdots (a1_e > a'1_e)(a2_e < a'2_e),$$
(5.15)

or

$$(a1_e)(a2_e) \cdots (T_p(a) \to a') \cdots (a'1_e)(a'2_e) \cdots (a1_e < a'1_e)(a2_e > a'2_e).$$
(5.16)

All of these specific consistent sequences may arise from situations within the numerical range of Q_s. Consequently, in all three cases, an attempt would be made to fit the same Q_s conservation rule

$$(x_s)(T_p(x) \to x') - -> (x_s = x'_s) \quad \text{or} \quad (x \overset{Q}{=} x').$$

The inconsistency of the results which would emerge from these attempts at predicting Q_e outcomes on the basis of a Q_s rule is evident and could only generate confusion for the system.

Three types of specific consistent sequences arise from line 5 of Table 5.1, including the sequence incorporating T_p, presented above.

$$(a1_e)(a2_e) \cdots (T_+(a) \rightarrow a') \cdots (a'1_e)(a'2_e) \cdots (a1_e > a'1_e)(a2_e < a'2_e)$$
$$(5.17)$$

$$(a1_e)(a2_e) \cdots (T_-(a) \rightarrow a') \cdots (a'1_e)(a'2_e) \cdots (a1_e > a'1_e)(a2_e < a'2_e)$$
$$(5.18)$$

$$(a1_e)(a2_e) \cdots (T_p(a) \rightarrow a') \cdots (a'1_e)(a'2_e) \cdots (a1_e > a'1_e)\, 'a2_e < a'2_e).$$
$$(5.19)$$

If each of these sequences arises from a situation within the numerical range of Q_s it will elicit an attempt to fit a different Q_s conservation rule. The three rules which would be elicited, listed in the order corresponding to the specific consistent sequences that activate them, are as follows:

$$(x_s)(T_+(x) \rightarrow x') --> (x_s < x'_s) \quad \text{or} \quad (x \overset{Q}{<} x')$$
$$(x_s)(T_-(x) \rightarrow x') --> (x_s > x'_s) \quad \text{or} \quad (x \overset{Q}{>} x')$$
$$(x_s)(T_p(x) \rightarrow x') --> (x_s = x'_s) \quad \text{or} \quad (x \overset{Q}{=} x').$$

The three different rules would result in the prediction of three different final quantitative comparison outcomes. The three specific consistent sequences, in contrast, yield the same outcome from the final quantitative comparison. Confusion is thus confounded. As will be indicated below, these conflicting results can only be avoided if the types of transformation are classified with respect to their effect on quantity, and if the ambiguties of the transformations that produce compensatory changes in two dimensions are resolved prior to the attempt to apply the Q_s conservation rules to Q_e.

The necessity of the generalization of the conservation rules from Q_s to Q_e and the impossibility of the construction of the rules by the system via Q_e and independent of Q_s can be easily demonstrated. The empirical regularities listed in Table 5.1 constitute the fullest possible informational base for the derivation of common consistent sequences and subsequent rule construction. In practice, common consistent sequences cannot be derived, and thus rules cannot be constructed. Attempts at detecting common consistent sequences would comprise searches for regularly recurring sequences of the form: (*transformation*) $\cdots$ (*final quantitative comparison outcome*). Such searches will lead to failure since, as Table 5.1 indicates, T_+ and T_- transformations can unpredictably give rise to any one of four possible final outcomes, whereas T_p can equally unpredictably produce any of three final results.

How does interaction between Q_s and Q_e lead to classification of the types of transformation listed in Table 5.1, resolution of the status of the ambiguous transformations, and generalization of the conservation rules to Q_e?

The solutions to all three problems are, in our view, pursued concurrently. As so often before, the key lies in those situations where both Q_s and Q_e can be applied. A collection is quantified by Q_s and Q_e and then undergoes a transformation. In the case of Q_s the outcome of the final quantitative comparison is determined by the operation of a conservation rule, while in the case of Q_e, a bidimensional requantification (e.g., length and density) of the collection is carried out and the results are compared with the corresponding symbols from the initial quantification to yield the final outcome. Since the same collection and transformation have been processed by Q_s and Q_e, the system establishes an equivalence between the final outcomes derived from the two quantification operators. By this procedure of double application to the same collections and transformations, all of the varied final outcomes obtained by applying Q_e to situations produced by T_p, listed in lines 1, 5, and 9 of Table 5.1, are established as equivalent to the same Q_s quantitative comparison outcome symbol. The establishment of this equivalence, in informal terms, constitutes a broadening of the semantic basis of the concept of "equal." In formal terms it is marked by the linking of the three Q_e final outcomes to the relational attribute symbol $\stackrel{Q}{=}$. For the purposes of this discussion it is assumed that the Q_s conservation rules already include relational attribute symbols as a result of the prior establishment of equivalence between Q_s and Q_c final outcomes. If this is not the case, the establishment of equivalence between Q_s and Q_e final outcomes will result in the emergence of the three basic productions linking quantitative comparison outcomes from the two quantification operators to relational attribute symbols. These relational attribute symbols will then be included in the Q_s rules and in consistent sequences derived from Q_e.

Empirical regularities in the application of Q_e to the environment give rise to three specific consistent sequences such as Sequences (5.14), (5.15), and (5.16) above. Let us assume that these sequences concern situations which fall within the range of Q_s. When Q_s is applied to these situations the same aspect of Q_s will operate in all three cases. The aspect in question is the production rule

$$(T_p(x) \rightarrow x') \,-\!-\!> (x \stackrel{Q}{=} x').$$

Since the same collections and transformations have been processed by Q_e and Q_s, the system establishes equivalence between the final outcomes obtained. The establishment of equivalence takes the form of modifications of the Q_e specific consistent sequences: Sequences (5.14), (5.15), and (5.16) become

$$(a1_e)\,(a2_e) \cdots (T_p(a) \rightarrow a') \,\cdots\, (a'1_e)\,(a'2_e) \cdots (a \stackrel{Q}{=} a') \qquad (5.20)$$

$$(a1_e)\,(a2_e) \cdots (T_p(a) \rightarrow a') \,\cdots\, (a'1_e)\,(a'2_e) \cdots (a \stackrel{Q}{=} a') \qquad (5.21)$$

$$(a1_e)\,(a2_e) \cdots (T_p(a) \rightarrow a') \,\cdots\, (a'1_e)\,(a'2_e) \cdots (a \stackrel{Q}{=} a'). \qquad (5.22)$$

These modifications, in turn, establish that all three specific consistent sequences include a transformation of the same type. Note that, as a result, specific consistent Sequences (5.21) and (5.22) cease to belong to the categories of empirical regularities (lines 5 and 9 of Table 5.1) which feature ambiguous transformations.

As the pattern of events just outlined occurs with reference to an increasing number of Q_e specific consistent sequences featuring T_+ and T_- as well as T_p transformations, the twin problems of classifying the types of transformation listed in Table 5.1 and resolving the status of the ambiguous transformations are concurrently resolved. This opens the way for the generalization of the Q_s conservation rules to Q_e. With modified Q_e specific consistent sequences of the type illustrated above, the process of generalization could proceed by the direct fitting of Q_s rules to Q_e specific consistent sequences. Since this would involve very many repetitions of the rule-fitting process, it would be more in accord with the processing economy principle if common consistent sequences were first derived from the Q_e specific consistent sequences and Q_s rules subsequently fitted to these common consistent sequences. The three modified specific consistent sequences presented above would, for example, give rise to a common consistent sequence of the form

$$(x1_e)\,(x2_e) \cdots (T_p(x) \rightarrow x') \cdots (x'1_e)\,(x'2_e) \cdots (x \overset{Q}{=} x'). \qquad (5.23)$$

This common consistent sequence would then be successfully fitted to the Q_s rule

$$(T_p(x) \rightarrow x') - \!-\!> (x \overset{Q}{=} x').$$

The final form of the associations between pairs of Q_e quantitative comparison outcomes and relational attribute symbols is indicated in Table 5.2. All of them must be established for the complete generalization of the Q_s conservation rules to Q_e. Once this has taken place the appropriate quantitative relational attribute symbols can be predicted directly on the basis of the conservation rules, although children sometimes refer to the pairs of quantitative comparison outcomes in justifying their predictions: "They are still the same because this one is longer but that one is thicker."

An appreciation of the association between the transformations discriminated into three categories and the pairs of Q_e quantitative comparison outcomes presumably underlies the capability to make the type of observation proposed by Halford (1970):

(a) Whenever material is poured from A to B and nothing is added or subtracted, if there is any change in the material then there will be another change as well.

(b) ... where a change occurs in one dimension, but not in any other, something will be added or subtracted [p. 305].

Observation (a) is represented by lines 2 and 3 of Table 5.2 and observation (b) by lines 5, 6, 10, and 11.

Once the process just outlined has taken place in "common" situations to which both Q_s and Q_e can be applied, and the applicability of conservation rules to the operations of Q_e has been established, the rules are applied to other situations involving continuous quantity. Such extensions follow the order of the phenomenal similarity of the transformations involved to those in the common situations. Thus, situations involving judgments and transformations on discontinuous quantity precede application to continuous quantity (e.g., Smedslund, 1964; Brainerd & Brainerd, 1972), while within continuous quantity plasticene may be dealt with successfully prior to water (e.g., Uzgiris, 1964).

OPERATIONAL CONSERVATION OF QUANTITY

When the applicability to Q_c and Q_e of the conservation rules detected in the functioning of Q_s has been established, the child has attained the criterion for "operational" conservation. The rules will be employed in making terminal judgments when any of the three quantification operators are employed. The adoption of this criterion has important implications. It leaves much more room for individual variations in the course of the development of conservation than, for example, the traditional Genevan approach which implies that the pace of development may vary but the sequence is the same for all. This emphasis on individual variation is consistent with a number of empirical findings. Gréco (1962), for example, reports that some of his subjects, when undergoing EC trials with two rows of discontinuous elements, continue to give classic nonconservation responses on the terminal quantitative judgments. However, when questioned on the numerosity of the terminal collections, they are able to respond correctly that "You have six and I have six," or "There were five before." This distinction between *quotité* (number name) and *quantité* (numerical quantity) can be interpreted in terms of our criterion, that is, as stemming from subjects who are employing the conservation rules in making terminal judgments when Q_c is in operation, but whose Q_e is still functioning on a unidimensional, and thus inconsistent, basis.

Further evidence of individual differences in the relative rates of development of Q_c and Q_e is provided by Churchill (1958). In an acceleration study she found that, on tests of equivalence conservation of discontinuous quantity, some of her subjects based their correct responses entirely on "numerical" features of the situation (Q_c), while others relied purely on "perceptual" features (Q_e). In a study aimed at tracing the course of individual development of conservation of discontinuous quantity, Wallace, (1972a, pp. 169–170) has also detected a number of threads of development which can be identified as Q_e-led or Q_c-led

TABLE 5.2

Final Regularities for Equivalence Conservation Based upon
Two-Dimensional Estimation[a]

Line	Transformation	Relation between x_e and y'_e on Dimension 1	Relation between x_e and y'_e on Dimension 2	Quantitative relation between x and y'
1	T_p	=	=	=
2	T_p	>	<	=
3	T_p	<	>	=
4	T_+	<	<	<
5	T_+	<	=	<
6	T_+	=	<	<
7	T_+	<	>	<
8	T_+	>	<	<
9	T_-	>	>	>
10	T_-	>	=	>
11	T_-	=	>	>
12	T_-	>	<	>
13	T_-	<	>	>

[a] From Klahr and Wallace (1973, Table 2).

developmental sequences. Finally, it should be mentioned that at present there are indications that the Genevan group is engaged in a major reappraisal of its theoretical position. The available evidence (Cellérier, 1972) suggests that the outcome may be the introduction of a much greater flexibility into the group's account of development, which would being it closer to the multilinear picture of the development of conservation presented above.

The model of "operational" conservation is consistent with other aspects of the experimental evidence. As Beilin (1971) has pointed out in reviewing the many training studies stimulated by Piaget's work,

> What emerges from the data is the striking fact that a wide variety of methods, in fact, practically every type of experimental method, leads to successful improvement in performance, even if not in every experiment [p. 113].

This is precisely the type of outcome from acceleration studies which our model would predict. The developmental progression of the detection of the conservation rules by Q_s and the subsequent concurrent attempts to establish their relevance to Q_c and Q_e presents a broad front to training. Almost any of the acceleration treatments which have been employed to date could be shown to be likely to facilitate the development of children at particular points in the protracted and complex process of attaining "operational" conservation.

PS.QC5: A MODEL FOR QUANTITATIVE
COMPARISON AND CONSERVATION

PS.QC5[1] is a PSG model that links the quantitative comparison facility of PS.QC2 and PS.QC3 with the conservation rules introduced in this chapter. Whenever quantitative comparison questions are posed, PS.QC5 first checks to see if it can apply any of the conservation rules and thereby avoid a requantification effort. The major extension is the addition of the conservation rules (Fig. 5.2, 7000–8700) corresponding to Rules (5.4) through (5.13). A secondary modification has been the introduction of additional generality in the kinds of relations with which the system can deal. Finally, a set of changes which fall between psychological theory and "pure" programming have been introduced to clean up the system and rationalize its use of variables.

Since PS.QC5 represents the most advanced (and most complex) model in this series, we will describe several of its features in detail. Our description rests upon the assumption that by now the reader is reasonably familiar both with PSG and with the essential psychological assumptions of the quantitative comparison models. First, we will describe each of the important features of the model as listed in Fig. 5.2, then we will present a trace.

LTM Structure

Although PSG has the facility for simple additions to LTM, none of our state models use it. The only use of LTM (other than the productions themselves, which of course reside there) is in some simple "semantic" hierarchies, listed in 2200–4500, and represented as trees in Fig. 5.3. Recall that in PSG, A can be defined as the name of a class with members B1 B2 B3 by writing A: (CLASS B1 B2 B3). If we then have production PD1: (A $--> $ Z), the production will fire if any one of the elements B1, B2, or B3 is in STM. For the duration of that production, A will be assigned the specific value of whichever one of its members was found. For example, in 4200, T.PER (the PSG equivalent of T_p —a perceptual transformation) is defined as a class with six members: EXPAND, COMPRESS, and so on. In 7200, the third condition element starts with T.PER, and it would be successfully matched with an element in STM that started with any of the members of T.PER, for example, (MOVE X (NEW X)) or (INVERT X (NEW X)). The elements in the domain of a class can themselves be class names; thus, a network of symbols is possible, although in PS.QC5 this never gets more than three layers deep. The psychological assumptions represented by these class variables will be discussed when we treat the specific productions that use them. Their most important feature is that they are one direct method of introducing generality to any given production. However, as

[1] There is no PS.QC4 in this volume. It was a tentative model which we abandoned.

```
1400 X:(VAR)
1500 Y:(VAR)
1600
1700          relate simulates (1) relative magnitude determination
1800                           (2) quant. relational attribute
1900 RELATE:(OPR CALL)
1950 SAT:(ACTION (* ==> +))
2000                         Semantic network
2200 WVAL:(CLASS RED BLUE SQUARE ROUND WOOD)
2300 VAL:(CLASS (WVAL) (V1 NOT V2))
2400 V1:(CLASS WVAL)
2500 V2:(CLASS WVAL)
2600 QUANTIFIER:(CLASS SUBIT COUNT ESTIMATE)
3200 XLM:(CLASS XDOT XRED XETC XELM VAL)
3300 REL.WORD:(CLASS MORE LESS LONGER SHORTER BIGGER SMALLER EQUAL SAME)
3400 CS:(CLASS LEFT RIGHT TOP BOTTOM THERE HERE WVAL)
3500 C1:(CLASS CS)
3600 C2:(CLASS CS)
3700 QREL:(CLASS QEQ QLT QGT)
3800 QEQ:(CLASS EQUAL SAME FAIR EQUAL.TO SAME.AS Q= )
3900 QLT:(CLASS FEWER SMALLER LESS LESS.THAN Q< )
4000 QGT:(CLASS MORE MORE.THAN BIGGER GREATER.THAN Q> )
4100
4200 T.PER:(CLASS EXPAND COMPRESS MOVE ROTATE TRANSLATE INVERT)
4300 T.ADD:(CLASS ADD POUR.IN)
4400 T.SUB:(CLASS SUB REMOVE EAT DELETE)
4500 TS:(CLASS T.PER T.SUB T.ADD)
4600
4700 VS.SETUP:(OPR CALL)     Create VSTM In Mid Run
4800 PDVS0:((GOAL * SUBIT XLM) (SEE XLM) ABS --> VS.SETUP)
4900 PDVS1:((GOAL * SUBIT XLM) (SEE XLM) (SEE XLM) ABS --> SAT (QS ONE XLM))
5000 PDVS2:((GOAL * SUBIT XLM) (SEE XLM) (SEE XLM) (SEE XLM) ABS --> SAT (QS TWO XLM))
5100 PDVS3:((GOAL * SUBIT XLM) (SEE XLM) (SEE XLM) (SEE XLM) (SEE XLM) ABS --> SAT (QS THREE XLM))
5500
5600 PSVS:(PDVS3 PDVS2 PDVS1 PDVS0)
5700
5800                         goal manipulation
5900 PA:((* GOAL) (* GOAL) --> (* ===> %))
6000 PZ:((* GOAL) ABS (% GOAL) --> (% ==> *))
6150 PQ:((* GOAL) ABS (% GOAL) ABS --> QUESTION.PLEASE)
6200                         verbal encoding
6300 PDV1:((REL.WORD) (V1) (V2) --> (HEARD **)(X ===> HEARD X)(Y ====> HEARD Y)(VALUE (V1))(VALUE (V2))(GOAL GET.REL V1 V2))
6600 PDV2:((REL.WORD)(NEW V1)(V2) --> (HEARD **)(X ===> HEARD X)(Y ====> HEARD Y)(VALUE (V1))(VALUE (V2))(* GOAL GET.REL V1 V2))
6800 PSVERB:(PDV1 PDV2)
7000                         conservation rules
7100                         .....equivalence conservation
7200 PD.CON4:((* GOAL CON) (OLD (C1 QEQ C2)) (T.PER C2 NEW C2) --> SAT (C1 QEQ NEW C2))
7400 PD.CON5:((* GOAL CON) (OLD (C1 QEQ C2)) (T.ADD C2 NEW C2) --> SAT (C1 QGT NEW C2))
7500 PD.CON6:((* GOAL CON) (OLD (C1 QEQ C2)) (T.SUB C2 NEW C2) --> SAT (C1 QGT NEW C2))
7800                         .....identity conservation
7900 PD.CON7:((* GOAL CON) (T.PER C1 NEW C1) --> SAT (C1 Q= NEW C1))
8000 PD.CON8:((* GOAL CON) (T.ADD C1 NEW C1) --> SAT (C1 Q< NEW C1))
8100 PD.CON9:((* GOAL CON) (T.SUB C1 NEW C1) --> SAT (C1 Q> NEW C1))
8200                         .....inequivalence conservation
8300 PD.CON10:((* GOAL CON) (OLD (C1 QGT C2)) (T.PER C2 NEW C2) --> SAT (C1 QGT NEW C2))
8400 PD.CON11:((* GOAL CON) (OLD (C1 QGT C2)) (T.SUB C2 NEW C2) --> SAT (C1 QGT NEW C2))
8500 PD.CON12:((* GOAL CON) (OLD (C1 QLT C2)) (T.PER C2 NEW C2) --> SAT (C1 QLT NEW C2))
8600 PD.CON13:((* GOAL CON) (OLD (C1 QLT C2)) (T.ADD C2 NEW C2) --> SAT (C1 QLT NEW C2))
8700 PD.CON.FAIL:((* GOAL CON) --> (* ==> -))
8800
9000                         main productions
9100 P1A:((* GOAL GET.REL X Y)(X QREL Y) --> SAT (NTC (X QREL))(OLD **) SAY.IT)
9200 P1B:((* GOAL GET.REL Y X)(X QREL Y) --> SAT (NTC (X QREL))(OLD **) SAY.IT)
9300 P2:((* GOAL GET.REL)(TS)(- GOAL CON) ABS --> (* GOAL CON))
9400 P4:((* GOAL GET.REL X Y) --> (* GOAL COMPARE X Y))
9650 P6:((* GOAL COMPARE) (X QREL Y) --> SAT)
9700 P7:((* GOAL COMPARE X Y) (QS X) (QS Y) --> RELATE)
10100 P9:((* GOAL COMPARE) (VALUE X) --> (VALUE ===> OLD VALUE) (* GOAL QUANTIFY X))
10300 P10:((* GOAL QUANTIFY X) (GOAL + QUANTIFIER X) --> SAT)
10400 P11:((* GOAL QUANTIFY X) --> (GOAL * SUBIT X))
10500
10900 SAY.IT:(ACTION (SAY X) (SAY QREL) (SAY Y))
11000
11100 QUESTION.PLEASE:(OPR CALL)
11200 SSTM1:(NIL NIL NIL NIL NIL NIL NIL NIL NIL NIL NIL NIL NIL NIL NIL NIL)
11300 VSTM1:(NIL NIL NIL NIL NIL)
11400 INIT.ACT:(QUESTION.PLEASE)
11500
11600 PS.CON:(PD.CON4 PD.CON5 PD.CON6 PD.CON10 PD.CON11 PD.CON12 PD.CON13 PD.CON7 PD.CON8 PD.CON9 PD.CON.FAIL)
11700 PSM2:(P1A P1B P2 P4 P6 P7 P9 P10 P11)
11800 PSEXEC:(PA PZ PSVERB PSVS PS.CON PSM2 PQ)
```

FIG. 5.2 PS.QC5.

mentioned in Chapter 2, the search for specific elements of a complex hierarchy of classes is buried in the PSG interpretive mechanism. When we discuss the general model in Chapter 7, we will treat such a search mechanism as a production system itself.

Variables

Lines 1400–1500 contain the only two free variables used by PS.QC5. Any STM element can match a free variable, and that value remains "bound" until the action is completed. Previous models defined X0, X1, X2, . . . , Xn as free variables.

Production Sequence and Conventions

PS.QC5 is written as a system consisting of subsystems and productions, but there is no hierarchic structure: the entire system is scanned at the same level. The sequence is determined by PSEXEC (11800), PSVERB (6800), PSVS (5600), PS.CON (11600), and PSM2 (11700), each of which contains a list of productions. The naming conventions are an arbitrary mixture of some mnemonics plus some consistency with earlier models. The conservation rules PD.CON4 to PD.CON13 correspond to Rules (5.4) to (5.13) in this chapter. P1, P3, P3A, . . . , and so on correspond roughly to the previous PS.QC models.

Goal Manipulation (5800–6100)

PA and PZ have been with us since PS.QC1, although PZ has now been moved up almost to the front of the production list. PQ has been added to keep the system attending (to the terminal) for input when no active or interrupted goals are around.

The Visual Encoding System (4700–5600)

PSVS is included in this model instead of PSCOUNT, as in PS.QC3, to demonstrate that it too functions appropriately in the larger context of quantitative comparison. Since (GOAL * SUBIT) must be in SSTM for any of the encoding productions to fire, any situation which does not ultimately fire P11 (10400) could not satisfy any of the PDVS rules. PDVS0 is included here to provide terminal control in the situation where subitizing has failed. The typical intervention here is to set up VSTM in some appropriate way.

Verbal Encoding (6300–6800)

PDV1 and PDV2 take the three linguistic elements and transform them into internal symbols and a goal of GET.REL with the target values determined by

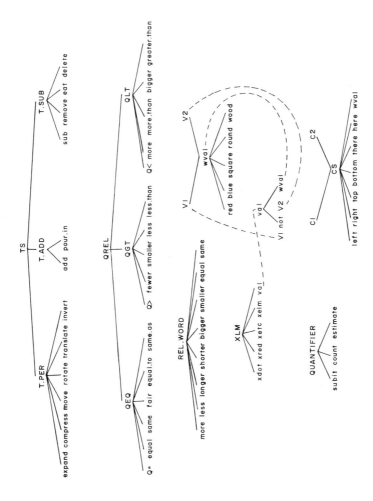

FIG. 5.3 Semantic memory for PS.QC5.

133

the two value terms. The old P3 is now included in PDV1 and PDV2. The format is

PDV1: ((REL.WORD) (V1) (V2)

         -->

         (HEARD **) (X ===> HEARD X) (Y ====> HEARD Y)

         (VALUE (V1)) (VALUE (V2)) (* GOAL GET.REL V1 V2)).

PDV1 fires if it finds a REL.WORD and V1 and a V2. Recall that these are defined as *class variables,* so that they can match on any of a small set of specific values in SSTM. REL.WORD will match against relational terms such as MORE, LESS, or BIGGER. V1 and V2 have been similarly defined to match on values such as RED, BLUE, WOOD, and so on. Thus, an input to SSTM such as (MORE) (RED) (BLUE) will be sufficient to fire PDV1. The actions in PDV1 do two kinds of things. First, they tag the three elements that fired PDV1 so that they are essentially inhibited from firing it again. Each element is tagged with the symbol "HEARD." Then three new elements are added to SSTM. Two of them are tagged as VALUE elements, with whatever particular value V1 and V2 have at that moment. The third new element is an active goal of determining the relationship between the two values: (*GOAL GET.REL RED BLUE). The psychological function of this production is to transform the auditory input from the question "Which is more, the reds or the blues?" into an imperative command to the system: "Get the relationship between the reds and the blues." PDV2 has been added to handle the conservation situation in which the question is either explicitly or implicitly in reference to a NEW (i.e., transformed) collection.

Conservation (7000–8700)

The conservation rules are PSG implementations of the numbered Productions (5.4) through (5.13). There are two basic forms of rules: identity conservation, PD.CON7–PD.CON9; and equivalence/inequivalence conservation, PD.CON4–PD.CON6 and PD.CON10–PD.CON13. The mapping between the PSG rules and the rules presented earlier in the chapter is straightforward. Consider Rule (5.4) and PD.CON4:

Rule 5.4: $(x \overset{Q}{=} y) (T_p (y) \to y') - -> (x \overset{Q}{=} y')$

PD.CON4: ((* GOAL CON) (OLD (C1 QEQ C2)) (T.PER C2 NEW C2)

        - -> SAT (C1 QEQ NEW C2)).

The first element in all the conservation productions is (* GOAL CON), an active goal of attempting to apply a conservation rule. This goal is created by P2 (9300) in its attempt to get the system to utilize information about transformations. If none of the conservation productions fire, then the CON goal fails (8700) and the system would do a "normal" pass through PS.QC3.

The second condition element is a template that searches STM for an OLD (C1 QEQ C2). C1 and C2 are class variables that can be either position names or value names, and QEQ is a class of quantitative relational attributes corresponding to equality. Any of the following, if tagged "OLD," would satisfy this second element: (RED EQUAL.TO BLUE), (THERE SAME.AS HERE), (SQUARE FAIR ROUND), and so on. The third condition element tests for any perceptual transformation upon C2. If the conditions are all satisfied, PD.CON4 fires, and two actions are taken. The conservation goal is satisfied, and a new element, containing information about the quantitative relational attribute that holds between C1 and NEW C2, is added to STM.

The mapping between the other PD.CON rules and the numbered productions described earlier is essentially the same, with the exception of the identity conservation rules. In these, the form of the relational attribute is not determined by the assignment from the corresponding STM element, but instead is determined directly by the rule. Thus Q=, although one of several symbols for quantitative equality, is produced only by the CON rules. The source of the other relational terms is RELATE, a terminal call that stimulates both relative magnitude determination and Conservation Rules (5.1)–(5.3) in this chapter.

Quantitative Comparison (9100–10400)

Although the basic logic of quantitative comparison has not changed from PS.QC2 and PS.QC3, several important refinements are included in this section. We will proceed in order of consideration, and with reference to PS.QC2. For convenience, the productions in PS.QC2 (Fig. 4.4) will be denoted by a prime. P1A and P1B correspond to P1' (that is, to P1 in Fig. 4.4); they test for a match between the goal and the relation. P2, discussed above, provides the point of departure for PS.QC5 to attempt "conserving." P4 is essentially the same as P4', but notice that since it occurs after P2, it is no longer generating a superfluous goal; that is, GET.REL no longer *invariably* generates COMPARE, for the conservation rules provide another possible way to determine relationships.

There is no P5 in PS.QC5. P5' was unnecessarily ad hoc in that it directly changed an interrupted goal to a satisfied goal, rather than go through the reactivation cycle (PZ). The satisfaction of GET.REL (previously MORE) is now handled by P1A or P1B. P6 is isomorphic to P6'. P7 is simpler than P7', since there is no need to mark the quantitative symbols OLD. P9 is isomorphic to P9'. P10 is a generalization of P10' because any satisfied quantification goal will satisfy the second condition. P11 directly links quantification to subitizing and, like P11', makes this model specific to a single quantifier. PS.QC5 in all other respects could work with the results of any of the quantifiers. Thus this particular model falls somewhere between preoperational and fully operational.

The extent to which it is operational depends partly upon the encoding simulated by the terminal calls, partly upon the LTM structure described above, and partly upon the variety of, and linkages to, additional quantification subsystems.

A Trace of PS.QC5 on a Conservation Task

Figure 5.4 shows an edited trace of the system's response to an inequivalence conservation trial. The top line shows the initial condition of SSTM and VSTM. SSTM starts with three elements representing a gross simulation of the system's initial representation of the query "Which is bigger, the red collection or the blue collection?" VSTM contains the representation for a display containing a collection including two blue things and three red things.

The rest of Fig. 5.4 is divided into three columns: the first contains the number of passes, or cycles, that have been made through the system, the second shows the name of the production that fired on that pass, and the third column shows the contents of SSTM after the named production fires and all its actions have been completed.

Given the initial conditions, the first production to fire is PDV1. It draws upon its knowledge that BIGGER is a symbol for a relational word, and that RED and BLUE are symbols for value words. PDV1 also marks the elements that fired it to indicate that it has attended to them. PDV1 takes five actions: two that modify existing SSTM elements and three that add information to SSTM. The net result of all this is shown in the third column. Next, on pass 2, P4 fires; notice that P2 does not fire here because its conditions are not satisfied. In this case the GETREL goal simply generates a subgoal of comparison. This new element goes to the front of SSTM, pushing all else down one slot.

Since there are two active goals in SSTM at this point, PA fires next, followed by P9, and then PA fires again. We can interpret SSTM contents in terms of what the system knows after the fifth pass:

It wants to quantify the red things,	(* GOAL QUANTIFY RED)
because it's trying to do a comparison,	(% GOAL COMPARE BLUE RED)
in order to determine a relationship;	(% GOAL GETREL BLUE RED)
it has already HEARD the terms	(HEARD BIGGER)
	(HEARD BLUE)
	(HEARD RED)
and it has used the value RED so far	(OLD VALUE RED)
but not the value blue.	(VALUE BLUE)

P11 responds to the quantification goal by inserting a corresponding subitizing goal into STM. Once SUBIT is active (pass 6), the system does a template match on VSTM to determine how many red things there are. PDVS3 SEES precisely three RED things. The net result of all this is the placement of a quantitative symbol, QS, in SSTM. (The value of the symbol is THREE, but the actual

```
Initial state    SSTM:((BLUE) (RED) (BIGGER) NIL NIL NIL NIL NIL)      VSTM:((RED) (BLUE) (BLUE) (RED) (RED))

n    pd                    STM contents after pd fires

1    PDV1      ((* GOAL GETREL BLUE RED) (HEARD (BIGGER)) (VALUE RED) (VALUE BLUE) (HEARD BLUE) (HEARD RED) NIL NIL NIL NIL NIL)

2    P4        ((* GOAL COMPARE BLUE RED) (* GOAL GETREL BLUE RED) (HEARD (BIGGER)) (VALUE RED) (VALUE BLUE) (HEARD BLUE)
               (HEARD RED) NIL NIL NIL NIL )

3    PA        ((* GOAL COMPARE BLUE RED) (% GOAL GETREL BLUE RED) (HEARD (BIGGER)) (VALUE RED) (VALUE BLUE) (HEARD BLUE)
               (HEARD RED) NIL NIL NIL NIL )

4    P9

5    PA        ((* GOAL QUANTIFY RED) (% GOAL COMPARE BLUE RED) (OLD VALUE RED) (% GOAL GETREL BLUE RED) (HEARD (BIGGER))
               (VALUE BLUE) (HEARD BLUE) (HEARD RED) NIL NIL NIL )

6    P11       ((GOAL * SUBIT RED) (* GOAL QUANTIFY RED) (% GOAL COMPARE BLUE RED) (OLD VALUE RED) (% GOAL GETREL BLUE RED)
               (HEARD (BIGGER)) (VALUE BLUE) (HEARD BLUE) (HEARD RED) NIL NIL )

7    PDVS3     ((QS THREE RED) (GOAL + SUBIT RED) (* GOAL QUANTIFY RED) (% GOAL COMPARE BLUE RED) (OLD VALUE RED)
               (% GOAL GETREL BLUE RED) (HEARD (BIGGER)) (VALUE BLUE) (HEARD BLUE) (HEARD RED) NIL)

8    P10, PZ, P9, PA, P11, PDVS2, P10

15   PZ        ((* GOAL COMPARE BLUE RED) (+ GOAL QUANTIFY BLUE) (GOAL + SUBIT BLUE) (QS TWO BLUE) (OLD VALUE BLUE)
               (+ GOAL QUANTIFY RED) (GOAL + SUBIT RED) (QS THREE RED) (OLD VALUE RED) (% GOAL GETREL BLUE RED) (HEARD (BIGGER)))

16   P7        ((RED MORETHAN BLUE) (* GOAL COMPARE BLUE RED) (QS TWO BLUE) (QS THREE RED) (+ GOAL QUANTIFY BLUE)
               (GOAL + SUBIT BLUE) (OLD VALUE BLUE) (+ GOAL QUANTIFY RED) (GOAL + SUBIT RED) (OLD VALUE RED)
               (% GOAL GETREL BLUE RED))

17   P6, PZ, P1B
                              ******** "RED  MORETHAN  BLUE" *******
20   PQ        ((EAT BLUE NEW BLUE) (OLD (RED MORETHAN BLUE)) (+ GOAL GETREL BLUE RED) (+ GOAL COMPARE BLUE RED) (QS TWO BLUE)
               (QS THREE RED) NIL NIL NIL)

21   PQ        (RED BLUE (BIGGER) (EAT BLUE NEW BLUE) (OLD (RED MORETHAN BLUE)) (+ GOAL GETREL BLUE RED)
               (+ GOAL COMPARE BLUE RED) (QS TWO BLUE) (QS THREE RED))

22   PDV1      ((* GOAL GETREL RED BLUE) (HEARD (BIGGER)) (VALUE RED) (VALUE BLUE) (HEARD RED) (HEARD BLUE)
               (EAT BLUE NEW BLUE) (OLD (RED MORETHAN BLUE)) (+ GOAL GETREL BLUE RED))

23   P2        ((* GOAL CON) (* GOAL GETREL RED BLUE) (EAT BLUE NEW BLUE) (HEARD (BIGGER)) (VALUE BLUE) (VALUE RED)
               (HEARD RED) (HEARD BLUE) (OLD (RED MORETHAN BLUE)))

24   PA        ((* GOAL CON) (% GOAL GETREL RED BLUE) (EAT BLUE NEW BLUE) (HEARD (BIGGER)) (VALUE BLUE) (VALUE RED)
               (HEARD RED) (HEARD BLUE) (OLD (RED MORETHAN BLUE)))

25   PDCON11   ((RED MORETHAN NEW BLUE) (+ GOAL CON) (OLD (RED MORETHAN BLUE)) (EAT BLUE NEW BLUE) (% GOAL GETREL RED BLUE)
               (HEARD (BIGGER)) (VALUE BLUE) (VALUE RED) (HEARD RED))

26   PZ        ((* GOAL GETREL RED BLUE) (RED MORETHAN NEW BLUE) (+ GOAL CON) (OLD (RED MORETHAN BLUE)) (EAT BLUE NEW BLUE)
               (HEARD (BIGGER)) (VALUE BLUE) (VALUE RED) (HEARD RED))

27   P1A       ((OLD (RED MORETHAN NEW BLUE)) (+ GOAL GETREL RED BLUE) (+ GOAL CON) (OLD (RED MORETHAN BLUE)) (EAT BLUE NEW BLUE)
               (HEARD (BIGGER)) (VALUE BLUE) (VALUE RED) (HEARD RED))
                              ******** "RED MORETHAN  BLUE" *******
```

FIG. 5.4   Trace of PS.QC5 on inequivalence conservation.

internal representation of it is obviously not assumed to be the word "three."
Like the names of goals, this particular name is chosen for the convenience of
people trying to understand the model: to the system they are just aribtrary
symbols.)

Thus, by pass 7, the system has managed to create one of the two quantitative
symbols it needs for the comparison. A sequence of goal satisfactions and
interruptions now ensues (P10, PZ, P9, PA, P11, PDVS2, P10, PZ). We pick up
the detailed trace again following pass 15, after two quantitative symbols have
been created. Notice that SSTM contains two satisfied (+) quantification goals

and two satisfied subitizing goals. At last P7 has what it needs, and it fires, calling upon the operator RELATE to determine the relative magnitude of the two quantitative symbols. Here, the system waits for human intervention from E to provide the hypothetical result from such a process. Thus, after pass 16, symbol (RED MORETHAN BLUE) is inserted into SSTM. A few more goal manipulations (P6, PZ) ensue, and finally P1B fires, "saying" the final result to the world after pass 19. By pass 20 nothing is active, all goals are satisfied, and the default production PQ responds to the absence of any active or interrupted goals by ATTENDing to the environment.

Thus far, the model has accounted for the first phase of a conservation experiment: the determination of the initial quantitative relationship between the two collections. In the case we have just simulated, this is an inequivalence trial, since the two collections are initially unequal. Next comes a transformation that is observed by the child. Let's assume that the child observes some of the blue things being eaten. In the production system, we represent the end result of an observed transformation by a single element with three components. In this case (pass 20), it is (EAT BLUE NEW BLUE). Once this information is inserted in SSTM, the system again fires PQ, which again waits for further input (pass 21).

Now "the" conservation question is posed, and PDV1 fires again. But this time the system has information about a transformation in SSTM: instead of P4 firing as before, P2 detects it, and inserts a goal of attempting to conserve (pass 23). On pass 25, a conservation rule, PDCON11, fires, producing new relational information. Having applied the conservation rule, the system goes through a series of cleaning up operations, similar to those on the initial quantification effort, and, having "said" the result, it quits.

CONSERVATION OF QUANTITY
AND THE STRUCTURE AND ORGANIZATION OF THE IPS

The theories of concrete operational performance on conservation of quantity and the developmental sequence of events underlying its emergence draw upon all of the structural and organizational modifications of the IPS required by the sufficient theories of preoperational and concrete operational CI performance. They also necessitate a further fundamental addition to the organization of the IPS. This is the capability to detect specific consistent sequences in the events arising from interaction with the environment, and subsequently, to derive common consistent sequences by detecting sequences of features shared by several specific consistent sequences. Common consistent sequences are used as a basis for the identification of redundant or unnecessary processing; as a result, rules are generated which obviate the necessity for such processing thereafter.

When rules are constructed the system attempts to generalize their application to as wide a range of its activities as possible.

The importance of this additional capability for a theory of transition from state to state in the development of the IPS is abundantly clear. We will return to a full consideration of its developmental implications in the discussion of transition in the final chapter.

6

Transitivity of Quantity

Since the term *transitivity* has been borrowed by psychologists from logic, it appears appropriate to begin our discussion of it by providing a brief, logical definition. Given three objects, A, B, and C, and a specific relation, r, which can hold between any pair of objects, the relation is transitive if the following is true:

$$(A \text{ r } B) \wedge (B \text{ r } C) \supset (A \text{ r } C).$$

That is, if the relation r holds between A and B, and between B and C, then it must hold between A and C also. Most of the developmental psychological studies of transitivity have dealt with the quantitative relations of equality (=), greater than ($>$), and less than ($<$). The discussion which follows will be entirely confined to logically necessary relationships. Relationships that are empirically transitive, but that are not logically necessarily transitive, will not be considered. This excludes, for example, preference relations, where A likes B, B likes C, so that A also likes C.

A type of performance indicative of complete command of transitivity of quantity is exemplified in a study conducted by Smedslund (1968). The adult subjects were shown cards with statements such as $ZR > PF$, $AN < PF$, informed that each pair of letters designated a quantity, and asked to find out which of the three quantities is the largest. Adults can easily perform these tasks.

In this chapter, we will attempt to explicate the development of the information-processing abilities underlying successful performance on transitivity tasks. The psychological studies relevant to this question can be divided into those primarily concerned with adult subjects, and those in which a developmental approach has been adopted. We will consider the import of the adult work first, and provide a model of transitive processing. Then we will turn to the developmental data and sketch a theory of the development of transitive processing.

TRANSITIVE PROCESSING IN ADULTS

All normal adults are capable of transitive processing. Experimental results indicate that they can cope successfully with a wide variety of transitivity tasks involving from three to seven elements (Wood, 1969). For adults, pass–fail data are comparatively uninformative and the main focus of the experimental studies is on latencies. Typically, subjects are instructed to provide answers to the transitivity problems as quickly as possible consistent with accuracy of their responses. Variations in latency with variations in the number and interrelationships of the elements in the problems are the crucial data. These are interpreted as being indicative of the nature of the processing underlying successful performance on transitivity tasks. The comparison of latencies is conducted at a global level and none of the studies has to date attempted to employ a more discriminating chronometric analysis of the type introduced in Chapter 3.

We will draw heavily on a recent review of Johnson-Laird (1972), which indicates that three aspects of the processing involved have been highlighted as possible sources of the variations in latency detected in the experimental studies: linguistic encoding, operations, and spatial representation. No attempt has been made by the researchers focusing on one or another of these aspects to demonstrate how it fits in with the structure and organization of the information-processing system as a whole. With a view to remedying this omission, we will discuss the three aspects of the processing in terms of the IPS which has emerged to meet the requirements of our work to date. The aspects will be considered in the order in which they are presumed to occur when a subject is confronted with a transitivity problem.

Linguistic Encoding

In the general experimental format adopted in the adult studies, processing commences with the subject reading or listening to the premises constituting the given in the situation, and the question which poses the transitivity problem. A typical problem is: "If John is better than Dick and Pete is worse than Dick, who is best?" The initial processing phase thus involves the encoding of visually or aurally presented verbal input. Clark (1969b) argues that variations in the difficulty of transitivity problems, as indicated in latency variations, are to be attributed to three general characteristics of the process of encoding linguistic material. The first of these is the nature of the base strings, or deep structure, that emerge as a result of encoding the surface structure of the sentences presented. Premises are similar or dissimilar in difficulty to the extent that they give rise to the same base strings. Clark's analysis, shown in Table 6.1, indicates that similarities in surface structure are not necessarily reflected in the base strings. Problems 1 and 2 are similar in surface structure except for the relational term, but they differ in deep structure; the same is true for Problems 3 and 4. Problems 1 and 3 differ in surface structure, but have the same deep structure; similarly for Problems 2 and 4.

The examples in Table 6.1 do not constitute the complete deep structure of the premises. They reflect the general principle of what Clark (1969b) calls the "primacy of functional relations." This asserts that the information most readily available from the encoding of a sentence is its underlying functional relations. In the case of comparative constructions, such as the premises in the transitivity problems, the functional relations comprise the subject–predicate relationship between each of the elements and the evaluative dimension included in the premise. These subject–predicate relationships are expressed in the two base strings to which each premise gives rise. "A better than B," for example, gives rise to two base strings: "A is good" and "B is good." These functional relationships do not represent the comparative information in the premise, and consequently it is presumed that the base structure includes an indication that the two strings are parts of a comparative construction. In accordance with the primacy of functional relations, Clark asserts that the two base strings are more readily available than the information that they belong to a comparison.

The encoded base structure constitutes the essential part of the interpretation of any sentence and therefore plays an important part wherever the interpretation is needed at a later time. This second general characteristic of the encoding process is exemplified in the differential effect on latencies of the nature of the relationship between the premises and the question in transitivity tasks. Clark argues that this is governed by the principle of congruence. Producing an answer takes less time if the base strings representing the premises are congruent with the base string derived from the question. This is illustrated in the longer latency generally obtained if the premises "A better than B" and "B better than C" are followed with the question, "Who is worst?" rather than "Who is best?" In Clark's view, absence of congruence results in an implicit reformulation of the question to produce it, and the reformulation takes time.

The two general characteristics of the linguistic encoding process described thus far are concerned with the form of the syntactic base structure. With the third characteristic highlighted by Clark, we move to the link between the syntactic and semantic aspects of language. He maintains that a feature of the lexicon or dictionary in LTM which defines the senses of words in syntactic base structure is the principle of lexical marking. This maintains that the senses of certain adjectives, like "good" and "long," are stored in the lexicon in LTM in a form that is less complex than the form in which the senses of their opposites,

TABLE 6.1

Base Structure of Premises in Three-Term Series Problems[a]

Form of problem	Base structure
1. *A* better than *B*	*A* is good
	B is good
B better than *C*	*C* is good
2. *A* not as bad as *B*	*A* is bad
	B is bad
B not as bad as *C*	*C* is bad
3. *C* not as good as *B*	*A* is good
	B is good
B not as good as *A*	*C* is good
4. *C* worse than *B*	*A* is bad
	B is bad
B worse than *A*	*C* is bad

[a] Adapted from Clark (1969b, Table 2).

"bad" and "short," are stored. The difference in complexity is attributed to the fact that "unmarked" adjectives like "good" and "long" can have one or two senses while "marked" adjectives like "bad" and "short" always have two senses.

The sense which is always possessed by unmarked or marked adjectives is the "nominal" sense. This indicates the name of the scale on which evaluative information is being provided. Unmarked adjectives can be used in a sense which names the scale but provides no additional information about absolute position on the scale. The question, "How good is X?" can simply be asking for an evaluation and the questioner will be satisfied if he is told that X is good or bad. In contrast, the question, "How bad is X?" conveys additional meaning. The questioner is understood to be aware that X is bad and to be asking about the extent of its badness. The distinction between the two sentences is due to the additional information about absolute position on the scale carried by the marked adjective "bad."

This additional information or second sense is termed the contrastive sense. Since they always carry two senses, it takes longer to store and retrieve the meaning of marked adjectives than unmarked adjectives. Also, it is assumed that, since operating with the contrastive sense lengthens storage and retrieval time, wherever the option is open, unmarked adjectives will be interpreted only in the nominal sense. The "good" underlying the premise "*A* better than *B*," for example, can be interpreted either nominally or nominally and contrastively. On the basis of the lexical marking principle, however, it is presumed that it will usually be interpreted in its simpler and less time-consuming nominal sense.

Clark cites a considerable amount of experimental evidence in support of the importance of the general principle of lexical marking for the performance of transitivity tasks in particular. On the basis of latency data and proportion of errors made in a fixed interval of time, it appears that transitivity problems involving the comparatives of "good," "much," "fast," "far," "tell," "happy," "warm," "deep," "old," and "high" are solved with less difficulty than problems featuring the comparatives of their opposites. This difference is consistent with the lexical marking principle since all of these adjectives are semantically unmarked and can thus give rise to a simple, nominal code in memory while their marked opposites cannot.

Since they would not be germane to our discussion, detailed comments on arguments adduced by Clark in support of his position will not be offered and we will confine ourselves to a few general remarks. Clark claims that the major importance of his analysis is the demonstration that performance on deductive reasoning tasks such as transitivity problems can be satisfactorily accounted for in terms of processes which are not specific to such tasks, but are quite general. These tasks, claims Clark (1969b), "are not meant to explain the solution of two- and three-term series problems alone, but to account for certain linguistic processes in understanding statements and answering questions wherever they occur [p. 403]." Reactions to this claim vary with the criteria applied in determining what constitutes a satisfactory explanation of performance in process terms.

Viewed from the standpoint adopted throughout this book, Clark's explanations founded on general linguistic principles throw little light on the information processing involved in transitive performance.[1] This general comment can be amplified if we consider his treatment of the comparative relations which are fundamental in all of the variants of the transitivity task. Recall that comparative information is carried in two features of the encoded representation. In addition to two strings, the base structure of each premise includes an indication that the strings are part of a comparative construction. This indication tells us nothing about the process basis of comparative relations. Indeed, its inclusion in the base structure is primarily related to decoding rather than encoding. It serves the function of indicating that in moving from the base structure of a premise toward its surface structure, the first transformation which should be applied is a comparative one. Application of this transformation to "*A* is good," "*B* is good," for example, produces the result "*A* is more good than *B* is good."

---

[1] Clark's approach (Clark, Carpenter, & Just, 1973) to the problem of relating language and perception has been criticized by Trabasso (1973) on similar grounds: "We see here where a failure to make explicit the process model underlying the linguistic-perceptual relationship as well as the necessary conditions for prior perceptual coding leads to possible misleading conclusions [p. 445]."

The second feature of the encoded representation that carries comparative information arises from the principle of lexical marking. If the lexicon entry for an adjective includes a contrastive sense, information about absolute position on the evaluative scale is represented. Such information does not determine the order on the scale of two items connected by a contrastive adjective, but indicates where each of them should be located in comparison with an underlying standard. Explanation in terms of the principle of lexical marking simply serves to highlight the importance of illuminating the aspects of the structure and organization of LTM which constitute the semantic basis of comparative relations as a whole. The nominal and contrastive senses of marked–unmarked pairs of adjectives and the ordinal sense of comparative adjectives in general are, presumably, to be attributed to the existence of processes in LTM whose function is operationally equivalent to the construction and maintenance of evaluative scales. The possible nature of some of these processes has already been discussed in the account of the quantification operations and quantitative comparison presented in Chapter 3, and it will be considered further in the present and succeeding chapters.

Neither of the features of the encoded representation carrying comparative information can account for the ordinal aspect of the examples of base structure provided by Clark. The comparative transformation is a decoding device, and lexical marking is concerned with contrastive rather than ordinal information. Nonetheless, as Table 6.1 indicates, Clark lists the base strings in order on the evaluative scale. Not only are the processes which account for the placing of pairs of items in order omitted, but the processing that orders the premises by considering the common item is also absent. Since this is the core of the transitivity principle, it is an important omission.

The importance of the relationship between the premises and the question in transitivity tasks has been highlighted both by Clark (1969b) and by Hunter (1957). The relative contribution of encoding and subsequent processing to variation in task performance has already been discussed in our consideration of class inclusion in Chapter 4, with particular reference to the work of Wohlwill (1968). The conclusion reached there seems to be equally applicable to transitivity performance. Although encoding difficulty is clearly a possible cause of slower, less accurate responses, it appears unlikely that it is a principal cause.

In concluding these general remarks, it should be mentioned that current trends in linguistics and psycholinguistics may undermine the basis of the general linguistic principles employed by Clark. These trends will be considered in greater detail in Chapters 7 and 8, but for the moment, the important point is that the necessity of the existence of the level of syntactic deep structure represented by the base strings is being questioned. Fillmore (1968) and McCawley (1968) have, for example, argued for a linguistic encoding process which proceeds directly from surface syntactic structure to semantic deep structure without the intervention of syntactic deep structure. Recent directions in developmental psycholinguistics are also at variance with Clark's approach. The view of cognitive development consistent with his explanation of transitivity is one in which the syntactic structure of language dominates the development of semantic structure. There is, however, an increasing amount of evidence (Macnamara, 1972) that children use independently attained meaning to discover at least certain syntactic structures that are of basic importance. It appears probable that the area of comparative relations—of which transitivity forms a part—lies within the semantic-led rather than the syntactic-led aspect of cognitive development.

Operations

Hunter (1957), as indicated above, resembles Clark in reporting data which support the importance of the relationship between the premises and the question in three-term series problems. His 65 11-year-old and 32 16-year-old subjects tackled 16 three-term transitivity tasks. Problems of the general form "A is taller than B, C is shorter than B;" "Who is tallest?" or "Who is shortest?" were found to be relatively easy for the 11-year-olds. Hunter attributes this to the form of the premises which suggest the correct answers to the questions. If the question is "Who is the tallest?" the answer suggested is the referent of the first premise, "A." Similarly, the referent of the second premise, "C," is suggested in answer to the question, "Who is shortest?"

Unlike Clark, Hunter does not regard the encoding of verbal input as the main determinant of variation in transitivity performance. In contrast, he accords major importance to the operations performed on the contents of semantic STM after encoding has taken place. The initial processing step involves transforming the premises, if necessary, until they are in linked isotropic order. Since the problems used did not include the "=" comparative relationship, the two possible outcomes of this phase are $(A > B)(B > C)$, or $(A < B)(B < C)$. A series $A > B > C$, or $A < B < C$ is then derived from the transformed premises by deleting the repetition of the middle term. This step involves a sequence of two inferences. The first of these involves the transitivity principle $(A > B)(B > C) \supset (A > C)$ and the second builds on this to yield the required series $(A > B)(B > C)(A > C) \supset (A > B > C)$. Answers to the scored questions can then be read from the series.

Variations in the accuracy and latency of responses are attributed to the different combinations of transformations required for successful processing of the premises. The two basic operations are *conversion* of a premise: $(X > Y)$ becomes $(Y < X)$; the *reordering* of premises: $(B \, r \, C)(A \, r \, B)$ becomes $(A \, r \, B)(B \, r \, C)$. Hunter assumes that the first premise establishes the direction of the series and predisposes the subject to convert the second premise if this is necessary to make it isotropic with the first. The second premise in $(A > B)(C < B)$ would be converted to yield $(A > B)$ $(B > C)$. Given the premises $(B < A)$ $(C < B)$, the second premise is reordered to yield $(C < B)$ $(B < A)$. With $(B < A)$ $(B > C)$ isotropy is achieved by one of two alternative procedures. The second premise is converted to $(C < B)$ and then reordered to yield $(C < B)$ $(B < A)$. Alternatively, the first premise is converted and $(A > B)$ $(B > C)$ is obtained. This transformation, in Hunter's (1957) view, also involves two operations. The first involves backtracking or returning attention to the first premise after a decision not to process the second premise, and the second is the conversion of the first premise. Hunter's prediction that the relative latencies obtained with individual problems would be consistent with the number of transformations required was supported by the results of the 16-year-olds and, with one exception, those of the 11-year-olds. The latter group found $(A > B)$ $(C < B)$ easier than $(A > B)$ $(B > C)$. This finding is, however, consistent with a prediction based on the type of interaction between the premises and the form of the question that was described above.

Spatial Representation

Hunter's account of transitivity performance does not indicate where the series resulting from the processing of the premises is stored or in what form it is encoded. The third approach to the explanation of the latency and accuracy variations in the transitivity data is based on a specific assumption about the representation of the series. De Soto, London, and Handel (1965) maintain that in solving transitivity problems, the subject constructs a spatial representation of the series underlying the two premises. This takes the form of a spatial image. The nature of the processing underlying the subjective experience of visual imagery is currently a source of controversy (Baylor, 1972; Chase, 1973; Pylyshyn, 1973). We will not become involved with this thorny question, however, since for our present purpose it is sufficient to point out that our interpretation of De Soto's approach involves the construction of a representation of the series in VSTM after the problem has been encoded in SSTM. He differs from Hunter in asserting that operations (on VSTM) required in constructing the spatial image account for variations in latency and accuracy rather than transformations carried out on the contents of SSTM.

De Soto and his colleagues argue that two principles explain variations in the difficulty of transitivity problems. Evaluative comparatives, even if they convey no explicitly spatial meaning, are represented in the form of *spatial images*. Some, like "better" and "worse," are consistently represented in the form of a vertical array. Others, like "wider" and "narrower," consistently gave rise to a horizontal array. In constructing vertical arrays, it is assumed to be easier to work from the top downward than from the bottom up, and in horizontal arrays from left to right rather than right to left. Thus, subjects have less difficulty in solving problems in which the premises follow a "top to bottom" or "left to right" direction. For example, (*A* is better than *B*) (*B* is better than *C*) is an easier form for array construction than (*C* is worse than *B*) (*B* is worse than *A*).

End anchoring is the second principle. De Soto *et al.* (1965) state it as follows: "It is helpful to the subject if the first element given in the premise is an end element in the ordering—so that the premise proceeds from one end toward the middle rather than from the middle toward an end [p. 516]." Thus, a premise is easier to represent in an array if its first item is an end anchor, an item that occurs at one end of the final array rather than as the middle item. This principle predicts that problems of the form (*A* is better than *B*) (*C* is worse than *B*) will be easier than those with premises like (*B* is worse than *A*) (*B* is better than *C*) or even (*A* is better than *B*) (*B* is better than *C*). It will be noted that the last prediction is at variance with Hunter's theory. Data derived from a series of experiments are interpreted by De Soto and his co-workers as supporting the validity of these two principles.

The centrality of constructing a spatial array in solving transitivity problems has been supported by Huttenlocher (1968) who suggests that it comprises images of words or abbreviations of words. However, she does dissent from De Soto on the end anchoring principle and argues that it is unnecessary. In her view, the experimental results consistent with the end anchoring principle can be more parsimoniously explained in terms of a feature of the relationship between verbal encoding and spatial array construction. She maintains that the construction of spatial arrays by adult subjects (in visual STM) is carried on in a manner similar to the construction of arrays by children in the external environment. Experiments conducted with 5-, 7-, and 9-year-olds (Huttenlocher, Eisenberg, & Strauss, 1968; Huttenlocher & Strauss, 1968) indicate that children find block manipulation tasks easier if the block to be moved is the subject rather than the object in the deep structure of the instructional sentence. Similarly, it is easier for an adult to construct a spatial array if a premise refers to an end item as the deep structure subject rather than the object. Predictions of relative problem difficulty based on this argument are identical to those derived from the end anchoring principle.

Further data consistent with spatial array construction are provided by Wood (1969) and Trabasso (Riley & Trabasso, 1973, 1974; Trabasso, 1975; Trabasso & Riley, 1973, 1975; Trabasso, Riley & Wilson, 1975). These studies pinpoint an important distinction between the processes involved in the *construction* of a spatial array and those which make *use* of the array to generate responses to transitivity questions. In one of the studies in the Trabasso series, Trabasso and Riley (1973) distinguish between two representations in memory which could be employed in a transitivity of length task. The "coordinate model" involves the subject storing in memory the outcomes of comparing the lengths of a number of pairs of sticks. The results are stored in the form of a list of ordered pairs such as: $(A > B) (B > C) (C > D) (D > E)$. When subsequently asked for example,

"Which is longer, *A* or *C*?", the critical pairs are retrieved and coordinated via the middle terms to yield the required response. The coordination process involves the application of the transitivity principles.

The alternative representation is the "spatial integration" model. The subject is assumed to integrate the information on relative length into a spatial array as he acquires it. The end pairs are found and used as anchors, and further elements are added to the array as they occur until all of the elements are ordered. When questioned, the subject identifies the critical elements in the array, notes their order, and makes the appropriate response.

The relative merits of the two representations were investigated in an experiment involving 36 adult subjects (Trabasso & Riley, 1973). In one case, subjects were trained to choose the longer of pairs of sticks selected from a series of six sticks in increasing length. The pairs selected were always adjacent in the length series. The sticks were color coded and the subjects were only allowed to use the colors to predict the length relation. No direct length comparisons were permitted, but feedback was provided on the accuracy of predictions. After training to criterion on each adjacent pair in a random order, the subjects were tested on all possible pairs without feedback. It was predicted that if the coordinate model underlay the subjects' responses, questions involving pairs of sticks which were further apart in the length series would result in longer latencies, since they would involve more inferential steps. On the basis of the spatial integration model, on the other hand, it was predicted that the further apart pairs of sticks were in the length series, the shorter would be the latency, since the subjects could access the spatial array and read the required response directly from this simple memory representation.

The latency results were found to be in accord with the spatial integration hypothesis and Trabasso and Riley conclude that their data afford no support for the coordination model. They assert that adults do not perform such inferential operations in transitivity tests but "use their knowledge that length is transitive, isolate the extreme ends of the scale, order each pair, and add single elements to a spatial array which is stored in memory for later use in answering 'transitivity' questions [Trabasso & Riley, 1973, p. 6]."

The situation does not appear quite so clear-cut when Trabasso and Riley's findings are considered in conjunction with the results obtained by Wood (1969). His adult subjects were presented with transitivity problems on slides, each of which contained both the premises and test question. The problems were of the following general type:

> *D* is taller than *E*
> *C* is taller than *D*
> *A* is taller than *C*
> *A* is taller than *B*
> *B* is taller than *C*
> Who is taller, *B* or *E*?

Latencies from the presentation of the slide to the subject's response were recorded. These data are diametrically opposed to Trabasso and Riley's results since they indicate a significant increase in latency the further apart the two names being compared are in the height series and the more inferential steps which are required to connect them.

It may be possible to reconcile these conflicting results by making the distinction, mentioned above, between the processes involved in the construction of a spatial array and those which operate on it to produce responses to questions. The latencies recorded by Trabasso and Riley reflect only the duration of the response-producing processes since the construction of the spatial array presumably took place while the subjects were being trained to criterion. Consequently, there is no basis for their assertion that the latency data demonstrate that the spatial array was constructed in accordance with the spatial integration rather than the coordination model. All that the results indicate is that the already existing array is searched in parallel from both the upper and lower ends to locate the two items required for the production of the reply to the transitivity question. There is nothing in Trabasso's data contradicting the indications in Wood's results that construction of the spatial array proceeds by means of a sequence of inferential steps involving application of the transitivity principles and in accord with the general process outlined by Hunter (1957).

A more compelling attack on the relevance of the transitivity principles to problem performance and on Hunter's account of the processes involved has been mounted by Huttenlocher (1968). She claims that the spatial arrays which subjects use are more concise than any transitive arrangements of the premises in linked, isotropic order $(A > B)$ $(B > C)$. The arrays do not include repeated items or relational terms. This aspect of her position is not widely at variance with Hunter's view, since he does not assert that transforming the premises to linked, isotropic order marks the end of the preparatory phase. It will be recalled that processing continues with the construction of a series by deleting the repetition of the middle term in the transformed premises. This series differs from Huttenlocher's array in two respects. The relational terms are retained and there is no assertion that the series is stored in the form of a spatial array in visual STM.

Huttenlocher differs fundamentally from Hunter on the methods employed in constructing the array. She argues that subjects do not produce arrays by initially transforming premises to linked, isotropic order and then deleting the repeated items and relational terms. This preliminary phase is unnecessary. Subjects construct arrays directly by arranging imaginary objects on a spatial axis just as if they were placing real objects in the external environment in order. Huttenlocher (1968) outlines the processes involved as follows:

> First S arranges the items described in the first premise, starting at the top or left of his imaginary space. If the relational term describes a dimension to which he assigns a particular orientation, this determines which item he places first. . . . After constructing

an array from the first premise, S uses the second premise to add the third item to his construction [p. 558].

Huttenlocher (1968) concludes that Hunter's analysis does not correspond to her subjects' descriptions of their strategies, since "almost universally, S's claim to create 'in their heads' a spatial array of items [p. 551] ." The force of this argument is reduced by the reservations which must accompany reliance on subjective reports and by comparison with other experimental results. Clark (1969b), for example, reports that only 49% of his subjects claimed that they made use of spatial imagery.

Furthermore, there appears to be a fundamental weakness in Huttenlocher's account of the transitivity problem-solving process. Is it plausible to assume that subjects construct arrays directly by arranging imaginary objects on a spatial axis *without* reference to the transitivity principles? It is clearly possible to order objects in the external environment without employing transitive inference, and Huttenlocher maintains that an analogous procedure can be adopted internally. However, this assertion is questionable.

Let us consider the first occasion on which a subject is asked to order three or more items purely on the basis of verbal information on the relationship between adjacent pairs and with no opportunity for direct comparison of nonadjacent pairs. As indicated above, Huttenlocher asserts that the subject begins by arranging the items in the first premise in his imaginary space. This is consistent with the directional influence accorded to the first premise by Hunter. She then asserts that "S uses the second premise to add the third item to his construction." Since Huttenlocher suggests that the items inserted in the array are words or abbreviations of words, "using the second premise" presumably does not involve the direct comparison of images of physical objects to enable the insertion of the third item in its appropriate position. Failing such direct comparison, it appears that the only way in which a naive subject can cope with the insertion of the third item is by applying the appropriate transitivity principle via a sequence of transformations such as those described by Hunter. The transitivity principles are available since they have been derived from the subject's experience of the outcomes of sequences of comparisons of objects in the external environment.

Huttenlocher's rejoinder to these comments on the mode of insertion of the third item lies in the second feature of her experimental data. She found that her subjects made more errors and yielded longer latencies when coping with problems of the type (A is taller than B) (B is taller than C) than with those in which the premises were in the form (A is taller than B) (C is shorter than B). These results are inconsistent with the employment of the transitivity principles since, if the transformational sequence suggested by Hunter was employed, the relative difficulty of these two types of problems would be exactly the opposite. They are, however, consistent with Huttenlocher's theory that construction of a spatial array is facilitated if a premise refers to an end item as the deep structure subject rather than the object. It will be recalled, however, that the data obtained by Hunter from his 16-year-old subjects supported his own theory and conflicted with Huttenlocher's view by indicating that $(A > B) (B > C)$ is the easier type of problem.

A Possible Reconciliation

In discussing the validity of Huttenlocher's argument, Wood (1969) comments on the differences in the experimental procedures adopted by her and by Hunter, and in the age of their subjects, which may well have affected the relative difficulty of types of problems. This comment may be appropriately expanded to cover the adult transitivity literature as a whole, since heterogeneity of procedures and subjects makes it extremely difficult to evaluate theories on a broader data base than that provided by the experimental results of their authors. A possible means of reconciling the opposed results of Huttenlocher and Hunter may, however, be offered by a feature detected by Johnson-Laird (1972) in his overview of the results of experimental studies to date. This is the relationship between the relative difficulty of the problems and the amount of experience subjects have had of tackling transitivity tasks. Huttenlocher (1968) and Clark's (1969a, b) subjects were relatively experienced and found $(A > B)$ $(C < B)$ problems easier than $(A > B) (B > C)$. Hunter (1957) and Handel, De Soto, and London (1968) gave their subjects fewer problems and found that $(A > B) (B > C)$ problems were easier than $(A > B) (C < B)$. As Johnson-Laird points out, judging by the number of errors that were made, De Soto *et al.* (1965) used relatively inexperienced subjects. Although their results indicated that $(A > B) (C < B)$ problems are easier than $(A > B) (B > C)$, the average difference in errors between the two types of problem is only 15% in comparison with Huttenlocher's comparable figure of 7%.

These results, viewed as a whole, suggest that naive adult subjects, when confronted with transitivity problems, initially employ an approach consistent with Hunter's proposals. With increasing experience they are able to devise strategies which are less generally applicable than the transitivity principles but take advantage of specific features of the form of the task to reduce the amount of processing required to produce an answer. Suggestions as to the nature of these more economic strategies already exist in the literature. Johnson-Laird (1972) describes a possible approach as follows:

> Likewise, the most natural modification in solving three-term series problems is to read the question *before* reading the premises. Of course, subjects may glance fleetingly at the premises to obtain a global impression of them, but it is suggested that their detailed interpretation will be guided by the nature of the question. The procedure resembles working backwards from the conclusion of an inference to its premises, and its great advantage is that it often renders it unnecessary to examine more than one premise in any detail. Where only one premise is congruent with the question, then this premise will be processed first; and once it has been interpreted and the item which is *more-X* stored (where X is the relevant attribute), there is a simple time-saving procedure. If the item does not occur in the other premise, it is the solution to the problem. Where both

premises have the same comparative, there is likely to be a natural tendency to interpret them in a standard order. The same technique of establishing the item which is *more-X*, where *X* is congruent with the question, can be used; and it is only necessary to interpret the other premise if this item is also mentioned in it [p. 81].

The strategy described by Johnson-Laird offers a method of deriving answers to certain three-term series problems without applying transitivity principles or constructing a spatial array. Wood (1969) provides the only direct experimental data on changes in subjects' strategies with increasing experience on transitivity problems. Unfortunately, for our purpose, the problems which he used all involved more than three terms and preserved the congruity of comparative relationships throughout the premises of any one problem. Wood's results are consistent with the occurrence of two sequential shifts in strategy aimed at achieving greater processing economy. Initially, his subjects appeared to construct a spatial array, including all of the items mentioned in the premises. After only two problems, on average, they abandoned this approach in favor of a focusing strategy. As Johnson-Laird suggests, this achieves economy by use of the information in the question. Only premises which may lie on the chain connecting the two items included in the question are processed and added to the array.

After some 50 problems, a few subjects provided evidence of an even more economic approach which avoids the necessity of constructing a spatial array. The first step involves checking to see if both items in the question, for example, "Who is taller, *A* or *B*?" occur on the left-hand side of the premises. If either does not occur, the other is announced as the answer. If both occur, then the chain leading from *A* is followed up. If this leads to *B*, then *A* is the taller; if it does not, then *B* is taller.

This scanning strategy can be easily applied to three-term series problems if the two premises have congruent comparative relations such as $(A > B) (B > C)$ since the two items in the question will never both occur on the left-hand side of premises. It cannot, however, explain the results from Huttenlocher and Clark's experienced subjects' indicating that $(A > B) (C < B)$ can be coped with more easily than $(A > B) (B > C)$. A specific strategy which is consistent with these findings takes the following form. Place the items mentioned in the first premise in order in the array. If the first item in the second premise has not appeared in the first premise, add it to the bottom of the array. If it has, process the entire second premise. This approach would lead to the prediction of greater difficulty and longer latencies for problems in which the first item in the second premise is the middle term.

Productions for Naive Transitive Processing

What is the importance of the adult studies that have been discussed for the development of transitivity in children? In light of the adult data, what processes constitute the basis of concrete operational performance in children on transitivity of quantity tasks? The performance of naive adult subjects seems to be the most relevant aspect of the experimental results. As indicated above, this is consistent with the employment of the transitivity principles and the type of transformations described by Hunter. Accordingly, in our information-processing analysis of transitivity of quantity, we have assumed that concrete operational performance in children involves the transforming of premises in semantic STM until they are in linked, isotropic order and the subsequent construction of a series by deleting the repetition of the middle term or terms. In some cases this series is stored in semantic STM while answers to questions are being derived; in others it is stored in visual STM and the subjects have the introspective experience of "operating on a spatial array in their heads."

On the basis of the definition which we have adopted, three groups of productions are required to enable children to perform at the concrete opera-tional level on transitivity of quantity tasks. The first group comprises three production rules which correspond to the transitivity principles outlined at the beginning of the chapter. The transitivity rules are presented in terms of the same symbols as the conservation rules described in Chapter 5:

$$(x \overset{Q}{>} y)(y \overset{Q}{>} z) \dashrightarrow (x \overset{Q}{>} z) \tag{6.1}$$

$$(x \overset{Q}{<} y)(y \overset{Q}{<} z) \dashrightarrow (x \overset{Q}{<} z) \tag{6.2}$$

$$(x \overset{Q}{=} y)(y \overset{Q}{=} z) \dashrightarrow (x \overset{Q}{=} z). \tag{6.3}$$

These rules enable generation of the appropriate quantitative comparison out-come without direct comparison of the first and third items, provided that the outcomes of the two initial quantitative comparisons are available in a form which matches the condition side of the production rules.

A second group of rules enables transformations to be performed on the initial quantitative comparison outcomes. These may result in the detection of a correspondence with the conditions of a transitivity rule not apparent prior to the transformations:

$$(x \overset{Q}{>} y) \dashrightarrow (y \overset{Q}{<} x) \tag{6.4}$$

$$(x \overset{Q}{<} y) \dashrightarrow (y \overset{Q}{>} x) \tag{6.5}$$

$$(x \overset{Q}{=} y) \dashrightarrow (y \overset{Q}{=} x). \tag{6.6}$$

Correspondence is obtained if the effect of the transformations (or "con-versions" in Hunter's terms) is to render the initial quantitative comparison outcomes in isotropic order.

If one of the transitivity rules operates, a state is produced in which the results of quantitative comparisons of all three items are simultaneously present in semantic STM. This constitutes the information required for construction of a series. A series is entered in semantic STM by a member of the third group of productions. The group comprises three productions:

$$(x \overset{Q}{>} y)(y \overset{Q}{>} z)(x \overset{Q}{>} z) --> (x \overset{Q}{>} y \overset{Q}{>} z) \qquad (6.7)$$

$$(x \overset{Q}{<} y)(y \overset{Q}{<} z)(x \overset{Q}{<} z) --> (x \overset{Q}{<} y \overset{Q}{<} z) \qquad (6.8)$$

$$(x \overset{Q}{=} y)(y \overset{Q}{=} z)(x \overset{Q}{=} z) --> (x \overset{Q}{=} y \overset{Q}{=} z). \qquad (6.9)$$

It will be noted that all of the production rules are expressed in terms of quantitative relational attributes rather than quantitative symbols. For full-fledged concrete operational performance, it is assumed that development has reached the point at which the results of quantitative comparisons carried out by all three quantification operators are represented in the form of quantitative relational attributes. The area of application of the three groups of production rules thus extends to the operations of Q_s, Q_c, and Q_e.

There is no implication that a child performing at the concrete operational level has available strategies involving optimally efficient sequences of application of the transformation production rules. On the contrary, it is assumed that such strategies only appear as a result of experience with transitivity problems. Hunter's (1957) evidence of the adoption of more systematic approaches and diminution in latencies as his 16-year-old subjects progressed through the sequence of transitivity problems can be attributed to the appearance of such strategies. Optimization of strategies based on generally applicable production rules precedes the derivation and adoption of the type of situation-specific (but relatively economic) methods of solving transitivity problems which were discussed in the previous section.

PS.QC6: A Model for Quantitative Comparison, Including Conservation and Transitivity Rules

PS.QC6 is a PSG model that adds transitivity rules to the model described in the previous chapter (PS.QC5). It includes rules and data structures sufficient to respond to any of the following tasks: direct quantification, subclass comparison, class inclusion, equivalence and identity conservation, and transitivity. As in previous chapters, the description of this model will treat first the model itself (Fig. 6.1), including both modifications of the immediately prior model and new productions central to the issues in this chapter, and then a trace of the model's behavior (Fig. 6.2). Only the new parts of PS.QC6 are shown; the other rules are identical to those in PS.QC5.

Main productions (11600–13600). These represent the final form of the old PS.QC1 (Fig. 2.1). P1A, P1B, and P2 are identical to those in PS.QC5. P2 provides the link with conservation rules, described in Chapter 5, and P3 uses a similar logic in attempting to utilize transitivity rules. Rules P4 through P10 are

```
03000    QUANTIFIER:(CLASS SUBIT COUNT ESTIMATE)
03100
03600    APPQUANT:(OPR CALL) simulate quant opr selection
03700             results in (GOAL * QQQQ(X)) where QQQQ
03800             is SUBIT, COUNT or EST
03900
04200    REL.WORD:(CLASS MORE LESS LONGER SHORTER BIGGER SMALLER EQUAL SAME)
07900
08000                  transitivity rules
08100    PTRAN:((* GOAL TRAN)(X QREL Y QREL Z) --> SAT (X ===> OLD X) SEREAD)
08200    PTR789:((* GOAL TRAN)(X QREL Z)(X QREL Y)(Y QREL Z) --> MARKREL (X QREL Y QREL Z))
08300    PTR1:((* GOAL TRAN) (X QGT Y)(Y QGT Z) --> (X QGT Z))
08400    PTR2:((* GOAL TRAN) (X QLT Y)(Y QLT Z) --> (X QLT Z))
08500    PTR3:((* GOAL TRAN) (X QEQ Y)(Y QEQ Z) --> (X QEQ Z))
08600    PTR.RE:((* GOAL TRAN)(X QREL Y)(Z QREL X) --> (NTC (Z QREL X)))
08700    PTR4:((* GOAL TRAN)(X QGT Y) --> (X ===> OLD X)(Y Q< X))
08800    PTR5:((* GOAL TRAN)(X QLT Y) --> (X ===> OLD X)(Y Q> X))
08900    PTR6:((* GOAL TRAN)(X QEQ Y) --> (X ===> OLD X)(Y Q= X))
09000    PTRAN.FAIL:((* GOAL TRAN) --> (* ==> -))
09100
09200    MARKREL:(ACTION (NTC (X Y)(OLD **)(NTC (Y Z)(OLD **)
09300         (NTC (X Z))(OLD **))
09400    SEREAD:(OPR CALL) read series for desired relation
11400
11600                  main productions
11700    P1A:((* GOAL GET.REL X Y)(X QREL Y) --> SAT (NTC (X QREL)(OLD **) SAY.IT)
11900    P1B:((* GOAL GET.REL Y X)(X QREL Y) --> SAT (NTC (X QREL)(OLD **) SAY.IT)
12100    P2:((* GOAL GET.REL)(TS)(- GOAL CON) ABS --> (* GOAL CON))
12200    P3:((* GOAL GET.REL)(- GOAL TRAN) ABS --> (* GOAL TRAN))
12300    P4:((* GOAL GET.REL X Y) --> (* GOAL COMPARE X Y))
12600    P6A:((* GOAL COMPARE X Y) (X QREL Y) --> SAT)
12700    P6B:((* GOAL COMPARE Y X) (X QREL Y) --> SAT)
12800    P7:((* GOAL COMPARE X Y) (QS (X)) (QS (Y))   --> RELATE)
13100    P9A:((* GOAL COMPARE X Y)(VALUE X) -->(VALUE ===> OLD VALUE) (* GOAL QUANTIFY (X)))
13300    P9B:((* GOAL COMPARE X Y)(VALUE Y) --> (VALUE ===> OLD VALUE)(* GOAL QUANTIFY (Y)))
13500    P10:((* GOAL QUANTIFY (X)) (GOAL + QUANTIFIER (X)) --> SAT)
13600    P11:((* GOAL QUANTIFY (X)) --> APPQUANT )
14500
14700    PS.TRAN:(PTRAN PTR789 PTR1 PTR2 PTR3 PTR.RE PTR4 PTR5 PTR6 PTRAN.FAIL)
14800    PSM2:(P1A P1B P2 P3 P4 P6A P6B P7 P9A P9B P10 P11)
14900    PSEXEC:(PA PZ PSVERB PSVS PS.TRAN PS.CON PSM2 PQ)
```

FIG. 6.1 PS.QC6, a model for quantitative comparison, including conservation and transitivity rules.

similar to earlier models of quantitative comparison. P9 is now more specific about which value it finds as an acceptable target for quantification, and P10 now can be fired by any satisfied quantification goal (also see line 3000). P11 has been generalized. Previously it always generated a specific quantification goal (e.g., SUBIT, or COUNT): thus all previous models could only call upon a given quantifier. Now P11 activates an operator called APPQUANT (for "Apply Quantifier"), which is an operator call simulating the decision about which of the three quantification operators to apply. At this point (GOAL * SUBIT) or (GOAL * COUNT) or (GOAL * ADD) could be inserted into SSTM.

Transitivity rules (8000–9400). The transitivity rules [(6.1) to (6.9) in this chapter], the process of reading quantitative comparison results from a series, and the process of reordering pairs of quantitative comparison outcomes to permit application of the transitivity rules are included in this section of PS.QC6. The transitivity rules, numbered (6.1) to (6.3) above, are represented in PS.QC6 by PTR1, PTR2, and PTR3. They operate when the TRAN goal is active and two quantitative comparison outcomes in isotropic order are also present in SSTM. The manner in which values are assigned to variables in matching the conditions with the current contents of SSTM prevents the activation of PTR1,

PTR2, or PTR3 when quantitative comparison outcomes are scanned in the order

$$(Y \quad QREL \quad Z) (X \quad QREL \quad Y).$$

This problem is overcome by the *reordering* production PTR.RE (8600), which simply inserts the second quantitative comparison outcome at the front of SSTM, thus ensuring that PTR1, PTR2, or PTR3 will be activated on the next pass.

Their activation may also result from the operation of one of the Conversion Rules (6.4) to (6.6). In PS.QC6 these are represented by PTR4, PTR5, and PTR6 (8700–8900). Consider PTR4, for example. When the transitivity goal is active and a quantitative comparison outcome of the general form (X QGT Y) is detected, the outcome is marked "OLD" and the transformed version (Y QLT X) is inserted at the front of SSTM.

The operation of PTR1, 2, or 3 produces a state in which three quantitative comparison outcomes covering paired comparisons of the same three items are present in SSTM. This state provides the conditions required for the operation of the series Construction Rules (6.7) to (6.9). These are represented in PS.QC6 by a single production PTR789 (8200), in which REL is a variable that can take on any relation (see 4200). The order of the three quantitative comparison outcomes on the condition side of PTR789 reflects the situation in SSTM that results from the action side of PTR1, PTR2, or PTR3, which place the third outcome at the front of STM. If these three conditions are satisfied in the presence of an active TRAN goal, the three outcomes are marked "OLD" and the appropriate series is inserted in SSTM. The process of reading the results of quantitative comparisons from series in SSTM is represented by PTRAN (8100).

When TRAN is active, and a series is present in SSTM, PTRAN marks the series "OLD" and initiates the operator SEREAD. This is an operator call which simulates the process of scanning the series for the requisite quantitative comparison outcome. If the necessary information is present it is inserted in SSTM in the general form (X QREL Y).

A trace of PS.QC6 on a three-term problem. In Fig. 6.2, at 0., we see the state of SSTM after the three-term problem "Blue is more than Green, Red is more than Blue; which is more, Red or Green" has been input to PS.QC6. First, PDV1 fires, as in previous models, and establishes the GET.REL goal and appropriate target values. Next P3 inserts the TRAN goal and the system is now essentially locked in the transitivity system (Fig. 6.1, 8000–9000). It can only exit with the TRAN goal satisfied, (PTRAN), or failed (PTRAN.FAIL). At 9., we see the state of SSTM upon entry to the transitivity section. This state leads to failure on PTR789, PTR1, PTR2, PTR3. Then PTR.RE fires, producing, after 10., the right conditions for PTR1 to make "the" transitive inference. PTR789 next produces the series, and PTRAN calls SEREAD to read off the desired relationship. PTRAN also satisfies the TRAN goal, and finally P1A wraps things up.

```
8.  SSTM: ((RED) (GREEN) (MORE) (BLUE MORE.THAN GREEN) (RED MORE.THAN BLUE) NIL NIL NIL NIL NIL NIL·NIL )

    PDV1: ((REL.WORD) (V1) (V2) --> (X ===> HEARD X) (Y ====> HEARD Y) (VALUE (V1)) (VALUE (V2)) (NTC (REL.WORD))
                                  (HEARD **) (* GOAL GET.REL V1 V2))

7.  SSTM: ((* GOAL GET.REL RED GREEN) (HEARD (MORE)) (VALUE (GREEN))
          (VALUE (RED)) (HEARD RED) (HEARD GREEN) (BLUE MORE.THAN GREEN) (RED MORE.THAN BLUE) NIL NIL NIL NIL )

    P3: ((* GOAL GET.REL) (- GOAL TRAN) ABS --> (* GOAL TRAN))
    PA: ((* GOAL) (* GOAL) --> (* ===> %))

9.  SSTM: ((* GOAL TRAN) (% GOAL GET.REL RED GREEN) (HEARD (MORE)) (VALUE (GREEN))
          (VALUE (RED)) (HEARD RED) (HEARD GREEN) (BLUE MORE.THAN GREEN) (RED MORE.THAN BLUE) NIL NIL NIL )

    PTR.RE: ((* GOAL TRAN) (X QREL Y) (Z QREL X) --> (NTC (Z QREL X)))

10. SSTM: ((RED MORE.THAN BLUE) (* GOAL TRAN) (BLUE MORE.THAN GREEN) (% GOAL GET.REL RED GREEN)
          (HEARD (MORE)) (VALUE (GREEN)) (VALUE (RED)) (HEARD RED) (HEARD GREEN) NIL NIL NIL )

    PTR1: ((* GOAL TRAN) (X QGT Y) (Y QGT Z) --> (X QGT Z))

11. SSTM: ((RED MORE.THAN GREEN) (* GOAL TRAN) (RED MORE.THAN BLUE) (BLUE MORE.THAN GREEN)
          (% GOAL GET.REL RED GREEN) (HEARD (MORE)) (VALUE (GREEN)) (VALUE (RED)) (HEARD RED) (HEARD GREEN) NIL NIL )

    PTR789: ((* GOAL TRAN) (X QREL Z) (X QREL Y) (Y QREL Z) ---> MARKREL (X QREL Y QREL Z))

19. SSTM: ((RED MORE.THAN BLUE MORE.THAN GREEN) (OLD (RED MORE.THAN GREEN)) (OLD (BLUE MORE.THAN GREEN))
          (OLD (RED MORE.THAN BLUE)) (* GOAL TRAN) (% GOAL GET.REL RED GREEN) (HEARD (MORE))
          (VALUE (GREEN)) (VALUE (RED)) (HEARD RED) (HEARD GREEN) NIL )

    PTRAN: ((* GOAL TRAN) (X QREL Y QREL Z) --> SAT (X ===> OLD X) SEREAD)

    ATTENDING :::::::: >(RED MORE.THAN GREEN)

23. SSTM: ((RED MORE.THAN GREEN) (+ GOAL TRAN) (OLD RED MORE.THAN BLUE MORE.THAN GREEN)
          (OLD (RED MORE.THAN GREEN)) (OLD (BLUE MORE.THAN GREEN)) (OLD (RED MORE.THAN BLUE)) (% GOAL GET.REL RED GREEN)
          (HEARD (MORE)) (VALUE (GREEN)) (VALUE (RED)) (HEARD RED) (HEARD GREEN) )

    PZ: ((* GOAL) ABS (% GOAL) --> (% ==> *))
    P1A: ((* GOAL GET.REL X Y) (X QREL Y) --> SAT (NTC (X QREL)) (OLD **) SAY.IT)

              **** READ MORE.THAN GREEN ****

32. SSTM: ((OLD (RED MORE.THAN GREEN)) (+ GOAL GET.REL RED GREEN) (+ GOAL TRAN) (OLD RED MORE.THAN BLUE MORE.THAN GREEN)
          (OLD (RED_MORE.THAN GREEN)) (OLD (BLUE MORE.THAN GREEN)) (OLD (RED MORE.THAN BLUE)) (HEARD (MORE))
          (VALUE (GREEN)) (VALUE (RED)) (HEARD RED) (HEARD GREEN) )
```

FIG. 6.2   A trace of PS.QC6 on a three-term series problem.

THE DEVELOPMENT OF TRANSITIVE PROCESSING

How do the production rules underlying concrete operational performance on transitivity of quantity tasks come into existence? How do transitivity rules based upon a particular quantification operator develop until they apply to all three quantification operators? The developmental studies of transitivity carried out to date provide a very limited empirical basis on which to attempt an answer to this question, since they deal almost exclusively with transitivity tasks drawing on Q_e. Transitivity of size or length is a favorite topic of study (Braine, 1959, 1964; Coon & Odom, 1968; Murray & Youniss, 1968; Piaget, Inhelder, & Szeminska, 1960; Smedslund, 1963a, b, 1964, 1965). Transitivity of weight (Smedslund, 1959, 1963c), large discontinuous quantities (Glick & Wapner, 1968; Smedslund, 1964), and distance and color intensity (Glick & Wapner, 1968) have all been studied as well.

At the outset of a typical investigation of length transitivity, two sticks identical in color but differing slightly in length (e.g., 8 inches and 8 $\frac{1}{8}$ inches) are placed before the child. They are positioned parallel to each other, with their ends coinciding, but sufficiently far apart to prevent the child from determining their relative lengths by visual inspection. A third, differently colored stick of intermediate length (e.g., $8\frac{1}{16}$ inches) is now introduced, laid alongside one of the intial pair, and the child is asked to indicate which stick is longer. The third stick is then placed alongside the second member of the initial pair and the question is repeated. After these two preparatory judgments, the child is asked which member of the initial pair he thinks is the longer.

A corresponding sequence of events is involved in the study of transitivity in the other content areas mentioned. Appropriate modifications are made to permit the making of the requisite quantitative judgments. When dealing with weight, for example, this is accomplished by using a beam balance.

What picture of the course of development of transitivity emerges from these studies? The dominant theoretical viewpoint is still that presented in the original discussion of transitivity by Piaget, Inhelder, and Szeminska (1960). They assert that transitivity, like so many other features of intellectual development in the concrete operational period, depends on the appreciation of reversibility. The particular example of reversibility involved is recognition that an object can be simultaneously longer than another object and shorter than a third. Appreciation of this form of reversibility first emerges in the context of seriation. Piaget maintains that understanding that, in a series of objects ordered from shortest to longest, each object is simultaneously longer than its predecessor and shorter than its successor, is a prerequisite for a grasp of transitivity. Once a child is aware of the reversible nature of an object, it is possible for him to infer the quantitative relationship of two objects from a knowledge of the relationship of both of them to a third object. It will be noted that this theoretical position, like the empirical studies which it has stimulated, deals primarily with the area of operation of the estimation quantification operator.

An attempt will now be made to provide a theoretical account of the development of transitivity. As in the discussion of conservation in the last chapter, this will involve a successive consideration of Q_s, Q_c, and Q_e in the course of tracing the development of transitivity to the point where the production rules are applicable to outcomes derived from any of the three quantification operators. It will be evident from the brief review above that a theoretical account ranging across the three quantification operators will inevitably go beyond the bounds of the available empirical evidence at many points. Use will be made of empirical evidence where possible as, for example, in considering the relationship between transitivity and conservation. Even in the total absence of empirical data, empirical criteria will not be lost sight of, since the theoretical account will generate clear empirical predictions.

The same systemic assumptions are made in the account of transitivity as in the discussion of conservation.

Detection of Environmental Regularities

As in the case of conservation, the basic hypothesis is that transitive processing is founded on the initial detection and storing in LTM of specific consistent sequences of events. Is it reasonable to assume that in his interaction with the environment the child experiences the type of sequences of quantitative comparisons that underlie the construction of the transitivity production rules? Unfortunately, there is a dearth of systematically acquired data which would enable a categorical reply to be given to this question. It is uncontestably true that the laboratory form of transitivity tasks is not a feature of children's everyday experience. However, it is not a necessary conclusion from this fact that concrete operational performance appears in the total absence of specific related experience. As indicated in Chapter 5, it seems probable that in the course of play experiences and other daily activities, children have ample opportunity to encounter consistent sequences of events embodying the principle of conservation of quantity. Some of the relevant sequences may, for example, occur during social interaction between children (Wallace, 1972a). While it may appear less likely that the more extended and elaborate sequences required to exemplify the transitivity principle occur fortuitously with any degree of regularity, only data acquired specifically for the purpose could resolve the issue.[2]

An alternative answer to the question can be formulated if an additional assumption is made about the organization of the IPS. In view of the existence

---

[2]Trabasso provides a delightful personal anecdote on a naturally occurring and *re*curring transitive sequence in his youth:

Whenever I recall childhood experiences or memories, a frequent and vivid recollection is that of being measured for height and being compared against other members of my family or myself at an earlier age. This quantitative experience was highly ritualized in my family. There was a strip of molding on a doorway leading into the kitchen upon which a score or more horizontal lines were drawn in pencil with notes such as: 'Mom: 62", June 2, 1942; Bud: 58", June 4, 1945; Tommy: 40", May 25, 1939, etc. . . . .

Year after year, this strip of molding remained in daily view and gave a graphic history of the relative heights of my mother, father, older brother, and sister and myself. . . . In effect, my family's concern with our respective growths provided sufficient information for us to acquire complete knowledge of the scale of length or height. We could, in effect, learn that height was ordered, that Dad was taller than Mom, Mom was (for a time) taller than Bud, Bud was taller than Joan, Joan (for a time) was taller than Tom. It is also true that we could reverse the relations: Tom was smaller than Joan, Joan was smaller than Bud, etc. Further, one could read directly from the spatial scale drawn on the molding other comparative relations of greater distance, namely, Dad was taller than Tom, etc. . . . [Trabasso, 1975]."

of formal operational activities such as hypothesis generation, it appears reasonable that the system should not entirely depend on direct interaction with the
environment to determine the sequence of events which it experiences. It should
also possess the ability to activate productions and production systems without
external intervention. A plausible criterion for selecting productions for activation would be previous membership of consistent sequences or rules, since this
might indicate further potential for consistency detection and achievement of
economic processing. On this basis, the productions and production systems
involved in the quantification operators, quantitative comparison, and the conservation rules would be likely candidates for systemic activation. This would
increase the probability of occurrence of specific consistent sequences which
would initiate the development of transitivity.

Direct environmental experience and system-initiated activity need not be
regarded as opposed explanations. Some children may acquire the necessary
specific consistent sequences via direct experience, while others reach the same
state as a result of systemic activation. It is also conceivable that in some cases
the common consistent sequences from which the transitivity rules are constructed may be derived from a pool of specific consistent sequences representing both sources.

We hypothesize that transitivity rules first get detected through sequences
involving outcomes of Q_s. The grounds for this proposal are the same as those
considered at length in our discussion of conservation and they will not be
reiterated here. Since the transitivity rules are founded on consistent sequences
of quantitative comparison outcomes, the development of quantitative comparison processes (as described in Chapter 3) constitutes an essential aspect of the
development of the transitivity rules. As indicated above, it is assumed that the
production rules underlying concrete operational performance contain quantitative relational attributes, for example, $(x \stackrel{Q}{=} y)$, rather than quantitative comparison outcomes expressed in quantitative symbols derived from one of the quantification operators, for example, $(x_s = y_s)$. It is possible, however, that in some
children's development, the initial construction of transitivity rules via the
functioning of Q_s may antedate the appearance of the productions linking the
results of subitizing quantitative symbol comparisons to quantitative relational
attributes. In these cases the transitivity rules would, at the outset, be expressed
in terms of subitizing quantitative symbols. This possibility will be recognized by
including both subitizing quantitative symbols and quantitative relational attributes in our account.

Linguistic Correlates

Clark's (1969b) account of transitive processing refers to linguistic data which
have interesting implications for the development of quantitative comparisons.
Viewed from a processing orientation, they suggest four developmental states

into which language is successively mapped. The first two of these processing states are both subsumed by the nominal sense of adjectives. Linguistic evidence of their presence is found in the children's protocols on transitivity tasks reported by Donaldson (1963). The first state is exemplified in the child who, when asked in the middle of a problem how he knew that Tom was four, replied, "Because it says that Tom is four years younger than Dick." Such a child has quantification processes capable of generating quantitative symbols onto which "age" has been mapped, but the relationship of quantitative comparison processes to these symbols has not yet been established. In the second "nominal" state the relevance of quantitative comparison processes to quantitative symbols for "age" has been established, but the application procedure has not yet been stabilized. This underlies the performance of children who appear to interpret "Betty is older than May," "May is older than Betty," and "Betty is younger than May" as all meaning "Betty is different in age from May."

When quantitative comparison processes can be reliably applied to quantitative symbols derived from the context area onto which an adjective is mapped, the adjective has acquired an ordinal in addition to a nominal sense. This event is marked by the appearance of correct use of comparatives such as "more," "bigger," "longer," "thicker," "higher," and "taller" (Donaldson & Wales, 1970). Attainment of the ordinal sense indicates that the content area designated by an adjective is ripe for the application of transitivity rules.

The fourth processing state is signaled by the appearance of the contrastive sense and correct use of comparatives like "less," "shorter," "thinner," and "lower." It appears developmentally later than the state underlying the ordinal sense since it involves the coordination of ranges of similar quantitative comparison outcomes onto which comparatives such as "less" and "lower" are mapped. Attainment of the processing state underlying the contrastive sense is not a prerequisite for the derivation and use of transitivity rules. The data cited by Clark (1969b), however, indicate that it does affect the relative difficulty of applying the transitivity rules in particular content areas.

Coordination of Quantitative Relations

In addition to reliable quantitative comparison processes, transitivity rules require processes for the coordination of quantitative comparison outcomes if the conjunction of outcomes represented in conditions such as $(x \overset{Q}{>} y) (y \overset{Q}{>} z)$ is to be successfully detected. Developmental evidence indicates that the main obstacles to effective coordination arise in the processing of the element common to the two quantitative comparisons. Trabasso and Riley (1973) found that 4-year-old children could not learn a list of linked relations such as $A > B, B > C, C > D,$ and $D > E$ when they were only asked the single question, "Which is longer?" about each pair. If asked both "Which is longer?" *and* "Which is shorter?" for each pair they succeeded both in learning the list and in making transitive inferences from it. The effect of the double question was, presumably, to ensure that the children stored two pieces of comparative quantitative information (C is shorter, C is longer) about the common elements, whereas the single question resulted in the storing of only a single piece of information (C is longer).

Another feature necessary for effective coordination is preservation of the qualitative identity of the common element. The effect of failure to do so is illustrated once again in Donaldson's (1963) protocols. Faced with the problem "Dick is shorter than Tom. Dick is taller than John. Which of these boys is tallest?" many children operated as if there were four children. One girl, for example, asserted "This Dick (second premise) is tallest, John is next tallest, Tom is third, and then it's Dick (first premise)." Retention of qualitative identity is represented in the transitivity rules by the use of the same symbol for the common element in the two premises in the conditions.

The extension of the consideration of identity of the common element from the qualitative to the quantitative dimension raises some interesting questions. It is evident that if the quantity of the common element is increased or decreased between the first and second quantitative comparisons, a prediction of the quantitative relationship between the other two elements based on the transitivity rules may be inaccurate. This eventuality could be met by the inclusion in the rules of a condition testing for a violation of quantitative identity. There are, however, many situations in which transitivity rules lacking such an additional condition can be successfully applied. These include all of the experimental situations reported in the literature in which transitive processing in adults or children has been investigated. Not a single study has varied the quantity of the common element between comparisons. Accordingly, it appears preferable to look to the interaction of the transitivity rules with the conservation rules rather than to additional conditions as a means of avoiding inaccurate predictions. If the conservation rules are assumed to be scanned prior to the transitivity rules when quantitative comparison is under way, the effect of any quantitative transformation will be detected by the identity conservation rules. As a result, symbols will be placed in semantic STM which will prevent the inappropriate operation of the transitivity rules.

The adoption of this view of the interaction between transitivity and conservation rules does not render the conservation rules a prerequisite for the development of transitivity. If a child experiences many sequences of quantitative comparison outcomes featuring common elements which remain free from quantitative transformations, the transitivity rules will be constructed regardless of the developmental status of the conservation rules. On the other hand, if experience arising from environmental interaction and/or systemic activation comprises many sequences in which transformations occur between comparisons, transitivity rules will not be derived until conservation rules have been constructed. There is some empirical evidence that suggests that the latter type of experience may be more general than the former. The clear-cut results which have emerged (Smedslund, 1964) strongly support the development of conservation before transitivity. Developmental primacy does not, of course, indicate that the former enables the appearance of the latter. Support for this contention is derived from studies in which attempts have been made to produce transitivity by training. Smedslund (1959), for example, found that training on conservation of weight was more successful in producing transitivity of weight on a delayed posttest than direct training on transitivity. More recently, in a study by Garcez (1969), an experimental treatment involving training on both conservation and transitivity of weight was found to be more effective in producing transitivity than training on transitivity alone. The juxtaposition of the conservation and transitivity tasks may have expedited realization of the relevance of the conservation rules to transitive processing.

Given the availability of reliable processes for quantitative comparison and the coordination of the results of comparisons which operate upon subitizing quantitative symbols (and, depending on experience, subitizing conservation rules), the construction of transitivity rules via the functioning of Q_s can proceed. The sequence of events closely parallels the account of the development of conservation rules presented in Chapter 5.

Let

$a,b,c \equiv$ internal symbols representing *specific* collections of discrete elements numerically within the range of Q_s.

$a_s,b_s,c_s \equiv$ quantitative symbols derived by submitting specific collections, a,b,c, to Q_s.

$RELATE_s \equiv$ an operator which determines the comparative relationship between two quantitative symbols produced by Q_s.

At the outset *specific consistent sequences* (specific CSs) of the following form are detected and stored in LTM[3]:

$$a_s \cdots b_s \cdots RELATE_s(a_s b_s) \rightarrow (a_s > b_s) \cdots c_s \cdots RELATE_s(b_s c_s) \rightarrow (b_s > c_s)$$
$$\cdots RELATE_s(a_s c_s) \rightarrow (a_s > c_s).$$

---

[3] As noted earlier (page 161), the sequences may be expressed in terms of either quantitative relational attributes $(x \stackrel{Q}{=} y)$ or outcomes of RELATE $(x_s = y_s)$. Thus all of the following sequences should, strictly speaking, be expressed in the form:

$$a_s \cdots b_s \cdots RELATE_s (a_s b_s) \rightarrow [(a_s > b_s) \; or \; (a \stackrel{Q}{>} b)] \cdots c_s$$
$$\cdots RELATE (b_s c_s) \rightarrow [(b_s > c_s) \; or \; (b \stackrel{Q}{>} c)] \cdots .$$

Since this is so cumbersome, we have eliminated the complex disjunctive term that includes both kinds of relational elements; such a disjunction should be understood in all the following sequences.

These give rise to the construction of a *common consistent sequence* (common CS):

$$x_s \cdots y_s \cdots \text{RELATE}_s(x_s y_s) \rightarrow (x_s > y_s) \cdots z_s \cdots \text{RELATE}_s(y_s z_s) \rightarrow (y_s > z_s) \cdots$$
$$\text{RELATE}_s(x_s z_s) \rightarrow (x_s > z_s).$$

Operation of the processing-economy principle results in the application of the prediction and verification processes to the common consistent sequence with a view to the possible elimination of the third operation of RELATE$_s$. Successful prediction culminates in the construction of a transitivity rule:

$$(x_s > y_s)(y_s > z_s) \dashrightarrow (x_s > z_s).$$

Similar sequences of events give rise to the other two transitivity rules.

As indicated above, groups of transformation production rules and seriation productions must be available in addition to the transitivity rules before concrete operational performance on transitivity tasks can occur. In the case of Q_s, transformation rules such as

$$(x_s > y_s) \dashrightarrow (y_s < x_s)$$

are derived from common consistent sequences of the type

$$x_s \cdots y_s \cdots \text{RELATE}_s(x_s y_s) \rightarrow (x_s > y_s) \cdots \text{RELATE}_s(y_s x_s) \rightarrow (y_s < x_s),$$

by elimination of the second operation of RELATE. The specific consistent sequences which result in the construction of the common consistent sequence are of the general form

$$a_s \cdots b_s \cdots \text{RELATE}_s(a_s b_s) \rightarrow (a_s > b_s) \cdots \text{RELATE}_s(b_s a_s) \rightarrow (b_s < a_s).$$

Note that these processes for entering a series in SSTM when the appropriate conjunction of quantitative comparison results is present do not involve redundancy elimination. The seriation production

$$(x_s > y_s)(y_s > z_s)(x_s > z_s) \dashrightarrow (x_s > y_s > z_s)$$

is derived from the common CS

$$(x_s > y_s) \cdots (y_s > z_s) \cdots (x_s > z_s) \cdots (x_s > y_s > z_s).$$

This common CS reflects the experience that if three collections, when quantitatively compared in pairs, yield the conjunction of results indicated, they can be arranged in a series. This can be put more concretely in terms of the application of Q_e rather than Q_s. If three sticks (L1, L2, and L3) are submitted to length comparison in pairs and the outcomes conform to the pattern (L1 $\overset{Q}{\gtrless}$ L2) (L2 $\overset{Q}{\gtrless}$ L3) (L1 $\overset{Q}{\gtrless}$ L3), then the sticks can be arranged in a line to form steps in a staircase. The seriation productions constitute generalized statements of their experience.

Mention of seriation of length provides an opportunity to make a general distinction of considerable importance. The present developmental account is concerned with the manner in which children become capable of engaging in transitive processing. This must be distinguished from aspects of children's behavior in which the transitivity principle is implicit but which do not necessarily require transitive processing. A typical seriation task provides an example. A collection of sticks arranged as a series in order of diminishing length constitutes a display conforming to the principle of transitivity. This does not mean that any child capable of producing such a series is able to carry out the sequence of steps which defines transitive processing. On the contrary, young children can achieve this end result by a protracted sequence of paired comparisons on a trial and error basis. Even in the case of older children exhibiting a methodical approach to the task (such as finding the longest, then the longest of those remaining, and so on), transitive processing cannot be assumed unless careful observation of the sequence of paired comparisons indicates that it is being used to avoid redundant processing steps. Detailed examples of the sequence of developmental states up to and including the application of the transitivity rules in length and weight seriation tasks are provided by Baylor and Gascon (1974).

Further examples of implicit transitivity are provided by Q_c and by equivalence conservation. The ordinal number system which provides the basis for the operations of Q_c conforms to the principle of transitivity. The ability to count a collection accurately does not, however, provide a reliable predictor of the attainment of transitive processing. Similarly, the fact that the transitivity principle is implicit in the formal description of equivalence conservation does not imply that in process terms the development of transitivity must precede that of conservation.

When Does Transitive Processing Appear?

There are two additional features of the developmental data which are worthy of comment. The first is concerned with determining the point in development at which transitive processing initially appears. This question has sparked considerable controversy over the years, particularly in relation to the relative merits of verbal and nonverbal approaches to determining the answer. As this literature has been reviewed elsewhere (Wallace, 1972a), we will confine ourselves to considering recent data. Studies conducted by Bryant and Trabasso (1971) and Riley and Trabasso (1973) have produced results suggesting that 4-year-old children are capable of making transitive inferences about the length of sticks. These findings contrast with the conclusion of studies in the Genevan tradition (Piaget, Inhelder, & Szeminska, 1960; Smedslund, 1963) that the average age at which children reveal a grasp of transitivity of length lies near 8 years. The most obvious reason for this disparity lies in a difference between the criteria of transitive inference adopted. Although direct verbal presentation of the scored questions was used in both groups of studies, in the Trabasso experiments responses were scored correct if the children selected the appropriate stick as "longest" or "shortest," while the Genevan criterion required, in addition, an explanation of the reasons for the responses in which references were made to both preliminary quantitative comparisons.

Reasons for the wide variation in results are also suggested if the experimental procedures are viewed in terms of our account of the development of quantification processes. The studies in the Genevan tradition required the children to make the preliminary judgments that $A > B$ and $B > C$ with the appropriate pairs of sticks displayed lying side by side. These quantitative comparisons involved the activation of Q_e, and, consequently, transitive inference would only be revealed when the transitivity rules initially derived via Q_s had been generalized to the operations of Q_e. Trabasso's procedure involved a preliminary training phase in which the children learned the relative sizes of pairs of color-coded sticks which were adjacent in a length series of five sticks. In one variant the subjects were provided with visual feedback on the accuracy of their choices. The choices involved selecting one of a pair of sticks of different colors, each protruding one inch from the top of a box. When the child made his choice, the experimenter drew out the rods and held them perpendicular to the table so that the child could compare lengths directly. Bryant and Trabasso (1971) criticize this visual feedback procedure on the grounds that it is possible that the children solved the *BD* transitive question not by making a genuine transitive inference, but simply by remembering from the training series that *B* was 6 inches and *D* was 4 inches. A modified procedure was devised to avoid this criticism. This involved replacing visual feedback by verbal feedback in the training phase. After making a choice, the child was simply told which of the pair of rods was the longer and which the shorter.

This procedure, unlike the Genevan approach, provides the results of quantitative comparisons *without activation of Q_e or any other quantification operator*. If the system has already derived the transitivity rules via Q_s, they are available for application to the quantitative comparison outcomes which have been directly provided. Indeed, it would be consistent with the processing-economy principle for rules derived from any of the quantification operators to be applied to suitable input arriving in semantic STM without links with any particular quantification operator. On this basis, Trabasso's procedure, unlike the Genevan approach, circumvents the absence of generalization of the transitivity rules to Q_e. Transitive inference occurs if the initial construction of the rules via the functioning of Q_s has taken place. A similar situation has already been described in Chapter 4 where Wohlwill's verbal presentation of CI problems resulted in significant improvement in performance. Since his subjects were directly provided with the necessary quantitative symbols, there was no need for any of the quantification operators to be applied. This improved CI performance because the major obstacle to success—the employment of inappropriate attentional grain during quantification—was avoided.

Task-Specific Shortcuts

The second feature of the developmental data that merits comment is concerned with the appearance of strategies that achieve processing economy by taking advantage of task-specific features of the form of tasks. As indicated above, adult subjects appear to adopt such specialized strategies in preference to applying the transitivity rules as they accumulate experience in tackling transitivity tasks in the laboratory. The results of developmental studies suggest that children are capable of devising such specialized, locally applicable strategies for tackling transitivity tasks before the generally applicable transitivity rules have been constructed and generalized to the three quantification operators.

   In the study already alluded to, Riley and Trabasso (1973) found that their 4-year-old subjects did not apply processes concerned with length relations when a more economic approach was sufficient to meet the requirements of the specific task. The design of the experiment called for them to learn the results of four comparisons, $A > B$, $C < B$, $C > D$, and $E < D$, so that they could select the element named by the relation; for example, select A when asked "Which is longer, A or B?" It was discovered, however, that what the children actually learned was the simple rule that A, C, and E are winners and B and D are losers.

   A second example is provided by Wallace (1972a) in a study specifically aimed at detecting children who were succeeding on transitivity of length tasks by employing nontransitive hypotheses. The procedure involved the recording of latencies and the including in the task sequence indeterminate problems—problems which did not permit the making of valid transitivity judgments. The results indicated that 10 of 19 subjects, aged from 4.10 to 6.4 years, who appeared to perform successfully on the transitivity trials were employing nontransitive hypotheses of the type $A > B \supset A > C$ or $A < B \supset A < C$. As in the Riley and Trabasso study, the basis of these children's performance was a strategy devised to fit the specific requirements of the task, having no wider relevance but maximizing processing economy.

Generalization from Q_s to Q_c and Q_e

How does the generalization of the three groups of productions required for concrete operational transitivity performance from Q_s to Q_c and Q_e take place? No attempt will be made to provide a detailed answer to this question for two main reasons. First, since the vast majority of empirical studies deal with aspects of transitivity which fall within the orbit of Q_e, there is a dearth of experimental evidence relevant to the developmental relationship between the quantification operators. In the absence of experimental evidence only a theoretical account can be offered. Second, our theory of how generalization proceeds in the case of transitivity is, *mutatis mutandis,* identical to the theory of the generalization of the conservation rules described in detail in Chapter 5. To avoid unnecessary repetition, therefore, only a few general remarks will be made at this point.

Consistent with the conclusions reached in our discussion of conservation, we hypothesize that generalization of the three groups of transitivity productions from Q_s to Q_c and Q_e occurs when specific consistent sequences detected in the operations of Q_c and Q_e on situations to which Q_s can also be applied give rise to the construction of common consistent sequences. Since the only difference in the sequence of events between the three groups is that common CSs rather than rules are generalized from Q_s to Q_c and Q_e in the case of the seriation productions, we will illustrate the process exclusively in terms of the group of transitivity production rules.

For generalization of the transivitity production rules to occur, the common CSs required from Q_c and Q_e are of the type

$$x_c \cdots y_c \cdots \mathrm{RELATE}_c(x_c y_c) \to (x_c > y_c) \cdots z_c \cdots \mathrm{RELATE}_c(y_c z_c)$$
$$\to (y_c > z_c) \cdots \mathrm{RELATE}\,(x_c z_c) \to (x_c > z_c).$$

Since the situations covered by the common consistent sequences lie within the compass of Q_s, the system attempts to assimilate the sequences to the transitivity rules. The rule relevant to the common CS example is

$$(x_s > y_s)\,(y_s > z_s) --> (x_s > z_s).$$

It is evident from a comparison of the rule and the common consistent sequence that the critical feature for successful assimilation is the establishment of the equivalence of quantitative comparison outcomes derived via Q_s, Q_c, and Q_e. This aspect of development has been discussed at length in Chapter 3, and we will only point out at this juncture that for the rule and type of common consistent sequence in the example the essential prerequisite is the derivation of the production

$$(x_i > y_i) --> (x \overset{Q}{>} y)$$

where

x_i, y_i = quantitative symbols for collections x and y derived from any one of the three quantification operators,

$x_i > y_i$ = quantitative symbol for x is greater than quantitative symbol for y,

$\overset{Q}{>}$ = quantitative relational attribute symbol indicating that collection x is greater in quantity than collection y.

For the reasons indicated in Chapter 3, establishing the equivalence of quantitative comparison outcomes derived from Q_s and Q_c is a relatively straightforward process. The situation is more complex in the case of Q_e. The establishment of equivalence between quantitative comparison outcomes from Q_s or Q_c and those produced by Q_e is not possible until Q_e is capable of generating consistent quantitative comparison outcomes. This in turn depends on the abandonment of unidimensional quantification by Q_e in favor of two-dimensional quantification. An account of the sequence of events underlying this transition has already been provided in our discussion of conservation.

Given that Q_e has attained the capability to produce consistent quantitative comparison outcomes via two-dimensional quantification, it might be predicted that the common CSs required for generalization of the transitivity rules to Q_e would be constructed more quickly than those necessary for generalization of the conservation rules. It was pointed out above that a child may experience many sequences of quantitative comparison outcomes featuring common elements that remain free from quantitative transformations between comparisons. If so, then the transitivity rules will be constructed regardless of the developmental status of the conservation rules. Such sequences appear more likely to occur in the content area processed by Q_e than in those served by Q_s and Q_c. Continuous materials are, in general, less likely to undergo quantity-altering transformations, $T_\pm$, between quantitative comparisons than discontinuous materials. This might be regarded as being offset by the fact that perceptual transformations, T_p, as indicated in Table 5.1, give rise to a variety of two-dimensional quantification outcomes which prevent consistent sequence detection. Many of the perceptual transformations within the content area of Q_e, however, result in the same two-dimensional quantification outcomes. This is the case, for example, in the sequences of quantitative comparisons of the length of sticks employed in many of the laboratory studies of transitivity. Since the sticks are composed of rigid material, the positional transformations to which they are subjected do not alter the results of submitting individual sticks to two-dimensional quantification via Q_e.

What is the evidence for the foregoing argument that common CSs (based upon Q_e) for transitivity appear prior to those for conservation? The experimental results are conflicting. The hypothesis gains some support from Brainerd's (1973) finding that transitivity appears before the conservation of length and weight. It is not supported by the results of studies described earlier (Garcez, 1969; Smedslund, 1959) which suggest that training conducive to the construction of conservation common CSs facilitates the appearance of transitivity common CS. Since both of these studies dealt with the weight of continuous materials, they deal with the content area of Q_e. The results are consistent with the view that either environmental interaction or systemic activation generates sequences in which transformations occur between comparisons involving Q_e. There are sufficiently many of these to prevent the construction of transitivity common CSs until conservation common CSs or rules have been derived.

Once the equivalence of quantitative comparison outcomes has been established as a result of the application of Q_s and Q_e to "common situations," generalization of the transitivity rules to the operations of Q_e on discontinuous material takes place as common CSs are assimilated to the corresponding rules. The extension of the transitivity rules to the operations of Q_e on continuous material proceeds in an order which reflects the amenability of the material to the generation of quantitative symbols by Q_e.

The nature of the quantitative symbols, or SASs, has already been discussed in Chapter 3. An extreme example of the differences in amenability is afforded by a comparison of the processing by Q_e which underlies comparisons on the "taller–shorter" and "happier–sadder" dimensions. Taller–shorter judgments lie in an area where the operations of Q_e overlap with the use of conventional measurement techniques and links between SASs and a standard measurement scale are easily forged. In contrast, there are no close relationships with measurement techniques to facilitate the operations of Q_e on the happier–sadder dimension. Determining a suitable basis for the generation of SASs poses intractable problems, and any standards constructed presumably vary much more widely between individuals and are more likely to include idiosyncratic features. This distinction continues even when the results of quantitative comparisons on these two dimensions are provided directly, without the necessity for any direct quantification of environmental input. Its operational effect is seen in Hunter's (1957) finding that transitivity problems posed in terms of happier–sadder judgments elicited significantly longer latencies from his 11-year-old subjects than structurally identical problems dealing with taller–shorter dimensions.

TRANSITIVITY OF QUANTITY
AND THE STRUCTURE AND ORGANIZATION OF THE IPS

Our account of the emergence of transitivity of quantity draws upon all of the structural and organizational features of the IPS required by the sufficient theories of preoperational and concrete operational performance on conservation of quantity tasks. In discussing the origins of the specific consistent sequences that initiate the development of transitivity, we suggested that an additional assumption about the organization of the IPS might be required. This would free the system from total dependency upon direct interaction with the environment to determine the sequence of events it experiences and accord it the capability of activating productions and production systems stored in LTM without external intervention. The implications of this powerful addition to the IPS for a theory of transition from state to state in development will be considered in the final chapter.

7

The Organization of the
Information-Processing System

In this chapter and the next, we offer a theory of cognitive development that is consistent with, but more general and less precise than, the specific aspects of the IPS that have been developed thus far. Recall that each of the previous chapters on quantification, class inclusion, conservation, and transitivity concluded with a brief statement of implications of the special requirements of each task for the general IPS. It is now time to integrate all these issues into an extended description of (a) the general structure of the adult IPS, and (b) the developmental processes that give rise to such a system. In this chapter we treat the former issue; in the next, the latter. We will limit the description of the adult system to the bare minimum necessary to provide a clear target for subsequent discussion of developmental mechanisms. Although the topic for this chapter is the structure of the IPS, we propose no major theoretical innovations here (although there are a few new wrinkles). Rather, this chapter should be viewed as providing the necessary background for the next chapter.

As we have indicated throughout this book, many parts of our theoretical viewpoint are speculative. However, rather than clutter this chapter and the next with caveats about the untested nature of various aspects of the view we are about to present, we will simply reiterate the point one final time. We have a complex system to describe, and it is presented in a form that may imply that we believe "that's the way things are."[1] We mean to imply no such audacious

---

[1] Indeed, one colleague, reacting to an earlier draft of Chapters 7 and 8, chided us for "a remarkable lack of critical attitude" and suggested that the description was "all generate and no test." "Unfair!" we cried, reminding him that Chapters 3, 4, 5, and 6 contain many examples of the general theory being proposed in Chapters 7 and 8.

certainty—only to attempt a comprehensive view. Where there is evidence supporting our view, we have cited it; where we can state our processes precisely enough, we have programmed them. The rest is to be read as an untested proposal for how cognitive development might proceed.[2]

MEMORY STRUCTURE

Short-Term Memory Buffers

The final form of the overall system architecture is depicted in Fig. 7.1. The system has five short-term buffers, and a long-term memory (LTM) which consists primarily of productions. These productions can test the contents of any of the buffers, and can act upon their contents or upon specified parts of LTM. Note that this system has obvious intellectual roots in the work of Broadbent (1970), Neisser (1967), and Newell (1973), and is similar to summaries by Hunt (1971) and others.

The multiple buffer model requires a slight elaboration in notation. We want to be able to refer explicitly to conditions and actions that involve specific buffers. Condition elements in a production may test iconic memory (IM), visual STM (VSTM), echoic memory (EM), auditory STM (ASTM), or semantic STM (SSTM); actions may be performed on the external environment (EXE) or upon VSTM, ASTM, or SSTM. Thus, the notation we will use for a prototype of a production that tests SSTM and VSTM, and then acts upon SSTM is ((SSTM) $\cdots$ (VSTM) $\cdots \rightarrow$ (SSTM)). The dotted arrows in Fig. 7.1 represent the functional flow of information from the external environment, through the sensory buffers, and eventually to SSTM. However, this flow is firmly under the control of productions in LTM, and the solid arrows indicate the "real" information flow. The system can respond to information in the buffers only via the conditions on productions, and it can modify the information in buffers only via the actions on productions. The functions assigned to the short-term buffers will be illustrated by considering the processing that ensues when stimulation from

---

[2] A caveat in a caveat: another intentional omission from these chapters—and from the book—is a comparison or evaluation of other recent "neo-Piagetian" views of cognitive development having an information-processing orientation; for example, Cunningham (1972), Osherson (1974), and Pascual-Leone (1970, 1973). We have briefly mentioned Baylor and Gascon (1974) and Young (1973), but we have not discussed their broad theoretical stance. Several of these viewpoints, as well as ours and some others, are presented in the volume edited by Van den Daele, Pascual-Leone, and Witz (in press). The absence of any extensive mention of these approaches in this book should by no means imply a judgment on our part as to their lack of either merit or relevance to our topic. Quite the opposite is true, but in order to keep this book within reasonable limits, we have confined ourselves to the telling of our own tale.

the external environment impinges on the sense organs. The present discussion will be confined to visual and auditory stimulation.

Visual input. If the stimulation is visual, it gives rise to a representation in iconic memory. This is an unselective form of memory for everything that strikes the visual sense organs. Information is stored in it in a very primitive and sensory form of representation which immediately begins to decay and vanishes in about half a second. During this time interval the contents of iconic memory are processed by visual encoding productions capable of making crude distinctions such as that between figure and ground. These productions select parts of the representation for further processing and preserve them by transferring them to visual STM. The general form of the visual encoding productions processing the contents of iconic memory is $((IM) \cdots \rightarrow (VSTM) \cdots)$.

Visual STM is a buffer of limited capacity (Murdock, 1960). There is also some evidence that information represented in it tends to decay with time (Broadbent, 1970). The visual encoding productions which process its contents give rise to "perceptual recognition." This takes place when the encoded information is transferred to semantic STM. The general form of the productions involved in the transfer is $((VSTM) \cdots \rightarrow (SSTM) \cdots)$. The information placed in SSTM by these visual encoding productions must be in a form such that it will match against the appropriate productions in LTM; that is, they must place enough properly encoded elements in SSTM to ultimately satisfy the LTM productions that correspond to meaningful recognition of the stimulus. This process involves complex discriminations based on representations in LTM of environmental attributes and their values.

Information transferred to SSTM becomes part of the current knowledge state of the system and is available as input to the productions which underlie human problem-solving. The method of operation of these productions has already been described in Chapter 1 and exemplified in Chapters 2 and 3. Semantic STM corresponds to the short-term memory that is an integral part of Newell and Simon's (1972) version of the human information-processing system and to the address store included by Broadbent (1970) in his account of memory. Information represented in it is not subject to decay with time, but the amount of information which it can hold is limited.

Auditory input. When the system is subjected to external auditory stimulation, a similar processing sequence ensues. By no means all auditory stimulation is speech, but since it is the most important aspect for our present concern, we will limit our discussions to the processing of speech. As in the case of vision, auditory stimulation produces a representation in an unselective memory store that, in accordance with Neisser's (1967) terminology, will be called echoic memory. Information stored in echoic memory is also immediately subject to decay. However, this is a more protracted process than in the case of iconic memory; estimates of its duration range from one to two seconds. During this

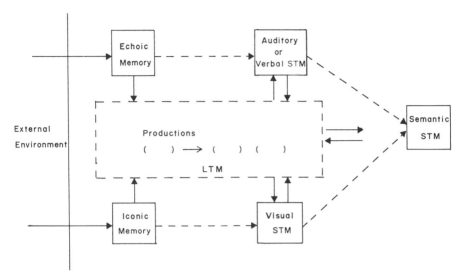

FIG. 7.1   General structure of the IPS.

period the sensory representation of acoustic events undergoes preliminary segmentation and phonological analysis.

The productions involved are of the general form $((\text{EM}) \cdots \rightarrow (\text{ASTM}) \cdots)$. Their function is to transfer segments of acoustic input to auditory STM. These segments are encoded in the underlying abstract level of representation within the sound system of the language which Chomsky (1970) refers to as lexical spelling. The encoding process involves the removal of surface phonetic variation which is attributable to the application of general rules of pronunciation to lexical spellings. The initial vowels in the words "nation" and "national," for example, are pronounced [ɛy] and [æ], respectively. These different vowels are generated by the application of pronunciation rules to a single vowel in phonological deep structure and in the encoding process are replaced by the lexical spelling for the single vowel.

Auditory STM is a store of limited but possibly greater capacity than visual STM (Broadbent, 1970). The general form of the productions that process its contents and transfer the encoded information to semantic STM is $((\text{ASTM}) \cdots \rightarrow (\text{SSTM}))$. Discussion of these productions raises some of the most contentious and intractable issues in psycholinguistics. Since these problems lie outside the scope of the objectives which we have set for this book, no attempt will be made to tackle them. However, some indication will be provided of the type of psycholinguistic solution that appears to be most compatible with our theory.

As indicated above, information stored in semantic STM must be encoded in a form recognizable by LTM. Accordingly, the productions that govern the transition from auditory to semantic STM must be capable of accepting acoustic input represented in the form of phonological deep structure and surface syntactic structure and converting it to semantic elements. But how is this to be done? Suppose that we accept Chomsky's (1965) view that the constituents of a grammar of a language include a syntactic base component, which specifies the membership of a class of potentially well-formed syntactic deep structures, a semantic component, which links these deep structures with their semantic representations, and a transformational component which links syntactic deep structures with their surface syntactic representations. Then the transition from auditory to semantic STM would involve representing the contents of auditory STM in syntactic deep structure and subsequently converting this deep structure to semantic representation. This appears to be a tall order.

Fortunately for the model of cognition being proposed, recent developments seem to be bringing psycholinguistic theory more into line with the type of transition from auditory to semantic STM outlined above. McCawley (1968), for example, argues that it is necessary to provide some justification for the hypothesis of a syntactic deep structure level between the levels of surface syntactic and semantic representation: "There is no a priori reason why a grammar could not instead consist of, say, a 'formation-rule component,' which specifies the membership of a class of well-formed semantic representations, and a 'transformational component,' which consists of rules correlating semantic representations with surface syntactic representations in much the same fashion in which Chomsky's 'transformational component' correlates deep structures with surface syntactic representations [McCawley, 1968, p. 165]." Fillmore's (1968) case grammar provides a further example of this trend. He asserts: "If it is possible by rules . . . to make these 'semantic deep structures' into the surface form of sentences, then it is likely that the syntactic deep structure of the type that has been made familiar from the work of Chomsky and his students is going to go the way of the phoneme. It is an artificial intermediate level between the empirically discoverable 'semantic deep structure' and the observationally acces-sible surface structure, a level the properties of which have more to do with the methodological commitments of grammarians than with the nature of human languages [Fillmore, 1968, p. 88] ."

The fundamental modifications proposed in transformational grammar would render it entirely consistent with the function ascribed to the productions regulating the transition from auditory to semantic STM. This, it will be recalled, involves encoding as semantic elements acoustic input represented in the form of phonological deep structure and surface syntactic structure.

More complex information flows. In the interest of clarity, the account has been presented thus far in terms of two distinct storage and processing chains entirely devoted to coping with incoming information. Of course, this is an oversimplification, since the operations of the system involve a two-way flow of information *along* the processing chains, and also a considerable amount of interaction *between* them.

The two-way flow of information in the visual chain is exemplified in the control exercised by the contents of semantic STM over the encoding productions processing visual STM. This control determines the features which are attended to and the level of detail at which they are processed. It might be implemented by productions that take their input from SSTM and place information on targets and attentional grain in VSTM; that is, $((SSTM) \cdots \rightarrow (VSTM)$ $(VSTM) \cdots)$. Since the presence of such control information is difficult to reconcile with the sensory nature of the VSTM store, an alternative method of achieving the same effect appears preferable. This is based on the assumption that each of the encoding productions comprises conditions on the contents of *both* SSTM and VSTM; that is, $((SSTM) \cdots (VSTM) \cdots \rightarrow (SSTM) \cdots)$. Adoption of this general form enables the contents of SSTM to influence the processing of VSTM by the encoding productions without the necessity of transferring control information from SSTM to VSTM. This was the approach used by PS.COUNT in PS.QC2 (Fig. 4.4) and by PSVS in PS.QC5 (Fig. 5.2). The subitizer in PS.QC5 includes a condition on SSTM as the first element to be tested in each of the subitizing productions, thus enabling the current value of the target to be quantified to be obtained from SSTM. This value of the target variable then carries over to the other elements and defines the parameterized discrimination production systems which process VSTM. A similar approach was adopted in the counting model used in PS.QC2 in Chapter 4. There, information on attentional grain was communicated from SSTM to VSTM.

A two-way flow of information is also essential to the functioning of the auditory chain. The productions that process the contents of auditory STM require information on the current semantic context in SSTM to enable the application of the rules linking surface syntactic representations with semantic representations: $((SSTM) \cdots (ASTM) \cdots \rightarrow (SSTM))$. Likewise, the preliminary segmentation and phonological analysis of the sensory representation of acoustic events in echoic memory cannot proceed without feedback on the current syntactic context in ASTM: $((ASTM) \cdots (EM) \cdots \rightarrow (ASTM) \cdots)$.

These examples illustrate the importance of a two-way flow of information in encoding visual and auditory sensory input. Informational feedback from SSTM to auditory and visual STM is also the basis of operation of the productions that decode and implement the system's responses to environmental stimulation. This is not to say that a transfer of information from SSTM is necessary for each response. In the case of the visual chain, for example, once the requisite control information regarding target features and attentional grain has been obtained from SSTM, a sequence of responses can be triggered by the subsequent contents of VSTM without further reference to SSTM. If a representation of a red object is obtained from SSTM as an attentional target, the responses involved in executing a visual search of the external environment are triggered and controlled by productions processing the contents of VSTM without further reference to SSTM.

Interaction between the functioning of the auditory and visual chains is the rule rather than the exception. For example, in the class-inclusion task the problem is posed in terms of a concrete situation to be processed by the visual chain and a question encoded by the auditory chain. The encoding of the question in SSTM involves the sequential application of two general types of productions: ((ASTM) $\cdots$ (EM) $\cdots \rightarrow$ (ASTM) $\cdots$), and ((SSTM) $\cdots$ (ASTM) $\cdots \rightarrow$ (SSTM) $\cdots$). This encoding process establishes a context which determines the nature of the target and attentional grain. Then this control information in SSTM is applied in the processing of VSTM by productions of the general type ((SSTM) $\cdots$ (VSTM) $\rightarrow$ (SSTM) $\cdots$).

Reading affords another example of such interaction. In a child still learning how to read, the printed or written letter symbols first give rise to a representation in iconic memory. This is processed by productions which employ grapheme–phoneme correspondence rules to generate overt vocal responses: ((IM) $\cdots \rightarrow$ (EXE) $\cdots$). The vocal responses provide auditory stimulation to be represented in echoic memory and subsequently undergo the two processing phases for speech outlined above. The two general production types are ((ASTM) $\cdots$ (EM) $\cdots \rightarrow$ (ASTM)), and ((SSTM) $\cdots$ (ASTM) $\cdots \rightarrow$ (SSTM)). This sequence alters when silent reading becomes possible. The overt vocal responses no longer occur and the grapheme–phoneme correspondence rules result directly in a representation in echoic memory; the production form becomes ((IM) $\cdots \rightarrow$ (EM)). As Chomsky (1970) has suggested, later in development there may well be a further modification in the interaction of the visual and auditory chains in reading. This involves the appearance of productions encoding the graphemic content of iconic memory as phonological deep structure and transferring it directly to auditory STM; that is, ((IM) $\cdots \rightarrow$ (ASTM) $\cdots$). Once this occurred, there would no longer be any need to employ grapheme–phoneme correspondence rules to ensure the representation of written material in SSTM.

Multiple buffers: Summary.   A description has been offered of the functioning of the visual and auditory chains in terms of productions stored in LTM, some of which operate upon a single buffer while others process the contents of one or two buffers and place the resulting output in another store. In some cases both buffers belong to the same chain while in others they are in different chains.

While maintaining the fundamental features of the overall system architecture, this multiple buffer model enables us to deal with many of the issues raised in Chapter 3. It appears likely that each of the buffers has a different configuration of parameters such as size, rehearsal rules, replacement rules, scanning rules, and timing assumptions. The multiple buffer approach also makes is possible to consider quite distinct matching rules and ways of resolving serial/parallel issues for VSTM and SSTM.

Long-Term Memory

The account of LTM presented here is shaped by our principal constraint, that of a plausible ontogenesis. In the next chapter, we present a developmental model for LTM: in this section we sketch the hypothesized form resulting from such a developmental process. The proposed structure is in the tradition of the LTM models of Quillian (1968, 1969), Collins and Quillian (1972), and Rumelhart, Lindsay, and Norman (1972), but differs from all of them in specific details.

LTM is assumed to comprise a complex list structure, but since, as Norman (1972) points out, there is a simple form equivalence between a list structure and a graph structure, in the interests of comprehensibility we will discuss LTM in terms of a complex graph or network. A description of how values, attributes, objects, and relations are represented in the LTM network will provide an indication of its general structure. Productions and production systems are the basic representational units. Consistent with Newell and Simon's (1972) approach, there is a single *type node* in the network at which is stored the complete representation of each production or production system. When additional representations are required in the network, they take the form of *tokens* which are pointers to the location of the appropriate type node. In addition to the productions stored at it, each type-node has a description list attached to it. This is a list providing information on its relationships with other nodes.

Objects. Objects, such as PS.OB3 and PS.OB6 in Fig. 7.2, are represented by type nodes at which are stored production systems composed of tokens representing the sequence of productions activated as a result of stimulation of the sense organs by the object. The description lists attached to these object type nodes contain tokens for production systems defining the characteristics of the objects. Qualitative attributes are represented by tokens pointing to the appropriate value type nodes. The tokens for round and square on the description lists of PS.OB3 and PS.OB6 provide examples.

In the case of relational attributes, such as those stemming from quantification, the value of an object is a symbol representing the outcome of inputting the object to the production system defining the attribute. For example, the attribute length is represented on the description list of PS.OB6 by a token pointing to PS.LENGTH, at which are stored the productions defining the attribute. These provide access both to the estimation and measurement production systems. The value, coupled with the attribute length on the description list of an object, is determined by which of these production systems has been employed. If estimation has been used, the value, as indicated in Chapter 3, will be a size analog symbol (SAS). This is presumed to be the situation in the case of PS.OB6. If measurement produced the value, it would be a numerical length symbol.

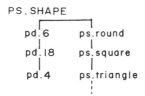

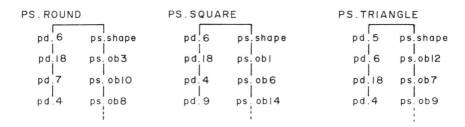

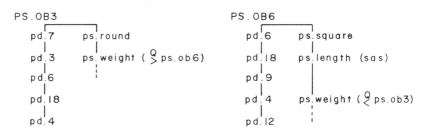

FIG. 7.2   Representation of attributes, values, and objects in LTM.

Attributes founded on quantitative measurement and other relational attributes provide information on the relationship between objects. Such information is added to the description list of an object under the appropriate attribute token representing the production system which established the relationship. The specific relationship is represented by a token pointing to the other object concerned and a token pointing to the specific outcome obtained by applying the production system to the two objects. The description lists of PS.OB3 and PS.OB6 contain attribute tokens pointing to the weight type node and quantitative relational attribute token and object tokens representing the outcome of a comparison of their relative weights.

Values. Type nodes for values (for example, square, round, red, green) are represented by production systems. These value production systems consist of the sequence of productions consistently triggered by the presence, in VSTM, of the representation arising from the stimulation of the sense organs by the sensory correlates of those values. Type nodes representing the values round, square and triangle are presented in Fig. 7.2. Each node contains both a production system (on the left) and a description list. On the description list of each value type node is a token for the appropriate attribute type node. In the case of the round, square and triangle type nodes, the token for shape appears on their description lists. Value description lists also include tokens for objects exhibiting the value. The difference between the function of the production systems stored at the type nodes and that of their description lists is exemplified in the difference between questions such as, "Is this object square?" (resolve by running PS.SQUARE on the object in question), "What is square?" (determine first item on description list of SQUARE), and "Can you name some square things?" (select a few items from SQUARE's description list.) Notice that these last two questions would require some rudimentary list processing production systems that could extract the appropriate information from these structures.

Attributes. At the attribute type nodes are stored production systems comprising sequences of productions that are common to the sequences which define the values subsumed by the attribute. In Fig. 7.2 the productions PD.6, PD.18 and PD.4 which are common to the value sequences are included in the production system at the shape type node. Tokens pointing to the locations of the appropriate values are stored on the description list of the attribute type nodes. Accordingly, tokens pointing to the round, square and triangle type nodes are among those on the description list of the shape type node.

The idea of representing objects, values, and attributes as production systems may be clarified by noting an important distinction between the kinds of conditions in two categories of production systems. One kind of production system, representing information up to and including the attribute level, consists of productions whose conditions test buffers other than SSTM. The other kind of production system represents higher levels of aggregation, and it has productions whose conditions do test SSTM (as well as other buffers). The former do not have goals in the conditions which must be satisfied for the production systems to become active. Their conditions deal only with predicate information. This predicate information is the input required by the "top" production in each system. By the time that the successvie consistent sequence detection processes leading to the construction of object, value and attribute have taken place, the productions remaining in the systems are unlikely to be of low discriminatory power. The performance of the systems is, however, monitored by systemic productions. They delete or add productions as the time line record indicates is appropriate and, also, modify the order of the productions to place those with greatest discriminatory power (most specific) at the top of the list.

Given this monitoring process, successful operation of an object, value, or attribute production system involves the successful functioning of all of the productions on the list. The culmination of successful operation is the placing of the token for the production system in SSTM. (In functional terms the process described is identical to the route through a discrimination net to a single terminal node, with testing being ended if any test is failed.) Verbal reference to objects, values or attributes results in the placement of their tokens in SSTM. If the import of the verbal input is a command or question, the token acquires the status of a goal and leads to a direct attempt to activate the production system. With the partial exception of this mode of activation, production systems scanning buffers other than SSTM are entirely confined to predicate-led functioning.

MEMORY DYNAMICS

The Time Line

In briefly describing the representation of values, attributes, objects and relations, we have alluded to sequences of productions stored at nodes. These sequences represent the outcome of the systemic process of consistency detection introduced in the accounts of conservation and transitivity. This process is explicated in Chapter 8, but in describing the organization of LTM it is necessary to outline the feature that makes the operation of the process possible. This is a *time line.* The basic idea of the time line was proposed by Penfield (1954; Penfield & Roberts, 1959), and is founded on the results of applying a gentle electric current to various places on the exposed cortex of epileptic patients undergoing brain surgery. In some cases this treatment led to subjective reports of vivid auditory or visual images of what appeared to be past events in the patient's experience. Penfield (1954) regards this as evidence of reactivation of a sequential record of specific previous experience and argues "–that the brain of every man contains an unchanging ganglionic record of successive experience [p. 14]." This attempt to demonstrate that there is a "permanent record of the stream of consciousness" by producing imagery as a result of direct brain stimulation has been effectively criticized by Neisser (1967). However, the more general view that humans lay down a temporally ordered coritcal record of their experiences has been adopted by Reitman (1965), and plays an important part in the structure of his Argus program which models performance on simple analogies problems. More recently, Tulving (1972) has suggested that a distinction may be usefully made between semantic memory and an episodic memory which "receives and stores information about temporally dated episodes or events, and temporal–spatial relations among these events [p. 385]." A time line is also of fundamental importance in our account of the structure and functioning of LTM.

How does the time line operate? As each type node (which can, of course, be the location of a single production or a production system) is activated, a token pointing to the type node and tokens representing the predicate input to the production system are placed in the time line. This creates in the time line a sequential record of production and production system activity. At the conclusion of a processing episode, details of the current goal state in SSTM and tokens representing the output placed in any STM store by the sequence are also inserted in the time line. The end of a processing episode is defined by (a) the attainment of the goal which initiated it, or (b) events in the external environment, or (c) events within the individual but external to the IPS. Thus, processing episodes are typically defined as the periods between distinct searches of LTM for the next node to process SSTM.

The activity of all of the productions and production systems in LTM is recorded in the same time line regardless of variations in the STM stores on which they operate. This feature of the functioning of LTM will undoubtedly pose considerable problems when the task of producing a sufficient, running version of our entire theory of cognitive development is undertaken. How are sequences of productions applied concurrently to different STM stores interlaced in the time line? How are the relationships between the termination of episodes in the five STM stores to be handled? These are only two examples selected from what will unquestionably prove to be a large number of difficulties. Why, then, are individual time lines for each STM store not included in the proposed structure? Such a proliferation of time lines would, in our view, not only be unparsimonious, but would create more serious problems than those it would solve. With separate time lines it would be extremely difficult to account for the development of sequences, including productions that operate on different stores; yet such sequences clearly occur and are of fundamental importance. The grapheme–phoneme correspondence rules required in the development of reading are derived from the detection of consistent sequences of productions operating on different STM stores. The same is true of the development of the rules which, it was argued in Chapter 5, underlie successful performance on conservation tasks. In general, the importance accorded in the proposed structure of LTM to productions taking their input from one store and placing their output in another would render the administration of multiple time lines dauntingly complex.

As subsequent discussion of the functioning of the time line will be confined entirely to a developmental context, it should be pointed out at this juncture that its contribution is probably not limited to the self-modification of the IPS. The information stored in the time line would, for example, provide a suitable basis for the type of responses regarded in an experimental situation as evidence of one trial learning. It would also be sufficient for successful performance on many laboratory memory tasks. As Tulving (1972) has indicated, a typical memory experiment in which a subject is asked to study and remember a list of familiar words or pairs of words is an episodic memory (time line) task. Since the subject has succeeded if he reproduces a copy of an input item on request, no access to information stored at type nodes is required and the tokens stored in the time line constitute a sufficient basis for success.

Hierarchy of Productions

Before turning, in the final chapter, to a discussion of the development of the type of LTM structure described, the question of how the sequences of productions are determined must be tackled. As already indicated, the entire repertoire of productions and production systems is regarded as being encoded in the complex list structure or network constituting LTM. Since the processing of the contents of the five STM stores proceeds concurrently, there are typically five parallel searches for and applications of the next appropriate production going on in the network at any point in time. One approach for determining which production to fire has already been considered in Chapters 1 and 3. It consists of beginning with the first production in the list and comparing the conditions of each production in turn with the current knowledge state. This approach, if generalized, would involve regarding LTM as a single long list of productions with five sequential searches of it proceeding concurrently. Although possessing the virtue of simplicity, this structure appears to be implausible in view of the wide variations in search latencies to which it would give rise.

The problems of implausible variations in search latencies can be met by adopting an LTM structure which permits the parallel matching of the conditions of all of the productions in the list with the knowledge state under consideration. As Newell (1972b) has pointed out, however, a reliance on parallel matching raises some difficult problems. There is "a strong interaction between the amount of parallelism and the sophistication of the matching process . . . with a complex match, involving variable identification and subsequent use within the match itself, the problems of carrying out an indefinite number of such processes simultaneously poses some difficulties [Newell, 1972b, p. 391]." If, as in our proposed LTM structure, not one but five searches involving parallel matching were proceeding concurrently, these problems would be all the more intractable.

A second difficulty highlighted by Newell stems from the fact that a sequential order of matching the conditions of productions is frequently critical for the selection of the appropriate production in a production system. In such circumstances, the adoption of parallel matching would lead to the difficulty of a multiple successful match or an inappropriate selection. Newell (1972b) comments that ". . . the functional aspect of the ordering appears to be that specific productions shield general (back-up) versions of related productions. Thus, the ordering is only effective in little strands, which may prove tolerable [p. 391]."

Newell (1972b) also expresses the view that "There is no dissonance (much less conflict) in a system being both highly serial and highly parallel at the same time (though not, of course, in the same respects) [p. 391]."

Consistent with this view, the answer which we propose to the question of how the sequence of productions is determined involves both serial and parallel search. LTM is divided into three *tiers,* and within each tier there are multiple levels (see Fig. 7.3). The tiers are searched in sequence, starting with Tier 1. *Within* each tier, each level is also tested sequentially. However, in a given level, the search which determines which production system to activate goes on in parallel. Finally, once a production system is activated, search is once again

Structure of LTM

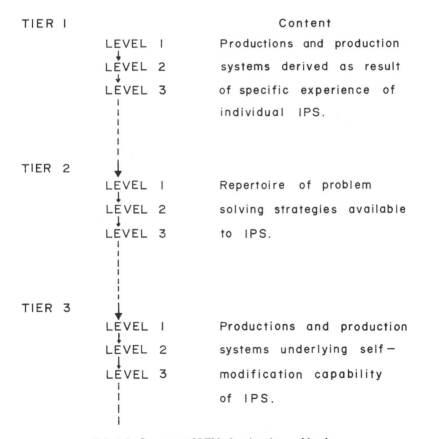

FIG. 7.3 Structure of LTM, showing tiers and levels.

sequential. (Recall that all our timing estimates were based upon analysis of activated production systems.)

As Fig. 7.3 indicates, the first tier to be processed differs from the others in the degree of differentiation represented in the conditions of the productions and production systems it contains. It comprises productions and production systems that have been added to the system's LTM repertoire as a result of consistent sequences detected in the sequential record of activity provided by the time line. Consequently, they are geared to the specific experience of the system. The processes involved in consistent sequence detection will be considered in the next chapter.

In its turn the first tier is made up of levels which, as mentioned above, are searched sequentially. Each of the levels is comprised of type nodes for productions and production systems which may represent specific or common consistent sequences derived from the time line or rules constructed by submitting common consistent sequences to a procedure aimed at the detection and avoidance of redundant processing. New type nodes created as a result of the specific experience of the IPS are added to LTM on the level immediately above the highest one containing any of the type nodes from which they are derived. In accordance with this principle, the objects in Fig. 7.2 are represented on a lower level than the values derived from them and the values, in turn, appear on a lower level than the attributes to which they give rise. A detailed example of the process of addition of new type nodes to the first tier of LTM will be provided in the final chapter.

When the search for an appropriate production proceeds beyond the first tier there is a significant qualitative change in the possible outcome. The productions and production system on Tiers 2 and 3 are all alike in being much less differentiated than those on the first tier. They represent possible modes of reaction in situations in which the previous experience of the system has not given rise to relevant consistent sequences. The production systems at the first of these more general tiers to be searched—Tier 2—constitute the system's repertoire of problem-solving strategies. These include such powerful techniques as means—end analysis.

When do the productions on these tiers get activated? We assume that during wakefulness, the search for appropriate productions will be almost totally confined to Tiers 1 and 2. However, there is an additional tier of generally applicable productions which may on occasion become operative during wakefulness. This tier, Tier 3, comprises the productions involved in the processes of detecting consistent sequences and rule generation. It is of fundamental importance, since it is the source of the productions underlying the self-modification of the system, and thus of cognitive development as a whole. Since these systemic productions use SSTM as a working memory during their operations, it is not inconceivable that their activity is largely confined to periods of sleep (see

Hartmann, 1973).[3] They may, however, operate during wakefulness if the system is engaged in environmental interaction which can be successfully conducted by productions that do not make use of SSTM. Many highly overlearned sequences of motor behavior fall into this category of interaction. The sections of the time line which are processed by the systemic productions during wakefulness may be those that are rendered salient by the outstanding motivational significance of the goals of the processing episodes. This would increase the likelihood of any consistent sequences detected in salient sections speedily giving rise to the addition of new type-nodes to the LTM network.

[3] For example, Hartmann (1973), summarizing the neurophysiological studies of sleep, notes that during D sleep (also called "desynchronized" or "dreaming" sleep, "Rapid-Eye-Movement" sleep, or "paradoxical" sleep):

... much of the forebrain is in a state similar to that of alert waking: the cortex shows desynchronized activity, blood flow is increased, there is a negative DC potential shift, and many species show prominent theta in the hippocampus. This last finding has been associated with alert waking during learning situations. ... The central portions of the sensory-processing motor systems are strongly active, while their usual inputs and outputs are blocked. This obviously suggests active central (possibly cortical) processing, perhaps involving learning or memory [p. 38].

8
The Development
of the Information-Processing System

In the previous chapter, we outlined some proposals about the mature form of the human IPS. In this chapter we consider the developmental processes which give rise to the adult system. The chapter is organized around the three tiers of productions described in Chapter 7. For each tier, we will describe first the innate state, and then some of the important developmental changes for the productions in that tier.

Before proceeding to a tier-by-tier analysis, a few comments are in order about our general position on the vexed question of innate endowment. The question is simply this: With what information-processing capability does the child enter the world? Piaget's (1968) answer to this question stresses the necessity of an innate point of departure in a theory of intellectual development. He argues that an innate neurological and organic *functioning* is required to permit the formation of the structures involved, for example, in conservation and quantification in general. No *structural* hereditary programming is presumed. Conservation is not regarded as being "wired in," but emerges as a result of the operation of a "functional kernel" via "a series of self-regulations and equilibrations in which even the errors play a functional success-promoting role [Piaget, 1968, p. 979] ." Piaget thus draws a distinction between the process of equilibration, which is presumed to be innate, and structures such as the groupings of operations underlying successful performance on class inclusion, conservation, and other operational tasks. The latter are constructed in the course of development as a result of interaction with the environment and the functioning of the equilibration process.

The process—structure distinction made by Piaget does not figure in our developmental theory. The indeterminate nature of such a distinction, when viewed in an information-processing context, has recently been demonstrated by Newell (1972a). The necessity of making it can be avoided in an account of development couched entirely in terms of productions. Piaget's structures are replaced by production systems, while the functions of equilibration are discharged by the generally applicable productions described in the previous chapter. All of these productions are features of the same organized process repertoire stored in LTM. They all have the same basic condition—action form. The only exceptions to this homogeneity stem from the variations in the memory stores from which they derive their input and to which they consign their output.

There is, however, a basic similarity between our account of the developmental process and Piaget's viewpoint: it lies in the acceptance of an innate "functional kernel." Innate productions are assumed to exist on all three tiers in LTM. We will begin our discussion of development by considering the tier of systemic productions which provides the basis of the system's self-modification capability, and thus of cognitive development.

INNATE SYSTEMIC PRODUCTIONS (TIER 3)

Innate systemic productions discharge the functions of consistent sequence detection and rule generation outlined in previous chapters. The operations of these productions conform to a fundamental principle assumed to govern the functioning of the system as a whole. This can be briefly described as a "least effort" or processing economy principle. The emphasis on minimizing effort does not imply that the most perferred state of the system is complete passivity. On the contrary, the principle is regarded as operating in a system strongly motivated toward the perpetuation of its own activity (Berlyne, 1965; Hebb, 1949; Stott, 1961; White, 1959). Although genetic programming has provided the neonate with a corpus of systemic productions, continuing activity is still necessary to permit the construction of the extended repertoire of productions required for increasingly effective interaction with the environment.

The construction of the requisite production repertoire imposes conflicting constraints on the system. If the effectiveness of environmental interaction is to be increased, the system must maximize the amount of information input which is processed. This maximization is necessary, since at the outset of development there is no experiential basis on which trivial information can be discriminated from input of considerable importance for effective interaction. Maximizing the amount of information processed minimizes the time required before the critical features of the informational input are determined.

Efficient Processing through Consistency Detection

The objective of maximizing informational throughput is constrained by the limited capacity of the visual, auditory, and semantic STM stores. Accordingly, there is a premium on processes which increase the amount of information being handled at any given moment in the limited STM work space. Such processes constitute the functional basis of the general principle of economy already mentioned. They conduct the search for invariants and the discovery of structure which Gibson (1970) regards as basic forces in cognitive motivation. In our model, these functions are performed by innate systemic productions that detect *consistent sequences* (CSs) on the basis of the time line record of the activity of the productions and production systems in LTM. As type-nodes representing *specific* CSs and, subsequently, *common* CSs are added to LTM, they permit the system to make use of information in an increasingly aggregated form. This augments the amount of information being processed in the STM stores at a given moment in time.

An example of the way in which specific CSs are first constructed and then give way to common CSs as guides to performance is provided in the work of Dienes and Jeeves (1970). Their experiments were based on the use of a forecasting machine very similar to a fruit machine or "one-armed bandit." There are three sets of symbols. One is termed "State" and is dictated by the machine; the second is termed "Play" and is chosen by the subject; the third is termed "Predict" and is also chosen by the subject as the forecast result of the interaction of the two other symbols. The task of the subject is to discover the logical pattern to which the machine is programmed. The logical patterns used by Dienes and Jeeves were those of mathematical groups of increasing size. Scores were obtained for the speed and accuracy with which the patterns were understood by children and adults.

For our purposes, the most interesting general result to emerge concerns the method of studying and understanding a logical pattern. In the early stages of a program, the subject seems to learn individual links and relationships in the pattern, for example, "When there are two stars, the third symbol will be a circle." But, as the *logic* of the program is grasped, what Dienes and Jeeves term "structural learning" takes place. This more advanced and effective process involves abstraction of the general pattern underlying the group from the previously learned individual links. In our terms, a common CS is derived from a number of previously detected specific CSs.

The direct consequence of CS detection is the extension of the production repertoire. However, another effect on this process—and the increased level of aggregation resulting from it—is the enhancement of the system's problem-solving capacity. Given the limited capacity of semantic STM, the more economically coded any given set of data are, the more easily may other relevant data be considered in the solution of a problem.

Efficient Processing through Redundancy Elimination

Our discussion of the functional characteristics stemming from the processing economy principle has been confined to the aggregation of information arising from the detection of CSs. Another functional feature attributable to the economy principle is the elimination of processing found to be redundant.[1] The removal of redundancy facilitates the system's interaction with the environment by ensuring that the limited STM work space available is devoted to productive processing. This function is discharged by innate systemic productions which monitor the common CSs added to LTM and, wherever possible, recast them as *rules* from which some redundant processing has been removed.

The avoidance of redundant processing by rule generation has played a prominent role in the accounts of the development of conservation and transitivity offered in preceding chapters. To provide additional clarification of what is involved, we offer examples drawn from experimental work on two other concrete operational tasks. The first is derived from a study by Smedslund (1968), which extended to adults the earlier investigations of addition–subtraction performance in children (Smedslund, 1964, 1966a, b, c). The basic task involves informing the subject that the words (L)eft and (R)ight written on a piece of paper before him represent two quantities which at the beginning of each trial are equal. Each trial comprises a sequence of three operations, in each of which a unit is added to or subtracted from one of the quantities. After the three operations the subject is required to indicate which of the quantities is the larger. He is urged to answer as quickly as possible. The emphasis is on speed, since adults, unlike children, make few errors on such items. Thus, reaction times provide the basic data for making inferences about the content and sequential order of the mental processes involved.

A particularly fine example of the elimination of redundant processing is provided by the detailed account of the performance of subject S1 on the sequence of items:

> . . . S1 improved steadily throughout the experiment. A closer study of the data revealed that S1 alone had a number of zero RTs; i.e., he anticipated the answer before the experimenter had finished reading the third element. The first zero RT appeared on the 11th repetition on item 31(+R, +R, −R). Subsequently, and until the end of the experiment, the items beginning with an identity yielded 38 out of 40 possible, or 95%, zero RTs, indicating a sudden insight which generalized to all items beginning with an identity. Then on repetition 14 a zero RT appeared for the first time to an item beginning with an asymmetry (−R, +L, +R). Subsequent items beginning with asymmetry yielded 19 out of 24 possible, or 79%, zero RTs, which also reflects a generalized, although not completely stable insight [Smedslund, 1968, p. 200].

---

[1] Note the function of abstract principles in the system: they serve to constrain, in a consistent fashion, the kinds of assumptions that are made about the functional aspects of particular processes. The principles are not *themselves* programs that cause things to happen. Rather, the programs will have general characteristics that conform to the principles.

During the first ten items beginning with an identity, S1 derives the correct answers by considering the effect of all three operations on the two quantities. His anticipation of the answer before the experimenter revealed the nature of the third operation on the eleventh identity item is consistent with the generation and use of a rule. The rule would be based upon recognition of the fact that when the first two operations are identical and applied to the same quantity, a difference of two between the quantities is established and the answer is thereupon uniquely determined. The third operation cannot effect the outcome, and consequently any processing arising from it is redundant and can be eliminated.

The appearance of a high proportion of zero RTs on asymmetry items suggests a partially successful attempt to apply a modified version of the rule to a wider range of items. The necessary modification would involve deleting from the condition side of the rule any reference to specific operations on specific loci and retaining the condition that the first two operations produce a difference of two between the quantities. Smedslund's discussion of these aspects of the data is entirely consistent with our analysis and with the importance we accord to the derivation of consistent sequences and subsequent rule generation:

> One outcome of this study is the demonstration that a subject may discover a logically possible shortcut, and that others may fail to do so even with very extensive experience. The conditions for discovering the logical constraints involved in a task are so far unknown. Perhaps performance first must become highly automatic and effortless (short RT) before reflection upon existing possibilities can take place, given a certain active and exploring attitude. With the present type of tasks, the subject may then discover that after an initial identity [e.g., L+, L+ or R+, R+] the answer is given, irrespectively of the nature of the third element. The explicit recognition that identity leads to a difference of 2 between the two quantities, may later on evoke recognition that the same occurs with an initial asymmetry [e.g., R+, L–]. The insight into a logical necessity that seemed to occur in subject S1 may in some respects be similar to what occurs, e.g., in young children when they acquire the notions of conservation and transitivity [Smedslund, 1968, p. 201].

The above example is of considerable interest since it provides a longitudinal account of the emergence of a rule in an individual case. However, the subject is an adult, and the course of events cannot be regarded as typical of the functioning of the general rule-generation productions. For example, the processes of CS detection and rule generation take considerably longer to operate in the course of development than is suggested by their rapid telescoped functioning in a sophisticated adult tackling a concrete operational task for a few minutes.

The second example of the avoidance of redundant processing by rule generation emanates from a developmental study involving cross-sectional data. Baylor, Gascon, Lemoyne, and Pothier (1973) have investigated children's performance on a weight seriation task and have produced theories to account for the performance of three individual children aged 6 years, 11 months, 8 years, 5 months, and 11 years, 4 months. These theories are presented in the form of production systems and their sufficiency has been established by computer simulation. The task involves confronting a child with seven cubes and a beam balance and inviting him to arrange the blocks from heaviest to least heavy by weighing not more than two of them at a time on the balance. The blocks are identically sized cubes identified by letter names.

Elimination of redundant processing is illustrated by a comparison of the method of operation of Louis (11 years, 4 months), with that of Pascale (8 years, 5 months). Both children succeed on the seriation task by using a "find the heaviest strategy" in which all of the blocks in the presented collection are weighed in turn. The heavier of the two blocks in each weighing is retained on the balance while the light one is laid aside in a file of weighed blocks and a new block from the presented collection is placed in the vacant pan on the balance. At the end of the episode, when no more unweighed blocks remain, the heavier of the two blocks in the last weighing is the heaviest of all and is positioned on the table to start the required series. This sequence of events is repeated with the remaining collection of blocks, and thus the remainder of the series is constructed block by block.

In comparison with Pascale's version of the "find the heaviest" strategy, Louis' approach reveals interesting evidence of processing economy. Having identified the heaviest block during the first part of the second episode, Louis discovers that $5 > 2, 3, 1$, and 4 and predicts aloud that block 5 is going to be the second heaviest in the final series. Suddenly, with the last weighing, it turns out that $6 > 5$, whereupon Louis places *both* 6 and 5 in their correct positions in the series. In essentially the same situation, Pascale placed only 6 in the series and proceeded to carry out a further episode of weighing before 5 was correctly positioned.

Although employing the same basic strategy, Louis makes only 16 comparisons in constructing the series, while Pascale requires 21 comparisons. Louis' relative processing economy is to be attributed to the presence in his production repertoire of a rule which prevents redundant comparisons. The functional characteristics of this rule have been described by Baylor *et al.* (1973):

> Louis' improvement over Pascale's behavior is essentially that he has added a test to take account of the effects of the final weighing of two blocks within an episode. More precisely, if the block that has been the heaviest of all up until the present moment (heaviest $block_{t-1}$) suddenly becomes the lighter block at $time_t$, then both the heavier $block_t$ and lighter $block_t$ can be moved into the final series [p. 186].

The contribution of the innate systemic productions involved in rule generation to the observance of the economy principle does not end with the recasting of common CSs as rules from which some redundant processing has been removed. Attempts are constantly made to extend the range of applicability of common CSs and rules. This may involve modification, as when Smedslund's subject applies the rule derived from identity items to asymmetry items.

On occasion, the pursuit of economy results in inappropriate extension of the area of application of common CSs or rules. Studies of language acquisition discussed, for example, by McNeill (1967) provide a particularly striking example of this phenomenon. It is well known that children regularize strong verbs in the past tense, producing such forms as *doed, comed,* and *runned.* Such regularizations are, however, a relatively late development in language acquisition. Children first produce strong verbs in the correct past tense form, saying *did, came,* and *ran* before *doed, comed,* and *runned.* Correctly formed strong verbs are, indeed, the first verb children mark for past tense. As McNeill points out, the reason for this is not difficult to see. Since the strong verbs are all frequent in parental speech, children are exposed to many examples of each of them. Having acquired these verbs in their correct past tense form, children also are afforded many opportunities to use them. The result, in our terms, is that specific CSs of productions corresponding to each of the strong verb past tense forms are detected, and new type nodes for each of them are added to LTM. These specific CSs are composed of productions whose function is to regulate the transition from SSTM to ASTM. This involves decoding semantic elements into ASTM input represented in the form of phonological deep structure and surface syntactic structure.

Type nodes for the past tense forms of weak verbs are added to LTM as a result of a similar process, although this takes longer to come about since the weak verb inflections occur less frequently in the parental speech heard by children. This is the prelude to the disappearance from the children's speech of the hitherto correct past tense forms of the strong verbs. McNeill attributes the instability of the strong verbs to the fact that ". . . each strong verb, although frequent, is unique unto itself, whereas the weak verbs, although infrequent, all exemplify a pattern. Apparently patterns weigh more heavily with children than frequency of repetition does, presumably because children search for linguistic features that can be expressed by rule. When the rule is formulated, it is applied wherever called for, contrary to past experience notwithstanding [McNeill, 1967, p. 465]." In our terms, the specific CSs corresponding to the weak verbs—unlike those corresponding to the strong verbs—give rise to common CSs. We would not use the term "rule" here, since this has been reserved for cases in which redundant processing in common CSs has been detected and removed. An attempt is then made to apply this common CS to the strong verbs as well as the weak verbs. The inappropriateness of this extension in pursuit of processing economy is determined by environmental feedback and a reversion occurs to operating on the basis of the relatively uneconomic specific CSs for the strong verbs.

This developmental cycle occurs in such a wide range of linguistic areas beyond strong and weak verb endings that Slobin (1973) has postulated it as a linguistic universal: "The following stages of linguistic marking of a semantic notion are typically observed: (1) no marking, (2) appropriate marking in limited cases, (3) overgeneralization of marking (often accompanied by redundant marking), (4) full adult system [Slobin, 1973, p. 205]." Such a linguistic universal is a consequence of our even more general notion of the system's search for efficient processing.

Local Organization of Subsystems

The examples above illustrate both appropriate and inappropriate extensions of the range of applicability of common CSs and rules. What is the nature of the developing relationships between sequences and rules? In answering this question we assume that the repertoire of productions stored in LTM comprises a number of subsystems. A subsystem is established when a common CS is derived from a range of specific CSs. If the common CS subsequently gives rise to a rule, then that rule's range of applicability is initially confined to the specific contexts subsumed by the common CS.

Relations between subsystems are governed by the processing economy principle. Innate systemic productions compare common CSs. If these are found to be compatible, an attempt is made to maximize the economy of both subsystems by imposing on one any rules which may have been derived from the operations of the other. The processing interface between subsystems is critical. Where subsystems are applicable to the same situations, recognition of equivalence of common CSs and the consequent transfer of rules are facilitated. The importance of such application overlaps is illustrated in the significance assigned to relationships between quantification subsystems in the account of the development of conservation and transitivity of quantity presented in Chapters 5 and 6. (Note that the common CSs and rules included in the quantification subsystems are derived from specific CSs that, in their turn, are comprised of subsystems incorporating common CSs and rules. The manner in which successive degrees of aggregation of information in development give rise to this situation will be outlined below.)

Individual variations in the nature of the subsystems which are constructed and in the developmental order of their appearance are regarded as being the rule rather than the exception. There are, however, some subsystems which feature in all cases of normal development and some sequential relationships between subsystems that are crucial for development. The processes underlying quantification provide examples. The three quantification subsystems described in Chapter 3 are regarded as essential features of normal development, and the initiation of the development of one of the subsystems, Q_s, is viewed as a prerequisite for the attainment of the status of reliable indicators of quantity by the other two subsystems.

Further examples of sequential relations between subsystems which are crucial for development are to be found in the course of language acquisition. The examples to be cited are from Macnamara's (1972) account of the cognitive basis of language learning. His view is entirely consistent with ours on the relationship between semantic units, syntax, and phonology. In our terms, his examples deal with the development of the subsystems comprising the productions which regulate the transition from SSTM to ASTM. These productions decode semantic elements into the surface syntactic structure and phonological deep structure suitable for ASTM input.

One of the tasks confronting the child is to detect the structures of syntax and relate them to semantic structures in a situation in which the consistencies and regularities of syntax are to some extent independent of those of semantics. How, then, does he relate the two? Macnamara's view, which we endorse, is that the child uses independently attained meaning to discover at least certain syntactic structures that are of basic importance. In our terms, syntactic common CSs are detected as a result of consistent relationships between syntactic sequences and previously established semantic subsystems.

Consideration of the following four sentences will illustrate the process:

1. a. Give the book to me.
   b. Give me the book.
2. a. The boy struck the girl.
   b. The girl struck the boy.

If the child is to form accurate syntactic structures, he must determine that the first two sentences represent stylistic variants while the second two do not. The only way he can do this is by the use of independently attained meaning. The decision to treat (1a) and (1b) as stylistic variants hinges on the child's appreciation that while books can be given to people, people cannot be given to books. Previously established semantic structure thus enables him to derive the notions of direct and indirect object and the alternative means of expressing them. Similarly, the basic syntactic device of using word order to express the subject–predicate relationship is presumably discovered as a result of observing what is happening when sentences such as (2a) and (2b) are uttered.

Two general qualifications must be added to the argument. Not all syntactic structures are derived via reliance on prior semantic structure. As Macnamara points out, the rule that determines the number of the verb on the basis of the number of the surface subject is surely a purely syntactic one. Although (3a) and (3b), for example, mean roughly the same thing, the number of the verb is different in the two sentences:

3. a. The boys strike the girl.
   b. The girl is struck by the boys.

It is clear that the child has great skill in detecting syntactic regularities regardless of whether they can be tied to meaning. This view is in line with our emphasis on the general importance of the derivation of consistent sequences in cognitive development.

The second qualification is necessary to prevent a possible misconception: that the argument advanced implies the child possess a complete set of semantic structures when he begins to learn language. All that is necessary for Macnamara's argument is that the development of certain basic semantic structures should precede the development of corresponding syntactic structures. Since the acquisition of syntactic structures is spread over a long period, there is no reason that the acquisition of the corresponding semantic structures should not also extend well into the period of language learning.

The above discussion has been confined to relations between syntax and semantics. A similar type of developmental relationship exists between phonology and syntax. Some phonological common CSs are only detected by way of consistent relationships between phonological sequences and syntactic structure, while others are derived independently of syntax. Language acquisition is thus characterized by essential interdependencies between subsystems, but also by much independent detection of consistent sequences.

Efficient Processing through Global Orientation

There is one final facet of the operation of the processing economy principle which must be mentioned in this overview. We call it an "initial global orientation." This is once again concerned with the avoidance of unnecessary processing. Unlike rule generation, which is aimed at the elimination of redundant processing from previously detected CSs, the objective of global orientation is the avoidance, *from the outset,* of the inclusion of unnecessary processing in CSs. Until either failure to detect CSs or informational feedback indicates its inappropriateness, the system functions on the "assumption" that environmental input can be effectively dealt with if each object is processed once—as a global whole, rather than as a set of dimensions—in a problem-solving episode. An operational example of this principle can be found in the control exercised by the contents of SSTM over the productions encoding the contents of VSTM.

The global orientation is effected through the setting of the level of attentional grain. When attentional grain is set to the level of global objects, each object is considered—as a whole—only once. When attentional grain is set to the level of dimensions or attributes, rather than objects, then multiple passes over a single object during a processing episode are possible. Since multiple passes over the same object may involve unnecessary processing, the preferred level of attentional grain is at the global object level, although this can be replaced with a dimensional grain when necessary.

In the "single visit" strategy, target values are regarded as indicating objects to be processed as discrete wholes. The task environment is considered to be divided longitudinally into object elements, not latitudinally into value dimensions. The way in which target values are interpreted as pointers to whole objects is clearly exemplified in the class-inclusion cases considered in Chapter 4. When

5-year-olds are asked to quantify the superset of a CI collection, they proceed to quantify only one of the subsets. The value on the second dimension of the first object quantified is added to the target (i.e., superset) value to define the discrete, whole objects to be quantified. The attentional grain aspect of the processing economy principle figured prominently in the accounts of the development of both CI and conservation performance offered in Chapters 4 and 5.

Consideration of the innate systemic productions has proved to be a protracted process. Perhaps this is inevitable in view of their function as the basis of the system's self-modification capability. Since the existence of innate productions is assumed on all of the tiers in LTM, an outline of the innate repertoire of productions on each of the other tiers will now be provided. In the course of the description some indication will be given of our as yet incomplete conception of the nature of the early development of cognition.

INNATE SPECIFIC PRODUCTIONS (TIER 1)

In the interest of clarity, the discussion will center on the storage and processing chain devoted to coping with visual information. It should be remembered, however, that there is also an auditory chain, and a considerable amount of interaction takes place between the two. We began by considering the last tier to be searched in LTM (Tier 3). The remaining two tiers in LTM can best be dealt with by considering them in the order in which they are searched. Although the first tier to be processed is comprised to productions and production systems arising from and geared to the specific experience of the system, it is assumed that here too an initial repertoire of innate productions is required. A convenient method of describing the function of these innate productions is to consider the processing sequence occurring when information enters the visual chain at the outset of cognitive development. (The developmental processes to be described in this section are summarized in Table 8.1).

Recall that visual stimulation gives rise to a primitive sensory form of representation on an unselective basis in IM. The visual encoding productions which select parts of this representation for further processing and transfer them to VSTM are assumed to be innate. Their function is confined to making crude distinctions, in particular that between figure and ground (Hebb, 1949).

In the adult, the visual encoding productions which process the contents of VSTM have been constructed mainly by the systemic productions via the operation of the time line. There are, however, a few productions which take their input from VSTM that appear to be required from the outset if cognitive development is to occur. These innate productions can be divided into two groups on the basis of their function. The first group are productions in which the condition side tests for the presence or absence of particular information in VSTM. These productions enable the making of gross discriminations such as the

TABLE 8.1

Successive Phases of Consistency Detection Resulting from Information
Entering via the Visual Information Processing Chain

Gross visual discrimination PRs ($C_{VSTM} \cdots \rightarrow A_{SSTM} \cdots$)
Attentional control PRs ($C_{SSTM} \cdots C_{VSTM} \rightarrow A_{VSTM}$)
Time line: PRGVD, PRAC, PRGVD, PRAC, PRGVD, PRACT . . . .

Outcome: Feature discrimination PSs, covering, for example, lines, angles, and colors. These are common consistent sequences abstracted from specific consistent sequences representing specific lines, angles, and colors.

Feature discrimination PSs ($C_{VSTM} \cdots \rightarrow A_{SSTM}$)
Time line: PS.FD1, PS.FD2, PS.FD3 . . . .

Outcome: Detection of 1. specific consistent sequences of PS.FD tokens corresponding to specific objects at specific distances;
2. subsequently, common consistent sequence of features shared by varying representations of same object gives rise to constant object type-node.

Constant object PSs ($C_{VSTM} \cdots \rightarrow A_{SSTM}$)
Time line: PS.CO1, PS.CO1, PS.CO1 . . . .

Outcome (a) — Detection of
1. Common consistent sequences representing values.
Value PSs ($C_{VSTM} \cdots \rightarrow A_{SSTM}$)
Time line: V.PS1, V.PS2, V.PS3
2. Common consistent sequences representing attributes.
Attribute PSs ($C_{VSTM} \cdots \rightarrow A_{SSTM}$)

Outcome (b) — Three interacting phases of consistent sequence detection.

1. Repeated episodes of common consistent sequence detection give rise to creation of type-nodes representing more aggregated classes of objects.
Time line: PS.C1, PS.C2 . . .

2. Repeated episodes of specific consistent sequence detection result in cardinal number type-nodes representing collections of objects belonging to the same class.
Time line: PS.1, PS.2 . . . .

3. Specific consistent sequence detection results in linking of cardinal number type-nodes in new production systems.
Time line: PS.12

199

light–dark distinctions associated with the edges of a figure. If the appropriate information is present in VSTM the action side of each production places its token in SSTM.

There is some empirical evidence consistent with the existence of such innate visual encoding productions. Salapatek (1968) traced visual scanning of geometric figures by newborn babies. His results indicate that a newborn baby will modify his visual scanning to fit the physical features of simple geometric figures placed in the visual field. This finding is also consistent with the existence of a further group of innate productions which process the contents of visual STM.

The second group of innate productions control the direction of movements of attention over the sensory information stored in VSTM. Linked to an action involving the movement of attention in a specific direction, each production comprises conditions based on the presence of relatively undifferentiated sensory information in VSTM in conjunction with an indication that one of the productions from the first group has fired most recently. For the reasons advanced in the previous chapters, the optimal method of administering such indications appears to be to assume that these attentional control productions include conditions on the contents of both SSTM and VSTM. The necessary control could be achieved by a condition testing SSTM for the presence of a "new" token representing a visual encoding production.

The first CSs detected by the systemic productions via the time line are composed of gross visual discrimination productions and attentional control productions. None of the productions which take their input entirely from SSTM are included in these sequences, since the tokens placed there by the gross visual discrimination productions do not constitute a sufficiently aggregated form of information to permit the detection of consistent relationships with the operation of semantic STM productions. This process is summarized in the top section of Table 8.1.

Consistency Detection Procedures

In this section we will elaborate upon the functioning of the consistency detection procedures. The reader should bear in mind the fact that these procedures are effected by systemic (Tier 3) productions, acting upon Tiers 1, 2, and even 3. The discussion will take us to the heart of our proposed model of cognitive development. First we briefly review the general nature of the developmental process, that is, the detection of specific and common consistent sequences in the time line. Since the proposed consistency detection process is essentially one of abstraction, we then propose an explicit functional description of what is meant by "abstraction," as well as how it occurs.

The sequential record of production and production system activity provided by the time line is composed of *specific situation sequences*. These specific situation sequences are simply the symbols inserted in the time line according to the procedure described in Chapter 7. They vary in the extent to which they recur consistently with the passage of time. *Specific consistent sequences* (specific CSs) are derived by systemic productions which detect recurring token sequences in the time line in a number of specific situation sequences. In some cases exact repetition of specific situation sequences occurs, but frequently partial repetition is encountered and abstraction of the recurring features is necessary for the derivation of specific CSs. Detection of a specific CS results in the addition to LTM of a new type node. At this new node is stored a production system composed of the tokens making up the consistent sequence of productions. As indicated in Chapter 7, the new type node is situated on the first tier of LTM to be processed during a search and, in particular, on a level immediately above the highest one that contains a type node for a token included in the specific CS.[2]

Abstraction of features is an essential component in the construction of *common* CSs. The occurrence of a token in the time line leads to a comparison of the production system stored at the corresponding type-node with the production systems represented by the other tokens in the current time line sequence. As common sequences are detected they are stored as production systems at new type nodes. These are added to the first tier of LTM, on a level immediately above the highest one, which contains a type node for a specific CS subsumed by the common CS in question. As indicated in the discussion of the representation of objects, values, and attributes in Chapter 7, the creation of a new common CS type node is accompanied by two kinds of cross referencing. The description list of the new type node gets tokens pointing to the type nodes from which it was derived, and the description list of each of those type nodes gets a token pointing to the new node.

The use of the term *abstraction* constitutes a verbal means of concealing one of the most intractable problems to be tackled if a sufficient information-processing theory of cognitive development is to be produced. When does the degree of commonality detected in specific situation sequences call for the construction of a specific CS? When should a common CS be derived from the production systems stored at type nodes? What processes decide these issues? The emergence of a specific or common CS is a discontinuous jump in a continuous process of accumulation of similarities. Continuous changes giving rise to discontinuous jumps are widespread in natural and artificial systems. How can we model them in an information-processing theory of development?

Catastrophe theory: Discontinuity in a continuous system. As Zeeman (1971) has noted, a general mathematical theory that can handle such discon-

---

[2] Throughout this chapter we will be referring to different kinds of sequences. They represent increasing higher levels of aggregation and abstraction of environmental regularities. A useful metaphor is the following: specific situation sequences: notes; specific consistent sequences: tunes; and common consistent sequences: themes.

tinuities has recently been invented by the French mathematician, René Thom. In this section we will indicate how such a theory encompasses the *functional* description of the relationship between continuous and discontinuous changes. In a subsequent section we will sketch a *process* description of the same phenomenon. Our treatment of Thom will be limited to those aspects which are relevant to common sequence detection. Readers desiring a more extended treatment should consult Thom (1974) and Zeeman (1972). The relevant features of Thom's work are clearly outlined in an example provided by Zeeman (1971), which we paraphrase below:

> Let x and y be, respectively, measurements of the rage and fear experienced by a dog at a given moment in time, and z a measure of the aggressive behavior of the dog. Positive z means attack, the more positive z is, the fiercer the attack. Negative z indicates flight, and when $z = 0$ neutral behavior occurs. Rage, x, and fear, y, influence behavior, z. Rage is expected to cause attack, and fear to cause flight, so that an increase in x causes an increase in z, while an increase in y causes a decrease in z. If both rage and fear are increased the least likely behavior is for the dog to remain neutral and the most likely behavior is attack or flight. Predicting whether attack or flight will occur leads to the consideration of probabilities. Figure 8.1 presents probability distributions for the following four situations: (1) rage only (attack); (2) fear only (flight); (3) neither (neurtal); and (4) both rage and fear (attack or flight).
>
> A three-dimensional graph of z as a function of x and y can be drawn by marking above each point (x, y) in the horizontal plane a point z which represents the most likely behavior as indicated by the corresponding probability distribution. By Thom's theorem, the outcome must be a surface similar to the cusp catastrophe illustrated in Fig. [8.2]. In the first situation included in Fig. [8.1] there is only rage and we obtain a single point marked (1) on the graph, indicating attack. Similarly, single points representing flight (2) and neutral behavior (3) are obtained from the second and third situations. Two points marked (4) on the graph are obtained from the fourth situation. These indicate the two peaks of the probability distribution. In addition, there is a third point, (4*), between these two indicating the least likely neutral behavior. By including least likely as well as most likely points on the graph a complete smooth surface is obtained. This is one of the consequences of Thom's theorem and it is important to remember when using the cusp catastrophe that the middle sheet, the underside of the overhanging cliff, always represents least likely behavior [paraphrased from Zeeman, 1971, p. 1557].

The remainder of the example can be best presented in Zeeman's (1971) words:

> We can now better understand the dog's behavior. As his drives vary in the horizontal (x, y) plane, his behavior varies over the surface above (except for the middle sheet). Suppose the dog is cornered and frightened so that he is on the lower sheet position (2). He will be in a retreating frame of mind and therefore cowering (with his ears back). Suppose we approach him, thereby causing his rage to increase until he reaches position (4) on the lower sheet; he will still be cowering (but his mouth may have opened ready to bite). Suppose we now continue to approach steadily, causing his rage to increase steadily, until at a critical moment he crosses the edge of the lower sheet (where it folds over into the middle sheet). When this happens he is forced to jump into the upper sheet to position (1) because there is nowhere else to go: suddenly he will switch from a

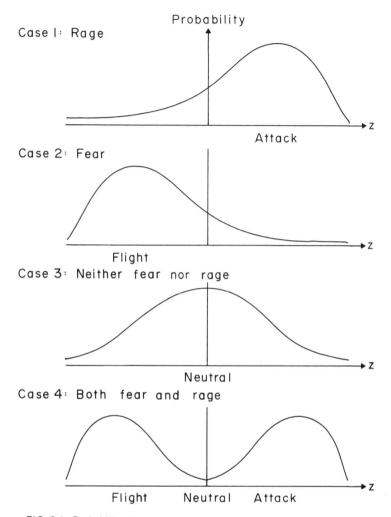

FIG. 8.1 Probability distribution for attack or flight. (From Zeeman, 1971.)

retreating frame of mind to an attacking frame of mind and consequently he will suddenly attack. Mathematically, what has happened is that the left-hand peak of the two-peak probability distribution of case (4) has been gradually getting smaller, and closer to the valley, until at the critical moment both peak and valley disappear, leaving only the one-peak distribution of case (1). Conversely if the dog is attacking fiercely and we gradually increase his fear, then at the critical moment he will fall off the overhanging cliff, suddenly switch to a retreating frame of mind, and disengage [Zeeman, 1971, p. 1557].

It is clear from this example that a fundamental feature of Thom's theory is that a gradual change in control can cause a sudden catastrophic change in

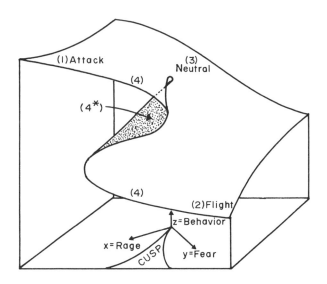

FIG. 8.2   Catastrophy surface. (From Zeeman, 1971.)

behavior. Indeed, this is why it has been christened catastrophe theory. As already indicated, the emergence of a specific CS constitutes a discontinuous jump in a continuous process of accumulation of similarities between specific situation sequences. It can accordingly be regarded as another example falling within the scope of Thom's theorem. The current estimates of the similarity and difference of the specific sequences being processed become x and y. The two most likely outcomes, z, are the construction of a specific CS or the continuation of the accumulation of information on similarities and differences. The least likely result, in view of the fundamental importance of the systemic productions searching for consistency in pursuance of the economy principle, is cessation of the processing of the time line. If a number of specific sequences with little in common are considered, the difference estimate will be high and the child can be regarded as being on the lower sheet at Position (2). The situation alters when subsequent specific sequences are found to be similar. As the estimate of similarity increases the child moves on the lower sheet toward Position (4). If Position (4) is reached and the similarity estimate continues to increase, he crosses the edge of the lower sheet and must jump to Position (1) on the upper sheet. As a result, the process of gathering information on similarities ceases and a new specific CS is added to LTM.

A process model of abstraction.   Thom's theorem provides an elegant description of the functional relationship between continuous and discontinuous changes. The determination by the system that there is a basis for abstraction is an example of such a jump from continuous to discontinuous processing. In this section we will sketch the outlines of a process model that makes such a determination.

The processing of the time line by the general systemic productions which carry out the consistency detection operations is similar for the derivation of both specific CSs and common CSs. The main distinction is that specific CS detection operates directly on the tokens in the time line while common CS detection operates on the tokens pointed to by the tokens in the time line. In this description, we concentrate on specific CSs. Table 8.2 summarizes the process.

The intial phase of the search for specific CSs involves segmenting into episodes the stretch of the time line which has appeared since the last search for consistency. To be compatible with the account of development offered in the present chapter, the consistency detection processes must be capable of coping with sequences that do not have the end of processing episodes marked by the

TABLE 8.2
Algorithm for Node Construction during
Time-Line Processing

Step 1. Segment time slice using table of partial-match templates under control of D.

Step 2. Compute instantaneous values of ccl on current segmentation. $ccl = f(d * n)$.

Step 3. Test: Is ccl = CCL (CCL is cumulative value of critical consistency level)?
　　　　If yes, go to Step 6.

Step 4. Revise CCL downward as function of ccl.

Step 5. Test: Is CCL below minimum level?
　　　　If yes, go to Step 8.
　　　　If no, return to Step 1.

Step 6. Create new node based upon current segmentation.

Step 7. Revise CCL upward as function of ccl.

Step 8. Move to new section of time line: create new time slice.
　　　　Go to Step 1.

---

insertion of tokens representing the current contents of SSTM in the time line. This is essential, since the construction of feature discrimination PSs antedates the presence of coherent end states (goals) in SSTM. This step in the consistency detection processes must therefore resemble a serial pattern detector (Klahr & Wallace, 1970a; Simon & Kotovsky, 1963). The contents of the time line do not exhibit the regular periodicity of letter series, but a basically similar approach to segmentation can be adopted.

The system needs to maintain information that will enable it to decide *when* to form consistent sequences. This decision is sensitive to both the cumulative past history of processing and the instantaneous situation. Three kinds of information are required: (a) information about the current sensitivity or responsiveness of the system to new information. We call this the critical consistency level (CCL); (b) informaton about the degree of similarity between segments of the time line (D); and (c) information about the frequency or number of similar instances discovered in the time line (N). CCL is a vector function of D and N, and D and N are revised after each attempt to abstract from the time line. The sequential steps are described below, but the general functional form is that D and N are modified on the basis of instantaneous values of the current time slice processing $(d$ and $n)$ and the magnitude of CCL; that is, $D' = f(\text{CCL}, D - d)$, $N' = g(\text{CCL}, N - n)$, and $\text{CCL}' = h(D', N')$, where f, g, and h are functions, as yet undefined, and the primed variables are the revised values of the corresponding unprimed variables. In addition, we assume that individual difference parameters control the responsiveness of CCL to differences between cumulative and instantaneous values D and N.

Step 1. Initially the time line is scanned, and all symbols for which multiple tokens exist are marked. This can be accomplished by initially comparing the first token with all the others in the time line and marking the location of all recurrences of it. This operation is then repeated with each successive token which has not yet been marked as a recurrence.

A possible segmentation process would proceed as follows:

a. Locate first repetition of first token in time line.
b. Take strip between first token and its first repetition and overlay it iteratively over remainder of time line.
c. Mark consistent sequences.
d. Take first token (after initial first token) not yet included in a consistent sequence
e. Repeat Steps a to c.

The matching process is controlled by the value of a parameter, D, indicating the current degree of commonality required for an acceptable match. The highest value of D requires perfect matching for two segments to be considered as repeated instances of each other. Lower values allow increasingly poorer matches to be accepted. *D* can be viewed as a pointer to a set of templates in a table indicating the general form of required matchings.

Step 2. Upon completion of the segmentation process, all those stretches of the time line that are candidates for the construction of CSs are reviewed. Values of *d* (the degree of commonality of the segments currently under consideration) and *n* (the number of segments with this value of *d*) are computed. From these two variables is computed the instantaneous value of the critical consistency level (ccl) for these segments. The general functional form is based upon the *product* of the values of *d* and *n*.

Step 3. The instantaneous ccl is compared to the cumulative CCL in order to determine whether a new node can be formed (Step 6) or whether further processing of the time line will be necessary (Step 4).

Steps 4 and 5. When ccl is insufficient to cause new node formation, CCL is revised downward. The size of the reduction in CCL is a function of both its current value and the value of ccl. However, there is some lower limit below which the system, instead of lowering CCL still further, abandons its attempts to find any regularity in the current time slice, and instead (Step 8) moves to a new section of the time line.

Step 6. If so indicated in Step 3, the system creates a new node. The details of this process are described elsewhere in this chapter.

Step 7. Upon creating a new node, the system revises upward the value of CCL. The size of the increase takes account of the current adaptation level (ccl).

These proposals clearly constitute only a crude starting point for a sufficient information processing analysis of "abstraction." Since the revision of *D* and *N* depends upon both individual parameters and the nature of the specific situation sequences, the proposals gain in plausibility as they are consistent with the appearance of variations between individuals in specific consistent sequence construction. Even when, as in training experiments, attempts are made to ensure that over a short period all of the subjects generate the same series of specific sequences in their time lines, variations, in adaption level ensure the continuation of individual differences.

Another aspect of individual variation which raised a fundamental problem involved in implementing the proposals is centered on the individual functions. Are the range of values of the parameters, and the form of functions *g*, *f*, and *h* subject to variation between individuals or are they constant? This in turn poses the more general question of how suitable forms for the functions are to be determined. Implementation of the proposals in the form of a running computer program would be a prerequisite for an attempt to answer these questions. It would enable comparisons of the incidence of discontinuous behavior when the functions are determined on a variety of schemes. Behavior generated by the program might also be compared with data obtained from experimental studies.

These would be training studies in which emphasis would be placed on obtaining a detailed trial by trial record of the performance of individual subjects to ensure the detection of the occurrence of discontinuities in their behavior. The tasks involved would also have to be carefully selected to exclude situations in which success depends on the derivation of rules from common CSs rather than on the construction of specific or common CSs.

In tackling the issue raised by the assigning of numerical values to these proposed functions and parameters, we may well be moving from the psychological level of information-processing analysis and computer simulation to analysis and simulation on the neurological level. Zeeman (1972), for example, argues that catastrophe theory is applicable to neural events in the brain, and thus provides a bridge between psychology and neurology. He suggests that behavior discontinuities on the psychological level may well coincide with similar discontinuities on the neurological level which might be detectable as observable phase shifts in EEG recordings.

Having considered at some length the process basis of the decision to construct a consistent sequence, this discussion of consistency detection procedures will conclude with two brief points concerned with the derivation of rules. It is presumed that the general systemic productions that give rise to rules are applied to common CSs as the tokens for the sequences occur in the time line. As a result, the more frequently that common sequences are activated, the earlier they will be reviewed as possible sources of rules.

It may be necessary for the construction of a sufficient theory of cognitive development to add an additional feature to the operations of the innate general systemic productions. Hitherto their function has been discussed entirely in terms of the search for consistency in the sequential information stored in the time line as a result of the child's interaction with his environment. However, there are rules governing aspects of human performance for which it is difficult to envisage a direct basis in environmental interaction. The transitivity rules discussed in Chapter 6 afford a specific example. Direct input to the time line, rather than input from environmental interaction, might come from innate general systemic productions which facilitate consistency detection. Such systemic productions would activate specific productions and production systems in LTM and thus generate sequences of tokens in the time line that could give rise to specific and common CSs and ultimately, perhaps, rules. The criteria for the selection of the specific productions to be activated would determine the content of the condition side of these additional systemic productions. A possible basis for effective criteria would be monitoring of subsystems that have already given rise to rules as indications of areas from which further rules might be derived. In the case of transitivity, for example, the prior existence of conservation rules might lead to the generation and exploration of sequences of tokens based on the quantitative comparison subsystems and the consequent derivation of the transitivity rules.

Development of Object Constancy

We return to our description of the processes that occur when information enters the visual chain at the outset of cognitive development. Recall that we assume the first specific CSs to be detected by the systemic productions are comprised of innate gross visual-discrimination and attentional control productions. The visual-discrimination productions take their input from VSTM, and the attentional productions take theirs from both SSTM and VSTM. These sequences of productions correspond to consistent features of the environment such as lines, angles, and colors. As new type-nodes—with these sequences stored at them—are added to the first LTM tier, the system acquires a repertoire of feature-discrimination production systems which process information in visual STM in a less crude and more aggregated form than the innate productions. This is summarized in the center section of Table 8.1.

If one of the feature-discrimination production systems is activated and successfully applied, its token is placed in SSTM. As in the case of the innate productions, these tokens do not represent a sufficiently aggregated form of information to enable the discovery of consistent relationships between the operation of the feature-discrimination production systems and that of the productions taking their input entirely from SSTM. However, the existence of the feature-discrimination production systems does make possible the detection of CSs that constitute a greater degree of aggregation of information. These sequences correspond to objects in the environment.

The first CSs corresponding to objects derived from the time line are representations of specific objects at specific distances. Multiple type nodes are created in LTM at which are stored production systems comprising the sequence of feature-discrimination production systems activated by stimulation arising from the same object viewed from different angles and distances. There is thus no object constancy. Object constancy arises from a further round of consistent sequence detection triggered by the inclusion in the time line of tokens pointing to the type nodes corresponding to different views of the same object. Processing of the production systems stored at these nodes by the general systemic productions leads to the detection of a common CS. This common CS includes the features shared by the varying representations of the same object. The addition to LTM of a type node at which this new common CS is stored marks the attainment of object constancy. The speed with which constancy is achieved in the case of particular objects depends upon the amount of variation in the stimulation emanating from each object. As Hebb (1949) asserts, "the more constant the stimulation from an object is, the more readily it will be identified and responded to [p. 94]."

Although feature-discrimination production systems are constructed early in cognitive development, values and attributes are not represented in LTM until somewhat later. The attainment of constancy of relevant objects is a prerequisite for the construction of value representations, since they are constructed via the application of consistency detecting productions to the information in the constant-object type nodes. As already indicated, this process occurs when tokens pointing to these type nodes are present in the time line. Evidence in support of the dependence of value representations on the prior existence of object representations is provided by language acquisition data. Children learn names for particular colors, shapes, and sizes after they have learned names for many objects. In general, names for entities are learned before names for particular values (Macnamara, 1972; Nelson, 1973). As we argued in the previous chapter, attribute representations are added to LTM as a result of the application of the systemic consistency detection process to the production systems stored at the value type-nodes. Once again, this takes place when tokens for values are included in the time line. The outcome of the process is the creation of attribute type-nodes at which are stored production systems containing the sequences of productions common to the consistent sequences defining the values subsumed by the attributes.

In discussing both the gross visual-discrimination productions and the feature-discrimination production systems it was asserted that the tokens which they place in SSTM do not constitute sufficiently aggregated forms of information to permit the detection of consistent relationships with the operation of the productions taking their input entirely from SSTM. The situation alters with the construction of the constant-object production systems, and the insertion in SSTM of their tokens. This gives rise to the discovery via the time line of specific CSs composed of tokens for constant-object production systems and tokens for SSTM productions. The latter point to type nodes at which are stored members of the child's innate repertoire of productions. These productions link largely undifferentiated conditions on the contents of SSTM with motor movements carried out on the external environment. In combination with the constant-object production systems, they provide the basis for sequences of behavior involving the manipulation of objects in the environment.

The developmental importance of the emergence of specific CSs comprising objects and motor movements is illustrated in the results of a longitudinal study carried out by Nelson (1973) of the acquisition of the first 50 words by 18 children between 1 and 2 years of age. A content analysis of the words referring to entities, which constituted the major portion of the children's vocabularies, revealed that with very few exceptions they are terms applying to manipulable or movable objects. Nelson concludes that "children learn the names of the things they can act on, whether they are toys, shoes, scissors, money, keys, blankets, or bottles as well as things that act themselves, such as dogs and cars. They do not learn the names of things in the house or outside that are simply 'there,' whether these are tables, plates, towels, grass, or stores [Nelson, 1973, p. 31]."

The representation in Table 8.1 further emphasizes the importance of the appearance of type-nodes representing constant objects. As LTM acquires constant-object type-nodes and corresponding tokens begin to figure in the time line, it becomes possible for the system to detect common CSs in object representations. As indicated above, some of these consistent sequences lead to the construction of type nodes in LTM representing values. These in their turn, when submitted to the systemic consistency detection process, yield common CSs which give rise to attribute representations.

Development of Q_s

The addition of value and attribute type nodes to LTM is only one consequence of the application of the systemic productions to object representations. Another consequence is the development of the subitizing quantification operator, Q_s. The presence, in the time line, of tokens pointing to constant-object type nodes leads to the detection of specific CSs composed of constant-object tokens. These sequences are an essential prerequisite for the construction of Q_s. We will now offer the account of the development of Q_s which was postponed during the discussion of quantification operators in Chapter 3.

The first specific CSs relevant to the development of Q_s are those derived from the child's experience with collections of identical objects. For example, re-peated experience on the simultaneous presence of two identical objects results in the creation of a type node for a specific CS. Located at this node is a production system containing two tokens pointing to the same constant-object type node. Even at this early point in development, such a production system is clearly a precursor of Q_s, since it is, in effect, a subitizing quantification operator limited in its field of operation to the cardinal number two and a single constant-object type node.

There are two reasons why we mention the beginnings of the representation of the cardinal number two prior to the corresponding events for the cardinal number one. The first is the existence of a small amount of empirical evidence suggesting that children construct a representation for two prior to one (De-croly, 1932). The second is that consideration of the cardinal number two provides a simpler initial example of the developmental events involved. Repre-sentation of the cardinal number one raises the question of the nature of the distinction between it and the corresponding constant-object type node. As Fig. 8.3a indicates, the distinction can be characterized as one between intensive and extensive properties. At the PS.OB1 type node is stored the common CS of feature discrimination productions which represents the intensive properties of the constant object. The PS.1 type node, in contrast, represents the extensive properties of a collection comprising a single object, PS.OB1. This intensive—extensive distinction will be accorded an essential function in the following account of the developmental events covered by Fig. 8.3.

Experience in dealing with collections of identical objects and the process of specific CS detection initially result in the construction of two type-nodes at which are located production systems respectively comprising one and two

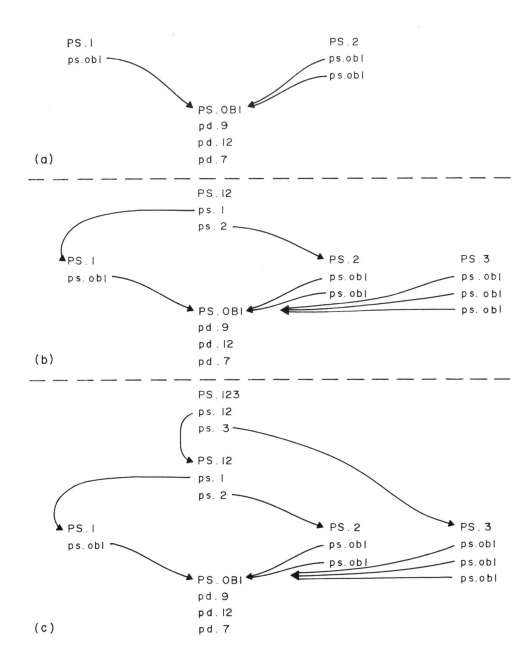

FIG. 8.3 The development of Q_s.

tokens pointing to the same constant–object type node. In accordance with the principle outlined above, these new type nodes are added to Tier 1 in LTM on a level immediately above the one containing the relevant-object type node. This is the situation depicted in Fig. 8.3a.

Continued experience with collections of the object PS.OB1 has two consequences which advance the development of Q_s. Scanning the collections results in repeated activation of PS.OB1 as individual objects are identified by their intensive properties. Application of the systemic productions to the sequences of tokens thus inserted in the time line leads to the detection of specific CSs. Their detection results in the construction of type nodes at which are located production systems comprising three (PS.3) tokens, pointing to the PS.OB1 type node. Figure 8.3b and c depicts the addition of PS.3 to LTM. As in the case of PS.1 and PS.2, the PS.3 type node is located on the level immediately above that containing PS.OB1.

Concurrent with the construction of further type nodes representing higher cardinal numbers of the same object, the type nodes representing the lower cardinal numbers become linked in specific CSs. Continued experience with collections of PS.OB1 not only produces scanning and successive identification of individual objects but also leads to the activation of type nodes representing extensive properties of the collections. Consider the developmental state represented in Fig. 8.3a. When a collection of two or more identical objects is presented, both PS.1 and PS.2 are activated, since they are on the same LTM level. Tokens pointing to these type nodes are inserted in the time line. Repetition of this sequence of events results in the detection of a specific CS and, as Fig. 8.3b indicates, the creation of a new type node, PS.12, at which are stored tokens pointing to PS.1 and PS.2. After the addition of PS.3 to LTM, repeated experience with collections comprising three or more of PS.OB1 leads to repeated activation of PS.12 and PS.3 since, as Fig. 8.3b illustrates, they are both on the "surface" level of the first tier of LTM. The outcome, presented in Fig. 8.3c, is the creation of a new type node, PS.123, at which are stored tokens pointing to PS.12 and PS.3.

With attainment of the state represented in Fig. 8.3c, the system has constructed a production system, PS.123, that is, in effect, a subitizing quantification operator with a maximum range of three items. All of these items, however, must satisfy the feature discrimination productions which compose PS.OB1. The account of the emergence of Q_s has been couched entirely in terms of a single object to facilitate explanation of the processes involved. In view of the time scale of the increase in the numerical range of Q_s presented in Chapter 3, it is highly improbable that a production system confined to a *single object*, rather than a class of objects, and with a numerical range as high as three is in fact ever constructed.

Explanation of the grounds for this assertion entails consideration of a third important result of the presence in the time line of tokens pointing to constant-object type nodes. As already indicated, it becomes possible for the system to detect common CSs in the representations of different objects. Some of these consistent sequences lead to the construction of type nodes in LTM representing values and later, attributes. Other common CSs give rise to new type nodes constituting representations of classes of objects. Successive applications of the consistency detection process to type nodes representing classes of objects, classes of classes of objects, and so on, result in the addition to LTM of type nodes representing increasing degrees of abstraction from the level of specific objects and, thus, subsuming categories of an increasing degree of breadth and heterogeneity at the specific object level.

Figure 8.4 depicts a simple example of the formation of class representations. Repeated applications of the consistency detection process to type nodes representing objects or classes of objects results in successive additions to LTM. The object type nodes PS.OB1, PS.OB2, PS.OB3, and PS.OB4 yield the class type nodes PS.C1 and PS.C2 which, in turn, give rise to PS.CC1, a type node

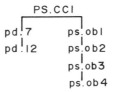

FIG. 8.4 Addition to LTM of type nodes representing classes of objects.

representing a class of classes. PS.CC1 subsumes both of the PS.C1 and PS.C2 classes and thus the variety of features at the specific object level represented by PS.OB1, PS.OB2, PS.OB3, and PS.OB4.

Before proceeding, it should be noted that common consistent sequences representing classes of objects are subject to the same kind of attempts at extending the area of application as were described earlier in this chapter. Examples of these efforts are provided by language development data which reveal inappropriate extensions of the range of applicability of such common consistent sequences. Nelson (1973), for example, reports many inaccurate generalizations such as the use of the word "ball" for light bulb and orange, and "shoes" for both shoes and socks.

The process of constructing type-nodes representing classes of objects of increasing breadth and heterogeneity proceeds concurrently with the creation of type-nodes representing cardinal numbers of the same object. It is the lengthy interaction between the results of the two processes that renders the construction of a production system confined to a single object and with a numerical range of four highly improbable. What is the outcome of their interaction in developmental terms? Early in development many production systems representing the cardinal numbers one and two, each confined to a single object, are constructed. As type-nodes representing increasingly broad and heterogeneous catagories of objects appear in LTM they give rise, via the time line and consistency detection processes, to production systems for the cardinal numbers having broader reference categories. By the point in development at which representations for three and four are derived, the system has a rich repertoire in LTM of type nodes representing broad categories of objects. Since these lie nearer the "surface" of LTM than the type nodes for the individual objects the categories subsume, the tokens from which the production systems for three and four are derived point to category rather than individual-object type nodes. Similarly, new representations for one and two with much wider reference are added to LTM. These prevent subsequent activation of their narrower predecessors lying on lower levels of Tier 1.

As the area of application of cardinal number type-nodes increases, there is a corresponding increase in the breadth of applicability of production systems of the type exemplified by PS.12 and PS.123 (Fig. 8.3). These production systems which link representations of the cardinal numbers are the direct predecessors of PS.SUB2. As development proceeds, type-nodes representing an increasing range of cardinal numbers, and with wider areas of application, are added to LTM and subsequently linked in single production systems. With the widening of the areas of application, the number of these single production systems on the current surface level of LTM diminishes. Previously constructed production systems dealing with subsets of the area of application of later systems are no longer activated, since they are located on lower LTM levels. Thus, the appearance of a production system PS.123 composed of cardinal number production systems based on the type node for the general category "animal" preempts the subsequent activation of the earlier constructed production systems referring to collections of specific animals now subsumed by the general category.

As the number of production systems of the PS.123 type on the surface level of LTM diminishes and the area of application of each production system widens, so the system comes closer to the developmental state represented by PS.SUB2 (see Chapter 3). This state is attained by the continuation of the interaction of the processes already outlined. The appearance of PS.SUB2 is contingent on the formation of a type node representing a category of such breadth and heterogeneity that cardinal number production systems derived from it are operationally equivalent to representations of abstract cardinal number: the "twoness of two." The initial version of PS.SUB2 is constructed by linking these abstract cardinal number production systems together in a single production system in the fashion indicated in Fig. 8.4.

One feature of newly constructed type nodes needs to be emphasized. Since these nodes represent consistent sequences derived from the time line, they are initially organized so as to reproduce the series that generated them. Thus, they function as if the underlying interpreter simply fired each production in sequence until a failure occurred. This would break the consistent sequence, and the sytem would terminate.

This sequential firing can be effected without any changes in the underlying production system interpreter. All that it requires is that each production directly point to the next via an action of the form (PD PX). For example, assume that we have a system like

P1:   (A B --> A1 A2 (PD P2) A3)
P2:   (C D --> A4 A5 (PD P3) A6)
P3:   (E F --> A7 A8 (PD P4) A9)
P4:   (G H --> A7 A8)

If P1 fires, it takes actions A1, A2, and then it tests P2. If P2 fires, it then takes A4, A5, and (PD P3). Suppose at this point that P3 fails. This would "complete" (PD P3), the third action in P2, and A6 would be taken. Then, since (PD P2)–the third action in P1–has been completed, the remaining action in P1, A3, would finally be taken. The sequence of actions would have been: A1, A2, (PD P2) A4 A5 (PD P3), A6, and A3.

A PSG model for initial Q_s. The explanation for the wide disparity between the latencies generated by the adult Q_s and the children's Q_s (see Fig. 3.8) lies partly in the above-mentioned character of newly formed type nodes. In the *adult* version of Q_s, represented by PS.SUB2 (Fig. 3.10), all redundant and unnecessary processing has been eliminated. Only one of the PDVS rules ever fires, due to the ABS condition which tests for precisely n elements in each rule. In the *initial* version of PS.SUB2, this is not the case (see Fig. 8.5). Notice that PDVS1, PDVS2, PDVSn will fire if there are at least $1, 2, n$ elements in VSTM.

```
00400   XLM:(CLASS ELM OBJ)
00500   X:(VAR)
00600   SATG:(ACTION (NTC (GOAL *))(* ==> +))
00700
00800   ;GROUP UNPACKER
00900   PDUNG:((SEE (GRP (XLM X))) --> (GRP (XLM X) =VS=> GRP) (IVS (XLM X)))
01000   PDUNGX:((SEE (GRP)) --> (GRP =VS=> OLD.GRP))
01100   PSUNG:(PDUNG PDUNGX)
01200
01300   PDVS0:((GOAL * SUBIT) --> (QS 0)(PD PDVS1) SATG)
01400   PDVS1:((GOAL * SUBIT) (SEE (XLM)) --> (QS 1)(PD PDVS2) SATG)
01500   PDVS2:((GOAL * SUBIT) (SEE (XLM)) (SEE (XLM)) --> (QS 2)(PD PDVS3) SATG)
01600   PDVS3:((GOAL * SUBIT) (SEE (XLM)) (SEE (XLM)) (SEE (XLM)) --> (QS 3) SATG)
01700   PSVS:(PDVS0)
01800   PSUBIT:(PDSUB)
01900   STMI:((GOAL * SUBIT) NIL NIL NIL NIL)
02000   PDSUB:((GOAL * SUBIT)(SEE (GRP)) --> (PS PSUNG)(PS.1 PSVS))
```

FIG. 8.5   PSG model for initial version of PS.SUB2.

Furthermore, the system is organized so that each production directly points to its successor in the manner outlined above. Thus all the PDVSs, up to and including the "correct" one, fire before a failure occurs and the sequence is broken.

The result of this organization is shown in Fig. 8.6, a trace of the initial version of PS.SUB2 quantifying two dots, and then one dot. (The corresponding trace for the adult PS.SUB2 is shown in Fig. 3.12.) From the accounting for ACT, VS, and PD, we see that the increments between 1 dot and 2 dots are $2*t_{ACT}$, $2*t_{VS}$, and $2*t_{PD}$. Summing these, using the estimates made in Chapter 3, we get a model slope of 150 + 15 + 30 = 195. This is identical to the estimate of 195 msec per dot for the children's subitizing rate, shown in Fig. 3.8.

How does the system go from the initial to the final version of PS.SUB2? In processing terms, the effect of the transition is to limit actions on SSTM to the insertion of the quantitative symbol representing only the final result of quantification. The redundant nature of the preceding actions is detected by the rule generating systemic productions described earlier in the present chapter. Their elimination is achieved by the insertion—in all of the productions—of the condition testing for the absence of a target object in VSTM. Implementation of this type of redundancy elimination would require considerable elaboration of the systemic productions beyond the complexity necessary for the straight-forward omission of redundant processing in the construction of conservation and transitivity rules.

INNATE STRATEGIC PRODUCTIONS (TIER 2)

The final tier of LTM that remains to be considered is the strategic tier on which are stored the innate productions governing the setting and general adminis-

```
ACT  VS  PD
00   00  00    SSTM: ((GOAL * SUBIT) NIL NIL NIL NIL NIL)
               VSTM: ((GRP (ELM DOT1) (ELM DOT2)))
00   00  01       PDSUB: ((GOAL * SUBIT) (SEE (GRP)) --> (PS PSUNG) (PS.1 PSVS))
01   00  02       PDUNG: ((SEE (GRP (XLM X))) --> (GRP (XLM X) =VS=> GRP) (ITE (XLM X)))
01   02  03       PDUNG: ((SEE (GRP (XLM X))) --> (GRP (XLM X) =VS=> GRP) (ITE (XLM X)))
01   04  05       PDUNGX: ((SEE (GRP)) --> (GRP =VS=> OLD.GRP))
02   05  08       PDVS0: ((GOAL * SUBIT) --> (QS 0) (PD PDVS1) SATG)
04   05  09       PDVS1: ((GOAL * SUBIT) (SEE (XLM)) --> (QS 1) (PD PDVS2) SATG)
06   05  10       PDVS2: ((GOAL * SUBIT) (SEE (XLM)) (SEE (XLM)) --> (QS 2) (PD PDVS3) SATG)
13   05  11    SSTM: ((GOAL + SUBIT) (QS 2) (QS 1) (QS 0) NIL NIL)
               VSTM: ((ELM DOT2) (ELM DOT1) (OLD.GRP))
```

(a)

```
00   00  00    SSTM: ((GOAL * SUBIT) NIL NIL NIL NIL NIL)
               VSTM: ((GRP (ELM DOT1)))
00   00  01       PDSUB: ((GOAL * SUBIT) (SEE (GRP)) --> (PS PSUNG) (PS.1 PSVS))
01   00  02       PDUNG: ((SEE (GRP (XLM X))) --> (GRP (XLM X) =VS=> GRP) (ITE (XLM X)))
01   02  04       PDUNGX: ((SEE (GRP)) --> (GRP =VS=> OLD.GRP))
02   03  07       PDVS0: ((GOAL * SUBIT) --> (QS 0) (PD PDVS1) SATG)
04   03  08       PDVS1: ((GOAL * SUBIT) (SEE (XLM)) --> (QS 1) (PD PDVS2) SATG)
11   03  09    SSTM: ((GOAL + SUBIT) (QS 1) (QS 0) NIL NIL NIL)
               VSTM: ((ELM DOT1) (OLD.GRP))
```

```
        Summary:   Act    VS    PD
                   13      5    11    2 Dots
                   11      3     9    1 Dot

                    2      2     2    (slope)
```

(b)

FIG. 8.6   Trace of initial version of PS.SUB2 on two dots (a) and one dot (b).

tration of goals. These productions can be divided into two categories, house-keeping productions and strategic productions proper.

Housekeeping productions deal with the interruption of goals to ensure that only one is active in SSTM at any given time. They also satisfy and delete goals when they have been attained. These productions are constantly active in the adult.

Strategic productions, in contrast, only come into operation when an impasse is reached on the first LTM tier. This occurs when none of the specific experience productions can accept the input currently available in SSTM in the service of the currently active goal. Strategic productions determine the way on in such a situation. They may, for example, lead to concentration on the currently active goal as distinct from the other contents of SSTM and initiate a search for a specific experience production to satisfy this goal. If such a production or production system is found, the next objective is to provide the requisite input for it by modifying the current contents of SSTM. Accordingly, productions to carry out the necessary modifications are sought. This strategy lies at the core of means–ends analysis.

An alternative method of tackling such an impasse involves concentrating on the contents of SSTM other than the currently active goal. An attempt is made to locate a specific experience production or production system that can accept this information as input. This strategy is termed *predicate-led* operation. Although recourse to it is infrequent in adults, we will attempt to show that it is of considerable importance in cognitive development.

In a developmental context, consideration of the functioning of the strategic productions raises a question of cardinal importance. How are goals established? The answer to this question is crucial since, at the adult level, the normal condition for productions taking their input from SSTM is the presence of an active goal plus additional semantic elements. We will now offer some suggestions as to how SSTM knowledge states acquire the status of goals.

Each goal comprises information on the end state created in SSTM by application of the production or production system in question. In the adult system, the end of processing episodes is largely determined by the attainment of the goals which initiated them. At the conclusion of an episode details of the current goal state in SSTM are inserted in the time line. Any resultant specific or common CSs include goal information, and thus enable the creation of new type nodes with goals in their initiating conditions. The consistency detecting systemic productions do not, however, designate end states as goals, and the presence of goal information is not a prerequisite for the establishment of new type nodes. This is exemplified in the development of the visual-discrimination production systems. Recall that they are initially constructed without goals in their activation conditions. Their operation is entirely determined by the presence of the appropriate predicate or input information in VSTM.

Predicate-led functioning is typical of early cognitive development. It is characteristic of all consistent sequences until those leading to the construction in LTM of type nodes representing objects have been detected. As already indicated, these sequences enable the discovery, via the time line, of CSs consisting of two kinds of tokens: tokens for object production systems, and tokens for innate productions linking largely undifferentiated conditions on SSTM with motor movements carried out on the external environment. These visual—motor sequences are the first to include goal information and thus to give rise to production systems with goals in their activation conditions. In order to explain the source of this goal information, we must consider the events marking the end of processing episodes.

Up to this point in development, the end of processing episodes is defined by environmental events or physiological motivational states. Both of these sources are "external" to the IPS. Information on the current state of the physiological system may enter SSTM. When the information corresponds to an aversive physiological condition such as hunger, its removal functions as a goal. This enables the innate housekeeping and strategic productions to operate as soon as the first consistent sequences leading to the attainment of physiological goals have been detected. These are the visual–motor sequences described in the previous paragraph. As already indicated, these consistent sequences are not detected until object type nodes have been constructed in LTM.

The situation is much less clear-cut when we consider the origin of goals internal to the IPS. Some tentative proposals will be outlined. To enable effective interaction with the environment, the child should possess as extensive a repertoire as possible of productions and production systems linked to specific goals. Some aspects of the behavior of young children suggest that the setting of end states as goals—independent of information from either the physiological system or the environment—is an innate feature of the cognitive system.

The prevalence of imitation is one such aspect. A sequence of behavior occurring in the environment in the child's view is processed by the visual encoding productions. As a result, tokens representing the sequence of productions activated are placed in SSTM, and also in the time line. Imitation arises from the conjunction of tokens in SSTM being accorded the status of a goal. A search of LTM ensues to locate productions that can generate behavioral sequences which, when processed by the visual encoding productions, will give rise to tokens in SSTM matching those comprising the goal. This, in functional terms, marks the attainment of the goal.

Recent evidence of the occurrence of imitative behavior early in development has been provided by Maratos (1973) in a longitudinal study of 12 infants from ages one to six months. Her tests of nonreinforced imitation of models presented via the visual, kinesthetic, or auditory sensory modalities indicate that a selective capacity to imitate models involving the head, mouth, and tongue exists during the first two months of life. From two months onward, auditory models and models involving arm and five finger movements are imitated and the imitative response increases with age.

Viewed from the standpoint we have adopted, observational learning is regarded as imitation in which the pursuit of the goal does not give rise to externally observable behavior. When the goal is attained as a result of external or internal imitation, the time line contains tokens for the sequence of productions which have given rise to tokens in SSTM matching the goal. Since this marks the end of a processing episode, details of the goal state in SSTM are inserted in the time line. The basis is thus established for the eventual addition to LTM of a type node at which is stored a production system containing this sequence of productions and including a goal in its activation conditions.

Before such a new type node is constructed, the sequence of productions must be repeated to enable its detection as a consistent sequence in the time line. Repetition of newly acquired sequences of productions appears to be another innate feature of the cognitive system. In conjunction with imitation, it facilitates consistent sequence detection and the addition to LTM of type nodes at which goal-linked production systems are stored.

The developmental function of the setting of end states as goals is not confined to imitative behavior. The prevalence and importance of predicate-led functioning in early cognitive development has already been asserted. (Recall that this involves the operation of productions on the basis of the presence in the relevant STM store of the appropriate predicate or input information without reference to goals.) Predicate-led functioning gives rise to a sequence of tokens in the time line and an end state in SSTM. The nature of the latter is determined by termination of the processing episode by environmental events. If the end state arising from predicate-led functioning is set as a goal, achieving this objective is much more straightforward than in the case of imitation. Attainment of the goal simply involves repetition of the most recent sequence of productions represented by tokens in the time line. As already indicated, repetition of newly acquired sequences appears to be an innate systemic feature. Like imitation, the combination of predicate-led functioning, goal setting, and repetition facilitates CS detection and the storing of goal-linked production systems in LTM.

Evidence in support of the important developmental role being assigned to this combination of processes is to be found in the literature on intrinsic motivation (Stott, 1961; White, 1959). Stott (1961), for example, studied the behavior of his son from birth to 18 months and found that much of it seemed to serve no immediate organic or social objective. The relational changes produced by this behavior could only be accounted for, in Stott's view, by postulating appraisal of the environment in terms of progressive effectiveness. The child continually sought new modes of effective action, and abandoned a mode once it had been exploited to the point of full mastery. This is exactly the type of externally observable behavior that would be predicted as the outcome of successive applications of predicate-led functioning, goal setting, and repetition sequence.

In the foregoing discussion a considerable amount of explanatory weight has been placed on the assumption that the setting of end states as goals is an innate feature of the developing cognitive system. This assumption may also prove of assistance in resolving one of the fundamental problems raised by language acquisition. The relevant evidence has been discussed by Macnamara (1972). How a child learns to categorize speech acts correctly is a mystery, except that this categorizing presupposes an ability to initially determine the nature of the acts independent of their syntactic form. For example, how are commands and questions categorized? Macnamara suggests that an angry tone of voice might come to be taken as an indication that the child is to do something or stop doing it. He cites evidence (Lieberman, 1967) for the existence of an innate tendency in babies to react positively to friendly tones of voice and negatively to angry tones.

Since, as already indicated, we are adopting Macnamara's view that in language acquisition the child uses independently attained meaning to discover basic syntactic structures, the question arises as to what constitutes the semantic basis for the discovery of the significance of the voice tone, pitch, and, later, syntactic cues for commands and questions. Macnamara proposes that such speech acts correspond to deeply rooted mental attitudes which are either innate or develop almost without benefit of learning. The child is on the lookout for means of expressing these attitudes, and thus comes to detect cues which distinguish different speech acts. Recourse of innate attitudes as a semantic basis for the discrimination of speech acts can be linked to the setting of end states as goals. Commands and questions are distinguished from other speech acts in that both have the effect of inserting an end state into SSTM and setting it as a goal. They are distinguished from each other by the nature of the end state. If, as was suggested above, the setting of end states as goals is an innate systemic feature, one important aspect of the processes underlying Macnamara's "mental attitudes" becomes more explicitly defined.

This discussion of the developmental origins of the goals included in the activation conditions of the productions and production systems stored at the type nodes in LTM concludes our consideration of the strategic level where innate productions governing the setting and general administration of goals are stored. The strategic level is the final LTM level to be considered in outlining the information-processing capability the child brings with him into the world.

CONCLUSION

In concluding this account of the general cognitive developmental framework underlying our model, it should be reiterated that the developing system is strongly motivated toward the perpetuation of its own activity. Continuing activity is required to permit the construction of the extended repertoire of productions necessary for increasingly effective interaction with the environment. As indicated above, much of this activity in the early stages of development is predicate-led functioning. When SSTM is void both of goals and of the input required for predicate-led functioning, activity—the developmental process—does not cease. It is precisely in this situation that the systemic productions which detect consistent sequences via the time line and which generate rules become active and employ SSTM as a working memory.

In our first attempt to apply information-processing analyses to the problems of cognitive development, we studied children's performance on series completion problems. Such problems were intrinsically interesting, we argued, because:

The ability to detect environmental regularities is a cognitive skill essential for survival. Man has a propensity to seek and capacity to find serial patterns in such diverse areas as music, economics, and the weather [Klahr & Wallace, 1970a, p. 243].

In this chapter, we have proposed a theory of cognitive development that places the detection of sequential regularities at the core of self-modification—and hence, of cognitive development. These regularities come not only from those aspects of the environment that undergo temporal variation, but also from the system's regular interaction with environmental constancies.

We wish to close with two final observations on the notion of sequential regularity detection as a fundamental aspect of cognitive development. First, it is not a new idea, for it is implicit in the importance accorded the modern work on sequence detection (Gregg, 1967; Kotovsky & Simon, 1973; Restle, 1970; Simon & Kotovsky, 1963; Simon & Sumner, 1968), and it constituted the central theme in the first attempt to formulate developmental problems in information-processing terms (Simon, 1962). Furthermore, in its broadest form, the role of sequence detection in development was eloquently described long ago by Phillips (1897):

> Consciousness is not one continuous impression but an innumerable multitude of successive changes. Which one of the senses plays the first and most important part in the series-idea, we are perhaps unable to determine. . . . The tactile sense very early produces an endless series of changes in consciousness which soon become vaguely recognized as distinct both in time and space; sound continually plays its part after the first few hours of life; random noises, voices, ticking and striking of the clock, all contribute to the formation of the series-idea; the succession of night and day continues to greet the eye, objects come and go before the field of vision; hunger and satisfaction periodically occupy a place in consciousness; functional processes, especially circulation and respiration, play an important part; the movements of a child, first by others, then its own—all these, in process of time, establish firmly the series-idea which exists long before the number—name series. The earliest and most rudimentary form of knowledge in the cognitive sense is a knowledge of a series of changes. This precedes all external knowledge of things [p. 228].

The second point is that psychology has developed to a point where there are now powerful tools available for formulating precise models of both self-modification and sequence detection. Very recently, Waterman (1974) constructed a set of what he calls *adaptive production systems* for a range of learning tasks. These models learn simple addition, verbal associations, and complex letter series. Each model is written as an initial core of productions, some of which have the capacity to add additional productions to the initial core. The final "learned" system operates under the same control structure and system architecture as the initial system, and the learning rules are represented in precisely the same way as the new rules that are learned, that is, as productions. The environments in which Waterman's system do their self-modification are relatively simple, but we believe that the basic approach is extendable to richer contexts. In particular, the general model for the detection of specific and consistent sequences in the time line, described earlier in this chapter, should be amenable to such an approach.

The theory of cognitive development presented here rates low in regard to the formal evaluative criteria of sufficiency and precision. Since it does not yet exist in the form of a running computer program, its sufficiency has not been demonstrated, and it fares badly on the precision criterion. In view of these shortcomings, the universality to which it aspires smacks more of bravado than strength. However, we are convinced that a general theory of cognitive development is invaluable in preventing the results of the information-processing analysis of specific tasks from becoming too local and mutually incompatible. If all of the theories sufficient to account for success and failure on specific tasks are consistent with the same cognitive developmental framework, then we may attain the ultimate objective of producing a sufficient information-processing theory of cognitive development.

References

Achenbach, T. M. "Conservation" below age three: Fact or artifact? *Proceedings of the 77th Annual Convention of the American Psychological Association,* 1969, **4**(Pt. 1), 275–276.

Ahr, P. R., & Youniss, J. Reasons for failure on the class inclusion problem. *Child Development,* 1970, **41,** 131–143.

Averbach, E. The span of apprehension as a function of exposure duration. *Journal of Verbal Learning and Verbal Behavior,* 1963, **2,** 60–64.

Baylor, G. W. *A treatise on the mind's eye (Parts I, II, and III).* Unpublished doctoral dissertation, Carnegie-Mellon University, 1972.

Baylor, G. W., & Gascon, J. An information processing theory of aspects of the development of weight seriation in children. *Cognitive Psychology,* 1974, **6,** 1–40.

Baylor, G. W., Gascon, J., Lemoyne, G., & Pothier, N. An information processing model of some seriation tasks. *Canadian Psychologist,* 1973, **14,** 167–196.

Beckmann, H. Die Entwicklung der Zahlleistung bei 2-6 jührigen kindern. *Zeitschrift für angewandte Psychologie,* 1924, **22,** 1–72.

Beckwith, M., & Restle, F. Process of enumeration. *Psychological Review,* 1966, **73,** 437–444.

Beilin, H. Cognitive capacities of young children: A replication. *Science,* 1968, **162,** 920–921.

Beilin, H. The training and acquisition of logical operations. In M. F. Rosskopf, L. P. Steffe, & S. Taback (Eds.), *Piagetian cognitive developmental research and mathematics education.* Washington, D.C.: National Council of Teachers of Mathematics, 1971.

Berlyne, D. E. *Structure and direction in thinking.* New York: Wiley, 1965.

Bever, T. G., Mehler, J., & Epstein, J. What children do in spite of what they know. *Science,* 1968, **162,** 921–924.

Blair-Hood, H. An experimental study of Piaget's theory of the development of number in children. *British Journal of Psychology,* 1962, **53,** 273–286.

Braine, M. D. S. The ontogeny of certain logical operations: Piaget's formulation examined by nonverbal methods. *Psychological Monographs,* 1959, **73**(5, Whole No. 475).

Braine, M. D. S. Development of a grasp of transitivity of length: A reply to Smedslund. *Child Development,* 1964, **35,** 799–810.

Brainerd, C. J. Order of acquisition of transitivity conservation and class-inclusion of length and weight. *Developmental Psychology,* 1973, **8,** 105–116.

Brainerd, C. J., & Brainerd, S. H. Order of acquisition of number and quantity conservation. *Child Development,* 1972, **43,** 1401–1406.

Brimer, M. A. *The classification of qualitative data.* Unpublished manuscript, University of Bristol, School of Education, 1968.

Broadbent, D. E. Psychological aspects of short-term and long-term memory. *Proceedings of the Royal Society, London, Series B.,* 1970, **175**, 333–350.

Brown, R. Introduction. In Society for Research in Child Development (Ed.). *Cognitive development in children.* Chicago: University of Chicago Press, 1970.

Bryant, P. E. *Perception and understanding in young children: An experimental approach.* New York: Basic Books, 1974.

Bryant, P. E., & Trabasso, T. Transitive inferences and memory in young children. *Nature,* 1971, **232**, 456–458.

Bunt, L. N. H. *The development of ideas of number and quantity according to Piaget.* Croningen: Wolter, 1951.

Calhoun, L. G. Number conservation in very young children: The effect of age and mode of responding. *Child Development,* 1971, **42**, 561–572.

Carpenter, P. A., & Just, M. A. Sentence comprehension: A psycholinguistic processing model of verification. *Psychological Review,* 1975, **82**, 45–73.

Cavanagh, J. P., & Chase, W. G. The equivalence of target and nontarget processing in visual search. *Perception and Psychophysics,* 1971, **9**, 493–495.

Cellérier, G. Information processing tendencies in recent experiments in cognitive learning—theoretical implications. In S. Farnham-Diggory (Ed.), *Information processing in children.* New York: Academic Press, 1972.

Chase, W. G. (Ed.) *Visual information processing.* New York: Academic Press, 1973.

Chase, W. G., & Calfee, R. C. Modality and similarity effects in short term recognition memory. *Journal of Experimental Psychology,* 1968, **81**, 510–514.

Chi, M. T. C. *Subitizing without eye movements.* Paper presented at the 81st Annual Convention of the American Psychological Association, Division 3, Montreal, August 1973.

Chi, M. T. C., & Klahr, D. Span and rate of apprehension in children and adults. *Journal of Experimental Child Psychology,* 1975, **19**, 434–439.

Chomsky, C. Reading, writing, and phonology. *Harvard Educational Review,* 1970, **40**, 287–309.

Chomsky, N. *Aspects of the theory of syntax.* Cambridge, Massachusetts: MIT Press, 1965.

Churchill, E. M. The number concepts of the young child. *Leeds University Research and Studies,* 1958, **18**, 28–46.

Clark, H. H. Influence of language on solving three-term series problems. *Journal of Experimental Psychology,* 1969, **82**, 205–215. (a)

Clark, H. H. Linguistic processes in deductive reasoning. *Psychological Review,* 1969, **76**, 387–404. (b)

Clark, H. H., Carpenter, P. A., & Just, M. A. On the meeting of semantics and perception. In W. G. Chase (Ed.), *Visual information processing.* New York: Academic Press, 1973.

Collins, A. M., & Quillian, M. R. How to make a language user. In E. Tulving & W. Donaldson (Eds.), *Organization of memory.* New York: Academic Press, 1972.

Coon, R. C., & Odom, R. D. Transitivity and length judgments as a function of age and social influence. *Child Development,* 1968, **39**, 1133–1144.

Crowder, R. G., & Morton, J. Precategorical acoustic storage (PAS). *Perception and Psychophysics,* 1969, **5**, 365–373.

Cunningham, M. *Intelligence: Its organization and development.* New York: Academic Press, 1972.

Curcio, F., Robbins, O., & Ela, S. S. The role of body parts and readiness in acquisition of number conservation. *Child Development,* 1971, **42**, 1641–1646.

Decroly, O. Observations, expériences et enquétes sur le développment das aptitudes de l'enfant. In M. Lamertin (Ed.), *Études de psychogénése.* 1932.

Descoeudres, A. *Le développement de l'enfant de deux à sept ans.* Paris: Delachaux and Niestle, 1922.

De Soto, C. B., London, M., & Handel, S. Social reasoning and spatial paralogic. *Journal of Personality and Social Psychology,* 1965, **2**, 513–521.

Dienes, Z. P., & Jeeves, M. A. *The effects of structural relations on transfer.* London: Hutchinson, 1970.

Donaldson, M. *A study of children's thinking.* London: Tavistock, 1963.

Donaldson, M., & Wales, R. J. On the acquisition of some relational terms. In J. R. Hayes (Ed.), *Cognition and the development of language.* New York: Wiley, 1970.

Elkind, D. Piaget's conservation problems. *Child Development,* 1967, **38**, 15–27.

Elkind, D., & Schoenfeld, E. Identity and equivalence conservation at two age levels. *Developmental Psychology,* 1972, **6**, 529–533.

Ellis, S. H., & Chase, W. G. Parallel processing in item recognition. *Perception and Psychophysics,* 1971, **10**, 379–384.

Ernst, G. W., & Newell, A. *GPS: A case study in generality and problem solving.* New York: Academic Press, 1969.

Farnham-Diggory, S. Cognitive synthesis in Negro and white children. *Monographs of the Society for Research in Child Development,* 1970, 35(2, Serial No. 135).

Farnham-Diggory, S. (Ed.) *Information processing in children.* New York: Academic Press, 1972.

Farnham-Diggory, S., & Gregg, L. W. Color, form, and function as dimensions of natural classification: Developmental changes in eye movements, reaction time, and response strategies. *Child Development,* 1975, **46**, 101–114.

Feigenbaum, E. A. The simulation of verbal learning behavior. In E. A. Feigenbaum & J. Feldman (Eds.), *Computers and thought.* New York: McGraw-Hill, 1963.

Fillmore, C. J. The case for case. In E. Bach & R. T. Harms (Eds.), *Universals in linguistic theory.* New York: Holt, Rinehart & Winston, 1968.

Flavell, J. H. *The developmental psychology of Jean Piaget.* Princeton, New Jersey: Van Nostrand, 1963.

Flavell, J. H. Stage-related properties of cognitive development. *Cognitive Psychology,* 1971, **2**, 421–453.

Flavell, J. H. An analysis of cognitive-developmental sequences. *Genetic Psychology Monographs,* 1972, 86(2), 279–350.

Flavell, J. H., & Wohlwill, J. F. Formal and functional aspects of cognitive development. In D. Elkind & J. H. Flavell (Eds.), *Studies in cognitive development.* New York: Oxford University Press, 1969.

Gagné R. M. Contributions of learning to human development. *Psychological Review,* 1968, **75**, 177–191.

Garcez, P. Les notions operatiores de conservation et de transitivite du poids, leur moment d'apprition et leur apprentissage. *Enfance,* 1969, 1–2, 103–117.

Gascon, J. Modèle cybernétique d'une sériation de poids chez les enfants. Unpublished master's thesis, Université de Montréal, 1969.

Gascon, J., & Baylor, G. W. *BG Manual,* Working Paper M.C.P. 13. Montreal: University of Montreal, 1973.

Gelman, R. Conservation acquisition: A problem of learning to attend to relevant attributes. *Journal of Experimental Child Psychology,* 1969, 7, 167–187.

Gelman, R. Logical capacity of very young children: Number invariance rules. *Child Development,* 1972, **43**, 75–90. (a)

Gelman, R. The nature and development of early number concepts. In H. Reese (Ed.), *Advances in child development.* Vol. 7. New York: Academic Press, 1972. (b)

Gelman, R., & Tucker, M. F. Further investigations of the young child's conception of number. *Child Development,* 1975, **46**, 167–175.

Gibson, E. J. The ontogeny of reading. *American Psychologist,* 1970, **25,** 136–143.

Ginsberg, H., & Opper, S. *Piaget's theory of intellectual development.* Englewood Cliffs, New Jersey: Prentice-Hall, 1969.

Glaser, R., & Resnick, L. B. Instructional psychology. *Annual Review of Psychology,* 1972, **23,** 207–276.

Glick, J., & Wapner, S. Development of transitivity: Some findings and problems of analysis. *Child Development,* 1968, **39,** 621–638.

Gould, J. D., & Peeples, D. R. Eye movements during visual search and discrimination of meaningless, symbol, and object patterns. *Journal of Experimental Psychology,* 1970, **85,** 51–55.

Gréco, P. Quotité et quantité. In J. Piaget (Ed.), *Structures numériques elémentaires.* Paris: Presses Universitaires de France, 1962.

Gregg, L. W. Internal representations of sequential concepts. In B. Kleinmuntz (Ed.), *Concepts and the structure of memory.* New York: Wiley, 1967.

Gregg, L. W., & Simon, H. A. Process models and stochastic theories of simple concept formation. *Journal of Mathematical Psychology,* 1967, **4,** 246–276.

Groen, G. J. *An investigation of some counting algorithms for simple addition problems,* Technical Report 118. Stanford, California: Stanford University Institute for Mathematical Studies in the Social Sciences, 1967.

Groen, G. J., & Parkman, J. M. A chronometric analysis of simple addition, *Psychological Review,* 1972, **79,** 329–343.

Halford, G. S. A theory of the acquisition of conservation. *Psychological Review,* 1970, **77,** 302–316.

Handel, S., De Soto, C. B., & London, M. Reasoning and spatial representation. *Journal of Verbal Learning and Verbal Behavior,* 1968, **7,** 351–357.

Hartmann, E. L. *The functions of sleep.* New Haven, Connecticut: Yale University Press, 1973.

Hatano, G., & Kuhara, K. Training on class inclusion problems. *Japanese Psychological Research,* 1972, **14**(2), 61–69.

Hayes, J. R. The child's conception of the experimenter. In S. Farnham-Diggory (Ed.), *Information processing in children.* New York: Academic Press, 1972.

Hebb, D. O. *The organization of behavior.* New York: Wiley, 1949.

Hunt, E. What kind of computer is man? *Cognitive Psychology,* 1971, **2,** 57–98.

Hunter, I. M. L. The solving of three-term series problems. *British Journal of Psychology,* 1957, **48,** 286–298.

Huttenlocher, J. Constructing spatial images: A strategy in reasoning. *Psychological Review,* 1968, **75,** 550–560.

Huttenlocher, J., Eisenberg, K., & Strauss, S. Comprehension: Relation between perceived actor and logical subject. *Journal of Verbal Learning and Verbal Behavior,* 1968, **7,** 527–530.

Huttenlocher, J., & Strauss, S. Comprehension and a statement's relation to the situation it describes. *Journal of Verbal Learning and Verbal Behavior,* 1968, **7,** 300–304.

Inhelder, B., & Piaget, J. *[The early growth of logic in the child].* (E. A. Lunzer & D. Papert, translators). London: Routledge & Kegan Paul, 1964. (Originally published in 1959.)

Inhelder, B., & Sinclair, H. Learning cognitive structures. In P. J. Mussen, J. Langer, & M. Covington (Eds.), *Trends and issues in developmental psychology.* New York: Holt, Rinehart & Winston, 1969.

Jennings, J. R. Cardiac reactions associated with different developmental levels of cognitive functions. Unpublished doctoral dissertation, University of California at Berkeley, 1969.

Jensen, E. M., Reese, E. P., & Reese, T. W. The subitizing and counting of visually presented fields of dots. *Journal of Psychology,* 1950, **30,** 363–392.

Jevons, W. S. The power of numerical discrimination. *Nature,* 1871, **3,** 281–282.

Johnson, N. F. The role of chunking and organization in the process of recall. In G. H. Bower (Ed.), *The psychology of learning and motivation.* Vol. 4. New York: Academic Press, 1970.

Johnson-Laird, P. N. The three-term series problem. *Cognition,* 1972, **1,** 57–82.

Kaufman, E. L., Lord, M. W., Reese, T. W., & Volkmann, J. The discrimination of visual number. *American Journal of Psychology,* 1949, **62,** 498–525.

Klahr, D. An information processing approach to the study of cognitive development. In A. D. Pick (Ed.), *Minnesota symposia on child psychology.* Vol. 7. Minneapolis: University of Minnesota Press, 1973.   (a)

Klahr, D. A production system for counting, subitizing and adding. In W. G. Chase (Ed.), *Visual information processing.* New York: Academic Press, 1973.   (b)

Klahr, D. Quantification processes. In W. G. Chase (Ed.), *Visual information processing.* New York: Academic Press, 1973.   (c)

Klahr, D. Steps toward the simulation of intellectual development. In L. B. Resnick (Ed.), *The nature of intelligence.* Hillsdale, New Jersey: Lawrence Erlbaum Assoc., 1976.

Klahr, D., & Wallace, J. G. The development of serial completion strategies: An information processing analysis. *British Journal of Psychology,* 1970, **61,** 243–257.   (a)

Klahr, D., & Wallace, J. G. An information processing analysis of some Piagetian experimental tasks. *Cognitive Psychology,* 1970, **1,** 358–387.   (b)

Klahr, D., & Wallace, J. G. Class inclusion processes. In S. Franham-Diggory (Ed.), *Information processing in children.* New York: Academic Press, 1972.

Klahr, D., & Wallace, J. G. The role of quantification operators in the development of conservation of quantity. *Cognitive Psychology,* 1973, **4,** 301–327.

Koehler, O. Vorsprachliches Denken ond "Zahlen" der Vogel. In E. Mayr & E. Schuz (Eds.), *Ornithologie als biologische Wissenschaft.* Heidelberg: C. Winter, 1949.

Kofsky, E. Developmental scalogram analysis of classificatory behavior. Unpublished doctoral dissertation, University of Rochester, 1963.

Kofsky, E. A scalogram study of classificatory development. *Child Development,* 1966, **37,** 191–204.

Kohnstamm, G. A. An evaluation of part of Piaget's theory. *Acta Psychologica,* 1963, **21,** 313–356.

Kohnstamm, G. A. *Piaget's analysis of class inclusion: Right or wrong?* The Hague: Mouton, 1968.

Kotovsky, K., & Simon, H. A. Empirical tests of a theory of human acquisition of concepts for sequential patterns. *Cognitive Psychology,* 1973, **4,** 399–424.

Landauer, T. K. Rate of implicit speech. *Perceptual and Motor Skills,* 1962, **15,** 646.

Laurendeau, M., & Pinard, A. *La pensée causale.* Paris: Presses Universitaires de France, 1962.

Lieberman, P. *Intonation, perception, and language.* Cambridge, Massachusetts: MIT Press, 1967.

Lindsay, P. H., & Norman, D. A. *Human information processing.* New York: Academic Press, 1972.

Macnamara, J. Cognitive basis of language learning in infants. *Psychological Review,* 1972, **79,** 1–13.

Maratos, O. *The origin and development of imitation in the first six months of life.* Paper presented at the British Psychological Society Annual Meeting, Liverpool, April 1973.

Markman, E. The facilitation of part-whole comparisons by use of the collective noun "family." *Child Development,* 1973, **44,** 837–840.

McCawley, J. D. The role of semantics in a grammar. In E. Bach & R. T. Harms (Eds.), *Universals in linguistic theory.* New York: Holt, Rinehart & Winston, 1968.

McGhee, P. E. Cognitive development and children's comprehension of humor. *Child Development*, 1971, **42**, 123–138.

McNeill, D. The development of language. Michigan University Center for Research on Language and Language Behavior. *Studies in Language and Language Behavior*, 1967, **4**, 429–463.

Mehler, J., & Bever, T. G. Cognitive capacity of very young children. *Science*, 1967, **158**, 141–142.

Mehler, J., & Bever, T. G. Study of competence in cognitive psychology. *International Journal of Psychology*, 1968, **3**, 273–280.

Miller, G. A. The magical number seven, plus or minus two: Some limits on our capacity for processing information. *Psychological Review*, 1956, **63**, 81–97.

Miller, G. A., Galanter, E., & Pribram, K. H. *Plans and the structure of behavior.* New York: Holt, Rinehart & Winston, 1960.

Moynahan, E., & Glick, J. Relation between identity conservation and equivalence conservation within four conceptual domains. *Developmental Psychology*, 1972, **6**, 247–251.

Murdock, B. B., Jr. The immediate retention of unrelated words. *Journal of Experimental Psychology*, 1960, **60**, 222–234.

Murray, J. P., & Youniss, J. Achievement of inferential transitivity and its relation to serial ordering. *Child Development*, 1968, **39**, 1259–1268.

Neisser, U. *Cognitive psychology.* New York: Appleton-Century-Crofts, 1967.

Nelson, K. Structure and strategy in learning to talk. *Monographs of the Society for Research in Child Development*, 1973, 38(1–2, Whole No. 149).

Newell, A. Studies in problem solving: Subject 3 on the Crypt-arithmetic task DONALD + GERALD = ROBERT. Unpublished manuscript, Carnegie Institute of Technology, July 1966.

Newell, A. On the analysis of human problem solving protocols. In J. C. Gardin & B. Javlin (Eds.), *Calcul et formalization dan les sciences de l'homme.* Paris: Center National de la Récherche Scientifique, 1968.

Newell, A. A note on process-structure distinctions in developmental psychology. In S. Farnham-Diggory (Ed.), *Information processing in children.* New York: Academic Press, 1972. (a)

Newell, A. A theoretical exploration of mechanisms for coding the stimulus. In A. W. Melton & E. Martin (Eds.), *Coding processes in human memory.* Washington, D.C.: Winston, 1972. (b)

Newell, A. Production systems: Models of control structures. In W. G. Chase (Ed.), *Visual information processing.* New York: Academic Press, 1973.

Newell, A., & McDermott, J. *PSG Manual,* Revision PSG2.D11. Pittsburgh, Pennsylvania: Carnegie-Mellon University, Department of Computer Science, 1974.

Newell, A., & Simon, H. A. *Human problem solving.* Englewood Cliffs, New Jersey: Prentice-Hall, 1972.

Norman, D. A. *Memory, knowledge and the answering of questions,* Technical Report 25. San Diego: University of California, Center for Human Information Processing, 1972.

Northman, J. E., & Gruen, G. E. Relationship between identity and equivalence conservation. *Developmental Psychology*, 1970, **2**, 311.

O'Bryan, K. G., & Boersma, F. J. Eye movements, perceptual activity, and conservation development. *Journal of Experimental Child Psychology*, 1971, **12**, 157–169.

Olshavsky, R. W., & Gregg, L. W. Information processing rates and task complexity. *Journal of Experimental Psychology*, 1970, **83**, 131–135.

Osherson, D. N. *Logical abilities in children, Vol. 1: Organization of length and class concepts.* New York: Wiley, 1974.

Parkman, J. M., & Groen, G. J. Temporal aspects of simple addition and comparison. *Journal of Experimental Psychology*, 1971, **89**, 335–342.

Pascual-Leone, J. A mathematical model for the transition rule in Piaget's developmental stages. *Acta Psychologica,* 1970, **32**, 301–345.

Pascual-Leone, J. A theory of constructive operators, a neo-Piagetian model of conservation, and the problem of horizontal decalages. Unpublished manuscript, York University, 1973.

Penfield, W. *The permanent record of the stream of consciousness,* Technical Report 486. Montreal: Montreal Neurological Institute, 14th International Congress of Psychology, 1954.

Penfield, W., & Roberts, L. *Speech and brain mechanisms.* Princeton, New Jersey: Princeton University Press, 1959.

Phillips, D. E. Number and its application psychologically considered. *The Pedagogical Seminary,* 1897, **5**, 221–281.

Piaget, J. Le Mécanisme du développment mental et les lois du groupement des opérations. *Archives of Psychology, Genéve,* 1941, **28**, 215–285.

Piaget, J. *[The child's conception of number].* (C. Gattengno & F. M. Hodgson, translators.) New York: Humanities Press, 1952. (Originally published in 1941.)

Piaget, J. Logique et equilbre dans les comportements du sujet. In L. Apostel, B. Mandelbrot, & J. Piaget (Eds.), *Études d'épistémologie génétique: II Logique et équilibre.* Paris: Presses Universitaires de France, 1957.

Piaget, J. In J. H. Tanner & B. Inhelder (Eds.), *Discussions on child development.* Vol. 4. London: Tavistock, 1960.

Piaget, J. Quantification, conservation and nativism. *Science,* 1968, **162**, 976–979.

Piaget, J., & Inhelder, B. *[The psychology of the child].* (H. Weaver, translator.). New York: Basic Books, 1969. (Originally published in 1966.)

Piaget, J., Inhelder, B., & Szeminska, A. *[The child's conception of geometry].* (E. A. Lunzer, translator.). New York: Basic Books, 1960. (Originally published in 1948.)

Pinard, A., & Laurendeau, M. "Stage" in Piaget's cognitive-developmental theory: Exegesis of a concept. In D. Elkind & J. H. Flavell (Eds.), *Studies in cognitive development.* New York: Oxford University Press, 1969.

Posner, M. I. Abstraction and the process of recognition. In G. Bower & J. T. Spence (Eds.), *Advances in learning and motivation.* Vol. 3. New York: Academic Press, 1969.

Posner, M. I. Coordination of internal codes. In W. G. Chase (Ed.), *Visual information processing.* New York: Academic Press, 1973.

Pylyshyn, Z. W. What the mind's eye tells the mind's brain: A critique of mental imagery. *Psychological Bulletin,* 1973, **80**, 1–24.

Quillian, M. R. Word concepts: A theory and simulation of some basic semantic capabilities. *Behavioral Science,* 1967, **12**, 410–430.

Quillian, M. R. Semantic memory. In M. Minsky (Ed.), *Semantic information processing.* Cambridge, Massachusetts: MIT Press, 1968.

Quillian, M. R. The teachable language comprehender: A simulation program and theory of language. *Communications of the ACM,* 1969, **12**, 459–476.

Quillian, M. R., Wortman, P. M., & Baylor, G. W. *The programmable Piaget: Behavior from the standpoint of a radical computerist,* C.I.P. Working Paper 78. Pittsburgh: Carnegie–Mellon University, 1964.

Reitman, W. R. *Cognition and thought.* New York: Wiley, 1965.

Renwick, E. M. *Children learning mathematics.* Ilfracombe: Stockwell, 1963.

Resnick, L. B., & Glaser, R. Problem solving and intelligence. In L. B. Resnick (Ed.), *The nature of intelligence.* Hillsdale, New Jersey: Lawrence Earlbaum Assoc., 1976.

Resnick, L. B., Wang, M. C., & Kaplan, J. Behavior analysis in curriculum design: A hierarchically sequenced introductory mathematics curriculum. *Journal of Applied Behavior Analysis,* 1973, **6**, 679–710.

Restle, F. Theory of serial pattern learning. *Psychological Review,* 1970, 77, 481–495.

Riley, C. A., & Trabasso, T. Logical structure versus information processing in making inferences. Paper presented to the Society for Research in Child Development, Philadelphia, March 1973.

Riley, C. A., & Trabasso, T. Comparatives, logical structures and encoding in a transitive inference task. *Journal of Experimental Child Psychology,* 1974, **17,** 187–203.

Rothenberg, B. B., & Courtney, R. G. Conservation of number in very young children: A replication of and comparison with Mehler and Bever's study. *Journal of Psychology,* 1968, **70,** 205–212.

Rumelhart, D. E., Lindsay, P. H., & Norman, D. A. A process model for long-term memory. In E. Tulving & W. Donaldson (Eds.), *Organization of memory.* New York: Academic Press, 1972.

Salapatek, P. Visual scanning of geometric figures by the human newborn. *Journal of Comparative and Physiological Psychology,* 1968, **66,** 247–258.

Saltzman, I. J., & Garner, W. R. Reaction time as a measure of span of attention. *Journal of Psychology,* 1948, **25,** 227–241.

Schaeffer, B., Eggleston, V. H., & Scott, J. L. Number development in young children. *Cognitive Psychology,* 1974, **6,** 357–379.

Sigel, I. E., & Hooper, F. H. (Eds.) *Logical thinking in children.* New York: Holt, Rinehart & Winston, 1968.

Simon, H. A. An information processing theory of intellectual development. *Monographs of the Society for Research in Child Development,* 1962, **27**(2, Serial No. 82).

Simon, H. A. Motivational emotional controls of cognition. *Psychological Review,* 1967, **74,** 29–39.

Simon, H. A. On the development of the processor. In S. Farnham-Diggory (Ed.), *Information processing in children.* New York: Academic Press, 1972.

Simon, H. A., & Kotovsky, K. Human acquisition of concepts for sequential patterns. *Psychological Review,* 1963, **70,** 534–546.

Simon, H. A., & Newell, A. Human problem solving: The state of the theory in 1970. *American Psychologist,* 1971, **26,** 145–159.

Simon, H. A., & Sumner, R. K. Pattern in music. In B. Kleinmuntz (Ed.), *Formal representation of human judgment.* New York: Wiley, 1968.

Slobin, D. I. Cognitive prerequisites for the development of grammar. In C. A. Ferguson & D. I. Slobin (Eds.), *Studies of child language development.* New York: Holt, Rinehart & Winston, 1973.

Smedslund, J. Apprentissage des notions de la conservation et de la transitivité de poids. In A. Morf, J. Smedslund, Vinh-Bang, & J. F. Wohlwill (Eds.), *L'apprentissage des structures logiques. (Etudes d'Epistemologie gentique, IX).* Paris: Presses Universitaires de France, 1959.

Smedslund, J. Development of concrete transitivity of length in children. *Child Development,* 1963, **34,** 389–405. (a)

Smedslund, J. Patterns of experience and the acquisition of concrete transitivity of weight in eight-year-old children. *Scandinavian Journal of Psychology,* 1963, **4,** 251–256. (b)

Smedslund, J. Patterns of experience and the acquisition of conservation of length. *Scandinavian Journal of Psychology,* 1963, **4,** 257–264. (c)

Smedslund, J. Concrete reasoning: A study of intellectual development. *Monographs of the Society for Research in Child Development,* 1964, **29**(2, Serial No. 93).

Smedslund, J. The development of transitivity of length: A comment on Braine's reply. *Child Development,* 1965, **36,** 577–580.

Smedslund, J. Microanalysis of concrete reasoning. I: The difficulty of some combinations of addition and subtraction of one unit. *Scandinavian Journal of Psychology,* 1966, **7,** 145–156. (a)

Smedslund, J. Microanalysis of concrete reasoning. II: The effect of number transformations and non-redundant elements and some variations in procedure. *Scandinavian Journal of Psychology,* 1966, **7,** 157–163. (b)

Smedslund, J. Microanalysis of concrete reasoning. III: Theoretical overview. *Scandinavian Journal of Psychology,* 1966, 7, 164–167. (c)

Smedslund, J. Mental processes involved in rapid logical reasoning. *Scandinavian Journal of Psychology,* 1968, 9, 187–205.

Society for Research in Child Development (Ed.). *Cognitive development in children.* Chicago: University of Chicago Press, 1970.

Sperling, G. The information available in brief visual presentations. *Psychological Monographs,* 1960, 74(11, Whole No. 498).

Sternberg, S. Retrieval of contextual information from memory. *Psychonomic Science,* 1967, 8, 55–56.

Sternberg, S. Memory scanning: Mental processes revealed by reaction time experiments. *American Scientist,* 1969, 57, 421–457.

Stott, D. H. An empirical approach to motivation based on the behavior of a young child. *Journal of Child Psychology and Psychiatry,* 1961, 2, 97–117.

Thom, R. *Structural stability and morphogenesis: an outline of a general theory of models.* Reading, Massachusetts: W. A. Benjamin, 1974.

Trabasso, T. Discussion of the papers by Bransford and Johnson; and Clark, Carpenter, and Just: Language and cognition. In W. G. Chase (Ed.), *Visual information processing.* New York: Academic Press, 1973.

Trabasso, T. Representation, memory and reasoning: How do we make transitive inferences? In A. D. Pick (Ed.), *Minnesota symposia on child psychology.* Vol. 9. Minneapolis: University of Minnesota Press, 1975.

Trabasso, T., & Riley, C. A. *An information processing analysis of transitive inferences.* Paper presented at the Eastern Psychological Association, Washington, D.C.: May 1973.

Trabasso, T., & Riley, C. A. The construction and use of representations involving linear order. In R. L. Solso (Ed.), *Information processing and cognition: The Loyola Symposium.* Hillsdale, New Jersey: Lawrence Earlbaum Assoc., 1975.

Trabasso, T., Riley, C. A., & Wilson, E. G. The representation of linear order and spatial strategies in reasoning: A developmental study. In R. Falmagne (Ed.), *Reasoning: representation and process in children and adults.* Hillsdale, New Jersey: Lawrence Erlbaum Assoc. 1975.

Tulving, E. Episodic and semantic memory. In E. Tulving & W. Donaldson (Eds.), *Organization of memory.* New York: Academic Press, 1972.

Uzgiris, I. C. Situational generality of conservation. *Child Development,* 1964, 35, 831–841.

Van den Daele, L. D., Pascual-Leone, J., & Witz, K. G. *Neopiagetian perspectives on cognition and development.* New York: Academic Press, in press.

Von Szeliski, V. Relation between the quantity perceived and the time of perception. *Journal of Experimental Psychology,* 1924, 7, 135–147.

Wallace, J. G. *Stages and transition in conceptual development: An experimental study.* Slough, England: National Foundation for Educational Research in England and Wales, 1972. (a)

Wallace, J. G. *Class inclusion performance in children: Information processing theories and experimental studies.* Paper presented at the 20th International Congress of Psychology, Tokyo, August 1972. (b)

Wallach, L. On the bases of conservation. In D. Elkind & J. H. Flavell (Eds.), *Studies in cognitive development.* New York: Oxford University Press, 1969.

Waterman, D. A. *Adaptive production systems,* C.I.P. Working Paper 285. Pittsburgh: Carnegie–Mellon University, Department of Psychology, 1974.

Waugh, N. C., & Norman, D. A. Primary memory. *Psychological Review,* 1965, 72, 89–104.

Wertheimer, M. Untersuchungen zur Lehre von der Gestalt: II. *Psychologische Forschung,* 1923, 4, 301–350.

White, R. W. Motivation reconsidered: The concept of competence. *Psychological Review,* 1959, 66, 297–333.

Wilkinson, A. *Counting strategies and semantic analysis as applied to class inclusion,* Report 61. Ann Arbor: University of Michigan, Department of Psychology, Developmental Program, 1975.

Wohlwill, J. F. Piaget's theory of the development of intelligence in the concrete operations period. *American Journal of Mental Deficiency Monograph Suppliment,* 1966, **70,** 57–83.

Wohlwill, J. F. Responses to class-inclusion questions for verbally and pictorially presented items. *Child Development,* 1968, **39,** 449–465.

Wood, D. J. *The nature and development of problem-solving strategies.* Unpublished doctoral dissertation, University of Nottingham, 1969.

Woodworth, R. S., & Schlosberg, H. *Experimental psychology* (rev. ed.). New York: Holt, 1954.

Young, R. M. *Children's seriation behavior: A production-system analysis.* Unpublished doctoral dissertation, Carnegie–Mellon University, 1973.

Zeeman, E. C. The geometry of catastrophe. *Times Literary Supplement,* December 10, 1971, 1556–1558.

Zeeman, E. C. *A catastrophe machine.* Unpublished manuscript, University of Warwick, Mathematics Institute, Coventry, June 1972.

Author Index

Numbers in *italics* refer to pages on which the complete references are listed.

A

Achenbach, T. M., 113, *225*
Ahr, P. R., 82, 84, 85, 86, *225*
Averbach, E., 33, *225*

B

Baylor, G. W., x, 13, 147, 166, 173, 174, 175, *225, 231*
Beckmann, H., 63, 70, *225*
Beckwith, M., 32, 57, *225*
Beilin, H., 75, 113, 129, *225*
Berlyne, D. E., 189, *225*
Bever, T. G., 77, 78, 112, 113, *225, 230*
Blair-Hood, H., 82, *225*
Boersma, F. J., 121, *230*
Braine, M. D. S., 158, *225*
Brainerd, C. J., 78, 79, 128, 170, *225*
Brainerd, S. H., 128, *225*
Brimer, M. A., *226*
Broadbent, D. E., 173, 174, 175, *226*
Brown, R., ix, x, xi, *226*
Bryant, P. E., 77, 166, 167, *226*
Bunt, L. N. H., 115, *226*

C

Calfee, R. C., 43, *226*
Calhoun, L. G., 113, *226*
Carpenter, P. A., x, 144, *226*
Cavanagh, J. P., 43, *226*
Cellérier, G., 129, *226*
Chase, W. G., 43, 147, *226*
Chi, M. T. C., 38, 59, *226*
Chomsky, C., 175, 178, *226*
Chomsky, N., 176, *226*
Churchill, E. M., 128, *226*
Clark, H. H., 141, 142, 143, 144, 145, 151, 152, 161, *226*
Collins, A. M., 179, *226*
Coon, R. C., 158, *226*
Courtney, R. G., 113, *232*
Crowder, R. G., 8, *226*
Cunningham, M., 173, *226*
Curcio, F., 113, *226*

D

Decroly, O., *226*
Descoeudres, A., 121, *227*
De Soto, C. B., 147, 148, 152, *227, 228*

235

Subject Index

DATE DUE